IN
the
CORRIDORS
of
POWER

David
LIPSEY

—

IN
the
CORRIDORS
of
POWER

—

An
Autobiography

Biteback Publishing

First published in Great Britain in 2012 by
Biteback Publishing Ltd
Westminster Tower
3 Albert Embankment
London SE1 7SP
Copyright © David Lipsey 2012

ISBN 978-1-84954-216-6

10 9 8 7 6 5 4 3 2 1

A CIP catalogue record for this book is available from the British Library.

Set in Adobe Garamond Pro
Cover design by Namkwan Cho

Printed and bound in Great Britain by
CPI Group (UK) Ltd, Croydon CR0 4YY

CONTENTS

INTRODUCTION

Some are born great and some have greatness thrust upon them. I am not a great man, far from it. But I have had the privilege in my political life to have had greatness thrust upon me, in the shape of those for whom I have worked. I have served, by good fortune, not one but three great men: sequentially, Tony Crosland, Labour's philosopher-king; Jim Callaghan, Prime Minister; and Roy Jenkins, Home Secretary, Chancellor, President of the European Commission and Renaissance man. I have also been a member of three government advisory commissions: on electoral reform, on care of the elderly and on the BBC. Commissions are an important area of political life on which, so far as I can see, there is virtually no literature. I have been editor of a respected weekly journal, deputy editor of two national newspapers and political editor of *The Economist*. I have observed from various vantage points the ebbs and flows of public life, while also enjoying a varied private life. So, without any great thought of publication, I decided to write down what I could remember.

Soon after I had finished my draft, the marvellous diaries of Chris Mullin started to appear. He was himself a relatively junior MP. They persuaded me of the wisdom of a *Guardian* leader: 'For sheer enjoyment, you need chroniclers who never reach the top table.' I certainly qualified under that head.

So, somewhat nervously, I sent my manuscript to two fellow peers: Kenneth (KO) Morgan, the biographer of Callaghan and Foot, and Peter Hennessy, modern historian *extraordinaire*. Both, bless them, were more than encouraging. Felicitously, Hennessy suggested Biteback as a publisher and Sean Magee as the contact there. Magee is also a biographer, of my equine hero Arkle, and through our mutual interest in the turf we have known each other for years. I did not know it at the time but he is also a brave, decisive and inspiring publisher. And so, here we are.

I wish to thank the various researchers who have over its time contributed so much to ironing out the errors in the manuscript and in my prose: Kate Barker, Rishab Mehan and Steve Rizoli. I did much work on the manuscript and wrote the conclusion when on sabbatical at the Center for European Studies at Harvard University in the spring of 2011. I am very grateful to Trish Craig, the director, and her marvellous colleagues for their help and support; and to Professors James Alt, Jim Cronin and Peter Hall for their help with the last chapter on change in British politics, which draws heavily on an article I wrote for the admirable journal *Political Quarterly*.

This is a not a personal memoir, so the most important people in my life – my wife Margaret, my stepsons Dominic and Barney, our daughter Becky and my step-grandchildren Isaac, Mabel and Owen – do not much feature. Without them, my life would have been much less happy and this book much less likely to have appeared.

CHAPTER 1

AN EDUCATION IN POLITICS
1948–70

I should like to ascribe my lifelong affair with Labour politics to a hard upbringing – bread and dripping, outside loo, tin baths and whippets. Or, failing that, I should like to ascribe it to early exposure to people who were living in poverty, whose plight excited my conviction. Honesty compels, however, that I relate the true story.

I attended Wycliffe Preparatory School, which trained boys for the Methodist public school near my home in Gloucestershire. When the 1959 general election was called, naturally my friends went to the Conservative offices in Stroud to pick up posters for the Tory candidate Sir Anthony Kershaw. So did I.

I was nailing the posters to the fence by the entrance to our garage when my parents came out to see what the noise was. To my surprise they were not pleased by my display of eleven-year-old civic virtue. Indeed, not to put too fine a point on it, they were angry. Though I don't know how they then voted, they clearly did not want to show any public enthusiasm for the Tories.

Presented with this display of precocious innocence, Penny and Lawrence, my parents, set about providing me with a political education. This comprised attending a couple of election meetings. The television barely existed and its coverage of politics was thin. The internet and its offspring were thirty years away. In those days, politics was conducted at public meetings, quite similar to the hustings of Victorian times.

Stroud later became a rather radical place, with a Green council and, until 2010, an excellent Labour MP, David Drew. But then it was Tory heartland territory. Sir Anthony, a grandee, had a comfortable majority.

First, we went to hear Labour at Stonehouse. The candidate was Tom Cox, a young LSE graduate who by coincidence was later to be my MP when we lived in Tooting, London, and who became Father of the House. I cannot remember his speech but I can remember that of his warm-up act. Tony Benn would have been proud, indeed jealous, of the authentic Gloucestershire accent, rising to a crescendo of passion. 'And Sir Anthony Kershaw gallops over the fields with the gentry 'unting to 'ounds while the labourers starve in their 'ovels.' The roots of Labour's ban on hunting have always owed less to a concern not to compromise the welfare of the fox than to a desire to compromise the welfare of the rich.

From there we went to the packed Subscription Rooms in Stroud to hear Sir Anthony. Now, my father had given my brother Robin, aged nine, and me strict instructions as to how we were to behave. 'Listen politely,' he said. 'I don't want to hear any heckling.'

So the meeting began. Sir Anthony warmed smoothly to his themes. Then, as now, it was not long before he got to government waste.

Suddenly I was aware of my father's unmistakeable Canadian accent. 'Blue Streak!' he shouted, 'Blue Streak!' Blue Streak was a missile commissioned by the Conservative government which had singularly failed to work.

Stewards appeared. The Lipsey family was escorted from the hall to disapproving murmurs from the faithful. How after that experience could I not be Labour?

What my father had done defied middle-class norms. But then our family was a strange mixture of bourgeois convention and radicalism.

My father was Canadian and Jewish (though not a practising Jew). He had come to Britain to fight in the war. Canadians were not under any obligation to join up when he did and I would congratulate him on his courage. 'Courage? Courage didn't come into it. I joined to get away from working in Uncle Mac's insurance business in Toronto.' He pooh-poohed the terror of war. He was torpedoed in the Mediterranean – not an experience about which he would speak – and described the terrible battle of Monte Cassino where he came under heavy fire as 'better than firework night'.

His parents were friendly with my maternal grandmother and step-grandfather. It was through them, therefore, my father met my mother while the war was still on. Before long, they announced they would like to get married.

The Jewish half of the family was perfectly all right with this. The Christians were not.

They hadn't much to boast about. My grandmother once confided that when she was first married she had no clue what was happening on her wedding night and her husband a year later absconded to Rhodesia with the nanny. My step-grandfather, after a short period as Uncle Val on BBC radio's *Children's Hour*, never worked again in his life. He was a repressed gay in the days when homosexuality was illegal; after his death, we found his under-graduate love letters carefully preserved in his desk.

Perhaps in consequence, he drank his way through my grand-mother's substantial fortune. But that meant even more emphasis on keeping up appearances. My step-grandfather told my mother that, when my grandmother wheeled her pram down the streets of nearby Minchinhampton, people would cross the road to avoid her.

Christianity redeemed itself somewhat when my mother Penny's parents called in the local vicar to deal with their errant child. He met my father, and proclaimed that he seemed a perfectly decent chap. When the war was over, the marriage proceeded.

My parents were, to outside appearances, a conventional middle-class family. My grandfather was in the flock trade, whereby old clothes were shredded for stuffing. Today I suppose it would be called a recycling business. Lawrence established his own successful business on my grandfather's premises, Rooksmoor Mills.

It could hardly have been simpler. The business took bulk deliveries of kapok, a natural pillow stuffing, put it in bags and then sold them ready packed to Woolworth's. One customer, one product and perhaps a couple of dozen workers filling and sealing, but it provided my father with a decent living. To this day I can remember the factory with the women packing away to the strains of *Workers' Playtime*, BBC Light Programme's offering. They never complained about the boss's relative affluence – leastways, not to me.

Much modern controversy goes on about whether incomes are more or less equal than they used to be. The size of the Gini coefficient, the shape of the distribution curve, the ebbing, then flowing, of the super-rich: these are hotly debated by economists and politicians.

Yet my impression is that the subjective gap in those post-war years was much wider than it is today. My father's business was both modest and simple. He could go to work in the morning, come home for lunch cooked by my mother, return to work for the afternoon and finish for the day by five o'clock. They owned a four-bedroom Cotswold house, effectively half of a mansion, with a large garden and tennis court. They employed a cleaner, Mrs Day, and a part-time gardener, Hill. My father would buy a new car, perhaps a Jaguar or a Daimler, every year or two, though he was nowhere near the chauffeur class. They went on regular continental holidays, put two children through paid education and ate out (in so far as in those days there was anywhere worthwhile to eat out) as often as they chose. They had central heating, the first washing machine in the area, an early television and a dishwasher.

Mrs Day and Hill enjoyed none of those things. Hill lived in a cottage in the grounds of the house owned by the other half, my beloved godmother Frances Smith and her husband. I rarely put my head round the door but it was dark and cold. Mrs Day's house in Minchinhampton was little better. It was clear that there was another half and they did not live as we did.

My parents then enjoyed the trappings of bourgeois life. Much of their company was also bourgeois – the Orchards, the local builders and developers; the Leonard Joneses, prosperous jewellers; the Hayneses, nearby solicitors; the Keens, the vet.

Yet more than politics made my parents different. My father was not English, for a start. Although he had come over to Britain to study at Bristol Grammar School, his Canadian origin made a difference. My mother, an extremely intelligent woman, had been denied the opportunity to go into higher education. Yet, though she slipped into the life of a middle-class wife and mother superficially, she remained quite different from most of their friends.

My parents' friends mocked modern art. 'What is it supposed to be?' they would chortle when faced with a Picasso or a Hepworth. My parents, however, developed a remarkable eye. I write underneath a Peter Lanyon, St Ives School, purchased cheaply by my father in the 1950s. The family still owns two fine Lynn Chadwicks, obtained by my father, believe it or not, in exchange for some rush matting, after he had diversified from kapok into the furniture business. There is an Ivon Hitchens, a Lucy Willis, a Mary Fedden and more, mostly acquired before the artists were well known. The furniture business showroom also became an art gallery from which my father sold the best output of local talent.

My parents liked modern theatre. There was not much live, though we went quite regularly to the Royal Shakespeare at Stratford. But on the TV, *Play for Today* presented modern classics in the days when the BBC took its cultural responsibilities more seriously than it does today.

They went to the opera. My father's ambition was to sit with friends listening to the complete Ring cycle. They later established a local group to invite well-known intellectuals to lecture, the George Street Club. I remember, for example, Christopher Mayhew, a controversial Labour MP, staying with us, and my parents became friends with the Oxford poet John Wain. By Stroud standards then – this was before the town became trendy – this was high-brow stuff.

My parents therefore defy categorisation. Perhaps that is why I have always had difficulty fitting into ready-made categories myself. I spent for example the 1970s and 1980s working to make the Labour Party a moderate and electable party. Then as the Blair and Brown years went by, I wanted it to be less moderate and more radical. We didn't take much for granted by way of ideas in my family, which made it a stimulating place to be. I should have been more successful in politics if my background had been duller and my views therefore more consistently mainstream; but that would not have been a price worth paying.

My parents' radicalism did not extend to sending us to state school, though my brother later rebelled against boarding and attended sixth form at Marling, the local grammar. After Wycliffe, I was sent to Bryanston, a public school in Dorset.

If I was to go private, Bryanston was a wise choice. I suppose I could have gone to one of the posher public schools – the fees were no higher – though not of course to Eton, for which I was not qualified by class. But Bryanston was more appropriate. Established in the 1920s, it had a kind of Bohemian veneer to it, which made it the school of choice for the children of better-off creatives. Indeed Peter Lanyon's own son went there until his father was killed in a tragic glider crash and he had to leave.

Bryanston was a curious mixture. It was, for example, serious about sport as all public schools were. A former Olympic 800-metre runner was chosen to train the athletes, rugby was taken seriously and so too was tennis, of which the headmaster, Robson Fisher, was a fine player. It was compulsory of a Saturday afternoon to go and support the school team at rugby, hockey or cricket.

But what distinguished Bryanston from the rest was that it put at least as much emphasis on non-sporting attainment. Music was of a high standard. The school boasted a fine orchestra, an ex-professional pianist to teach, regular singing contests and so on. Mark Elder, the superstar British conductor, was a contemporary of mine.

Bryanston did not despise intellectuals. Not only the staff but the pupils respected outstanding minds. I was fortunate in having a number of talented teachers in the subjects in which I was most interested – I think of the splendid history teacher Peter Brewin or of Ronald Hird, who taught me economics. My housemaster, John Griffin, alas, taught Latin, at which I was a waste of space, but he too fostered intellectual ambition, as did my tutor, Rev. Dr Ronald Pugh. Thanks to them my raw mind was sharpened and I emerged with a rare crop of 'A' level grade A's and an Exhibition to Magdalen, Oxford. Despite being an intellectual, I also rose to be head boy – not a role in which I shone but a useful practical counterweight to study.

It was at Bryanston that I had my first experience of journalism. The school produced a most worthy publication of the kind traditional to all such schools, the *Bryanston Saga*, but it had little to appeal to pupils. My friend David Tuckett and I determined to start a pupils' newspaper. We called it the *Federalist*, indicating our sympathies in the American civil war though what relation this bore to Bryanston life now escapes me. It appeared on sheets duplicated on an ancient Gestetner, a primitive machine, which restricted its length. Hence its motto was 'Multum in Parvo'.

The school authorities thought long and hard as to whether to allow our paper to exist. The compromise was that we could so long as a member of senior staff, in our case Pugh, acted as censor. Pugh was (from our point of view as editors) an inspired choice. He was an iconoclast of a liberal disposition. He appreciated anything we published which discomforted other members of staff, with whom he was generally at war.

I must even then have had something of the journalist about me, for the paper immediately began to make waves. First, we reported an interview with the professional brought in to raise funds for the school. He frankly described the hierarchy according to which money would be sought: potential big donors first and then so on down the widening pyramid. Neither he nor we realised that those not approached in the first wave might take offence at the implicit slight to their wealth and standing. We were nearly shut down.

Another of our stories hit the national newspapers. It was a minor incident really. A young boy from the school had been ribbed by the Blandford locals. Hearing of this, a group of large and senior boys set off bent on giving the upstarts a bloody nose. A fight resulted in which – at least according to the biased *Federalist* – our boys emerged victorious. The *Daily Express*, fed the story by a local stringer, agreed. 'Bryanston School, motto "Multum in Parvo", its page lead began. It was not to be the last story I wrote that made a national newspaper.

Another story did not make the nationals, luckily since it might have sunk my career. Anthony Crosland, then Labour's Education Secretary, visited the school to talk about his plans for public schools, which he hoped to abolish. I interviewed him for the *Federalist* and asked if his policy extended to prep schools. 'Stinking breeding grounds of sodomy,' I heard the great man reply, and so we reported.

It may indeed have been what he said. Years later, however, I came across a reference in one of his works to the prep schools: 'stinking breeding grounds of snobbery'. I don't to this day know if it was 'sodomy' or 'snobbery' he said and, indeed, as he was slightly pissed at the time, it might not have been altogether clear. However, as I was not carrying a tape-recorder, I should have been in some difficulty had that quote been picked up by the national press.

I fought two mock elections as Labour candidate, coinciding with the national general elections of 1964 and 1966. The experience was encouraging enough for me to get my betting boots on. I invested a penny to win a million pounds with a friend, Chris Moss, that I would one day be Prime Minister. I kept the increasingly dog-eared piece of paper recording the bet in my wallet for some years. Mr Moss, who became a judge, would no doubt have been a little surprised if ever he had had to pay out! By the second of those elections I was old enough – seventeen – to join the real Labour Party, attending in great excitement meetings of the Minchinhampton branch. Oxford, the next stage of my political career, lay ahead.

There was, however, an interlude, and one which did have a real influence in cementing my political faith. I had stayed an extra year at Bryanston, partly because I calculated correctly that that was necessary if I was to make it to head boy. My father agreed to this – and the cost – on one condition only: that I did something in the period before I went up to Oxford that would widen my social experience. So it was that I applied to Community Service Volunteers, an organisation which arranged such things. In the winter of 1967, I arrived at the YMCA hostel in Bradford, Yorkshire, with a remit to assist in teaching English to newly arrived immigrant children.

As a society we have become accustomed to – though not altogether reconciled to – mass immigration. It is thus hard to recall what a shock it could prove to recipients in those early days. Bradford, still a textile town, was reeling from a large-scale influx from the Asian sub-continent: people from various parts of India and Pakistan – good for its businesses, and indeed good for reviving a city in danger of decay through lack of energy, but a tremendous challenge for the authorities.

Today, for a city education authority, the presence of large numbers of ethnic minorities in schools is standard issue. But then Bradford was simply overwhelmed. I was supposed to be help-ing a trained teacher of English as a second language in an inner city school. But needs must: somehow the local authority had to discharge its statutory obligation to educate the newly arrived children. Within weeks I was extracted from my first and sent to another school. I was in sole charge of a classroom full of children of late primary age, who had not a word of English between them.

They were suffering from culture shock – but then so was I. Somehow I was supposed to instil in them some grasp of English. Armed with a second language textbook I did my best but by the last period of the day I was so exhausted that I could do nothing but play football with them. I remember one weekend sleeping from Saturday lunchtime until Sunday afternoon.

School was not the only shock. Sharing a room with two evan-gelical Christians was not my cup of tea and I soon extracted myself from the YMCA. But my basic bedsit, just off Lumb Lane, the immigrant centre of the town and then the epicentre of Yorkshire streetwalkers, was a lonely place to be. I was warned in no uncertain terms not to walk down the lane after dark as I should be set on by gangs of Asians and robbed. By the time of the warning, I had been walking down it at night for many months without incident. Thus do urban myths take root.

I had no friends. The staff at the new school did not take me under their wing. There were a few concerts at St George's Hall and there was football, the only time in my life I have taken any interest, with Bradford boasting two league teams, City and Park Avenue. There was Bradford Northern rugby league. There was jumping at Wetherby and flat racing at Pontefract. There was the pub and fish and chips. With the exception of a sad older man, who lived with his mother and doubtless fancied me, I had practically no company for the whole of my time in Bradford.

I survived and I learned. I learned how the worst-off lived, about poverty of aspiration, about deprivation and about degradation. But I also learned about human resilience. I still remember one boy in my class, Jasvinder Singh. His parents had aspirations and had managed to acquire a pub in the town. They were so grateful for my efforts with their boy that one night they plied me with beer to the extent that I barely staggered home for dawn. Jasvinder, whatever his handicaps of class and race, had application and a good mind. Sadly I never found out what happened to him, but I bet he made it.

The same, however, could not be said of one of his class mates, Ali. I now recognise that he was a boy with learning difficulties. Then, however, I did not know what that meant. He learned no English. He went through classes patiently and affectionately but rarely comprehending. He was, I suspect, bullied. I do not know what happened to him either.

I had gone to Bradford already a Labour supporter. I left Bradford as a Socialist.

Young people about to go to university are often in an agony of indecision. Where should they go? What should they read? How should they live?

In 1967, I too faced a difficult decision. Which Oxford Labour club should I join?

There were two: the Labour Club and the Democratic Labour Club. I took advice from my Gloucestershire friend, John Rodgers, already at Oxford. 'Of course you will want to join the Democratic Labour Club. It's not as left wing.'

I stumbled over this argument. I thought I was pretty left wing. I was against racism and I wanted Ho Chi Minh to win in Vietnam. I wasn't opposed to a bit of nationalisation and was still filled with fury at the thought of the gentry following hounds.

I had not understood what the terms 'left' and 'right' meant in an Oxford context. In particular, I had not understood what they meant in the run-up to *les événements* of 1968 and the sporadic rioting by students that took place across the world.

The Labour Club was the home of the students who were appearing all over the newspapers. They were Marxists. It is true that they were libertarian Marxists, forever explaining where the Soviet Union had gone wrong under Stalin and what a blissful place it could have been if Trotsky had dodged the ice pick. But theirs was the pure language of class war. They did not seem to be much troubled by the fact that they themselves were invariably of prosperous middle-class backgrounds. For class was of course a matter of your relationship to the forces of production and, as they didn't own sweatshops, their class interest was that of the workers. How wonderful it is what a first-class Oxford mind can persuade itself of!

I was never that kind of left wing though, and it turned out that the Democratic Labour Club, which was officially affiliated to the Labour Party, was the only choice for me.

For one thing, I thought that a Labour government, even one in the wretched state of Harold Wilson's government in 1968-9, was better than a Tory government. Indeed, I and my colleagues even worked for it. Buses were despatched to by-elections – I remember Wellingborough in 1969 where Peter Fry took a marginal Labour seat on a 9.7 per cent swing. In my mind, it is always raining in Wellingborough.

Meanwhile, we were closely involved in Oxford politics, where the Labour Club president (and later Labour Lord), Bill McCarthy, was the leading light. Bill taught industrial relations at Ruskin, the college set up to take working people who had left school without an education and turn them into graduates. More important, he was the research director for the Donovan Royal Commission on Industrial Relations, which endorsed the British approach of minimum legal regulation of trade unions. He himself was born without a gilded spoon in his mouth. He was completely devoted not just to the Labour Party but to Labour in all its forms, unions, co-ops – the components which made up what speaker after speaker at the Labour Party conference would describe as 'this great movement of ours'.

His wife Margaret was an Oxford councillor. Bill and Margaret became lifelong friends. She was a great party organiser. From her committee rooms, I learned the art of filling up Reading (or Mikardo) sheets, the duplicated sheets where you marked your supporters and then on polling day went out on the streets to persuade them to go to vote.

Grassroots activity was quite different then than it is today. For one thing, party workers were instructed never to talk to the voters. It took up time and you never convinced anyone. Your job was to identify those who would definitely vote Labour if they voted at all, and do everything you could to get them to the polls.

The idea that you would ring someone up to ask for their vote would have seemed wholly implausible. For one thing, a great many of our supporters did not have phones. For another, party loyalties were firm if not entrenched. You would go up to the door of a council house in, say, Blackbird Leys, and ask if they were planning to vote Labour. If the woman came to the door, the normal response was 'I'll ask my husband'. If the man, you'd get a 'we're all Labour here' or perhaps a 'you're all right, son'; even the occasional 'sorry, mate'. You marked your Mikardo cards and moved on. In more middle-class areas, you usually did not bother to canvass. Labour voters were too rare.

My experience in Bradford made me wonder if this really did constitute sufficient political activity to ensure the long-run vitality of our party. I therefore organised members of the Democratic

Labour Club to do a certain amount of what today might be called community work. We would give tuition to deprived immigrant children, even organise expeditions for them. Such activities would have been scorned by members of the more leftist Labour Club. They had more important work to do to 'heighten the contradictions' of capitalism, end the Vietnam war, expropriate the banks, and generally to advance the interests of socialism and the working class – incidentally advancing their own careers in the process.

Even if I had not had profound ideological differences with these people, I should have found this *insouciance* towards improving conditions in the real world difficult. Revolutionary ideology was all very well, but it did not suit my practical bent.

This was perhaps best illustrated by the visit to Oxford of Enoch Powell in 1969. Enoch Powell had been a Tory junior Treasury minister who resigned because the government refused to cut spending enough. He was famous at this time for a series of speeches pointing out the perils of immigration. 'Like the Roman, I seem to see the River Tiber foaming with much blood,' as he put it.

Curiously, despite his addiction to impenetrable classicisms, he built up a strong following among the British working class, the London dockers in particular. They were not keen on increased competition in the jobs market. They didn't like the priority given to immigrants for housing, often ahead of indigenous families, and they felt that they had a culture which they valued and which was under threat. Many of course were also straight racists.

The Oxford left was united in wanting to stop Powell coming; and if he came, to stop him speaking. Its forces, democratic and otherwise, were assembled to plan the demonstration to stop him.

Christopher Hitchens, later a contrarian controversialist who sadly died in 2011, was then the leading light of the far left. He was no mean orator as well as no mean writer, and he launched into a Marxist analysis of the significance of the Powell visit and of the demonstration.

As I joined the meeting, I had noticed that four prominent members of the Oxford Conservative Association were sitting in the back row. They included my friend Stephen Milligan, who died in 1992 in tragic circumstances soon after being elected an MP. The Tories had notebooks in their hands.

Hitchens eventually ended his revolutionary exegesis and turned to the job in hand. 'Now, comrades, let us turn to our plans to defeat Powell and his capitalist lackeys.'

'Chris,' I said, 'before we discuss our tactics, ought we not to ask those Tories to leave?'

Hitchens turned to me with the full force of his later legendary scorn. 'Comrade Lipsey,' he said, 'do not be so theoretical.'

When the demonstration took place, the far-left Labour Club carefully arranged its supporters at the back. It was the moderates, the Democratic Labour supporters, the Liberals and the even softer left who found themselves at the front, facing the fairly fierce policemen.

I of course acquit the far left of any lack of courage. By putting the soft left up front, they were allowing them to witness at first hand the heightened contradictions between the liberal society to which they belonged and the forces of law and order. That the 'loony' lefties avoided all risk of arrest or injury was entirely justified in the revolutionary cause.

It would be unfair to suggest that we Democratic Labourites were as pure as the driven snow. While the far left pursued their future by strutting their stuff in the national newspapers, we pursued ours in endless battles for election to high office in the Democratic Labour Club.

These were positions voted on by members of the club. However, this being Oxford, this was not as simple a proposition as it sounds. All political clubs were open, not only to supporters but also to members of other parties and none. In principle, this was because you could get to hear eminent speakers even though you disagreed with them, and therefore round out your political education.

That, however, was not the main reason why membership was large. Every member had a vote so it was quite common for supporters of one party to enrol members of another party in order that they might be available to vote for them for party office. Indeed, it is said that on occasion someone would actually pay for a supporter of another party to join the club.

In retrospect, I simply cannot believe how much of my time and effort I devoted to becoming chair of the Club. I made the huge mistake of standing in my first year. My rival was John Spellar, later an official of the electrical trades union and a Labour junior minister. Spellar was one of those rare cases of a man whose accent moved towards the common through life, and his Oxford education was largely airbrushed out of his CV. He had a good sense of humour and we were later friendly. But not during that election: Spellar, who had the organisational instincts that equipped him for his union, mercilessly crushed me.

A second failure followed, at the hands of another man who became a trade union official later in life, Giles Duncan. This hurt even more. I had the election, so I thought, in the bag. Though theoretically the vote was by individual ballot, in practice the most active member in each college decided whom it would support and voters went along with the verdict in a form of Labour democratic centralism. I had two big colleges on board, St John's and University, as well as my own college, Magdalen, which had an unprecedentedly large number of members.

Perhaps I got complacent. I do not know to this day what offer of advancement my rival made, but first my supporter organising University College ratted, then my supporter organising St John's. I simply did not have the votes.

Had I had any sense, I should have thrown in the towel. Instead, however, I decided on a desperate ploy. Against the conventions, I decided to visit each individual member of the club and try to persuade them to vote against their college organiser.

This was no small task. Remember, there were no telephones so there was nothing for it but to walk from room to room. When you got there, however, the other person might be in the library or with their girlfriends, and the visit would be in vain. Then of course, if they were in, not all of them were entirely thrilled to be greeted in their fastness by a bespectacled wimp canvassing their vote.

One took a terrible revenge. He was a surviving member of Moral Rearmament, an evangelical Christian movement started by Frank Buchman in 1938, particularly strong at Oxford. Though long since displaced by other unworldly institutions, such as the Labour Club, it retained a core of adherents. This particular one bugged me for months. Having initiated the contact, I could hardly just tell him to go away.

If my day time was filled canvassing, my night time was filled counting. I went through the names and colleges in my head, endlessly, repetitively, thinking here, thinking there, how a winning total might be assembled.

My campaign was surprisingly successful – but not successful enough. Duncan held on by four votes. If there was a reward, it was seeing his face practically grey when he realised at the count that his comfortable victory was proving anything but.

I did succeed at the third time of asking – curiously enough only just holding off a rival who adopted my college-to-college canvassing technique. The cost, however, to a rounded undergraduate life should not be underestimated. I never worked out how to hire a punt.

I don't think I resent it. For one thing, the chair was (for an undergraduate) a prestigious position. It commended occupants for future advance in the Labour movement. For another, we had many prominent visiting speakers. I can remember one night when Shirley Williams stayed too long at a meeting and missed the last train back to London. I drove her back in my little Fiat 500 (hidden, since undergraduates were forbidden cars, in the courtyard of a nearby pub). I went to bed in her flat at around two in the morning, leaving her still working through her boxes.

It was through Shirley that one of the more singular events of my undergraduate days was organised. Shirley was junior minister to Jim Callaghan, Labour's avuncular and traditionalist Home

Secretary. He was persuaded, goodness knows how, that he was not properly in touch with a new generation and its views. Shirley therefore was asked to assemble a group of political young people of my sort of age to meet with the great man. I cannot remember the full attendance list, though I do remember the presence of Jack Straw, then president of the National Union of Students, and invariably described in the national press as a 'firebrand'. We met over dinner – for which Callaghan paid – in the Bridge Tavern, opposite Westminster.

Callaghan had recently passed the Commonwealth Immigration Act 1968, a reaction to Kenya's expulsion of Asians, all of whom had the right under the law as it stood to emigrate to England. At a time when Powellism was rife, this was causing some unrest and considerable unpopularity for the government of the time.

We young people didn't give a fig for that. What the government was doing was morally wrong, so one by one we laid into Callaghan, in language which doubtless fell short of the respect one of his generation would expect for his office.

Eventually, he could stand it no longer. 'Well,' he said. 'I've listened to you all and let me tell you one thing. I am not having the number of black people coming into this country go up before the general election.'

Callaghan did not have a racist bone in his body, but he – unlike us at that stage – understood the society in which we all lived. We spilled into the night, sadder but wiser.

Only one thing competed with politics for my time at Oxford, and that was work. Magdalen had been a largely accidental choice of college, since my school tutor had thought it rather good when he was reading Theology at the university. But it was a great college for Politics, Philosophy and Economics, my subject.

The president of Magdalen was an economist of international repute, Keith Griffin, who was both a clear exponent and an enthusiast. Ken Tite, the senior politics fellow, was a superb tutor, making laconic comments on your essays through clouds of pipe smoke. Throughout his career people awaited the great book he undoubtedly had inside him, but they waited in vain.

Indeed, all my tutors were good. Bill Johnson, another politics tutor, was not only a clever left-leaning academic, but one who had contacts in the world outside Oxford. And he was not the only one. One fellow had combined teaching at Oxford with advising Ted Heath, the Tory leader. Oxford thought his tutorial work was more important.

Much speculation goes into why Oxford graduates do so well through life. Is it because Oxford chooses the brightest? Do they learn miraculous power of thought? Or is it all a matter of social networks? It is worth recalling that when I applied to be editor of *The Economist* in 1993, seven of the eight candidates had been to Magdalen, largely due to Johnson's unmatched talent for getting his more gifted pupils into journalism in general and *The Economist* in particular.

However, one aspect of an Oxford education may be relevant: if you take being a student seriously, it works you seriously hard. For PPE, I had to research and complete two essays of maybe 2,000 words each a week. I only ever dared threaten to be late with one, and then the reaction of my tutor when I told him made me work through the night to complete it. The result is that you get accustomed to concentrated effort, to doing exactly what you needed to do to get through, to avoiding all distractions, intellectual or other, and, most useful of all, to hitting deadlines. I have worked quite hard in my life on and off but never, I think, as hard as during my three Oxford years.

My mind was a typical Oxford mind, strictly logical and reductionist. I did pretty well. I jointly won the University Gibbs Prize in Politics at the end of my second year. This was a proud achievement for two reasons. I took the exam when just off the plane from America with jet lag. The plane had got back too late for me to sit for the economics prize, where I more strongly fancied my chances. And my co-winner was Frank Wright, a leading member of the far left and later a distinguished academic who died too young. Frank apparently thought he was sure of victory, and was relying on the prize to pay his bills. So it was a sweet political victory to deny him. From then on, it was pretty apparent I would get a first, though to this day I wake occasionally in the night dreaming I didn't. And with that would have gone a potentially wide choice of careers.

CHAPTER 2

UNION MAN 1970–72

After Oxford, I applied for just three jobs: at the Government Economic Service, at the TUC economic department and at the General and Municipal Workers' Union Research Department. However, enquiring of the GES whether there would be any inhibitions on my political activities if I joined the civil service – knowing (at least subconsciously) that the answer was yes – is an indication of what was to come. That application did not progress.

I must have been arrogant, for it didn't really enter my head that I might not succeed with either of the others. The TUC was a straightforward process where I was interviewed for a job in the economic department by the great Len Murray, a future general secretary and later a lovely colleague in the Lords.

The TUC was not yet at the height of its pomp, achieved in the early days of the 1974–79 Labour government. It then became an equal party with the government under the Social Contract, negotiating practically every aspect of public policy with the government and its Employment Secretary, Michael Foot. It was a give-and-take relationship. The government gave and the unions took.

In 1970, however, the TUC's position was more ambiguous. At first it was in direct confrontation with the Heath government over the Industrial Relations Act, a fated attempt to bring the law into play to cut union power. Then, as Heath U-turned to seek union help against inflation, it faced a difficult dilemma. Power was on offer but it in return required responsibility.

This was a dilemma that British trade unions found almost impossible to deal with. A transformationist wing wanted no truck with a capitalist government. An ameliorative wing was prepared to do business with anyone in the interests of its members. The TUC tried to balance the two. Jimmy Maxton, a prominent left-wing

MP, once said that if you weren't able to ride two horses at once, you shouldn't be in the circus. But this trick becomes more demanding when the horses are galloping in opposite directions.

Heath had put the TUC and its divided General Council into an agonising position. The General Council was animated by the old Labour movement slogan: 'Unity is Strength.' The trouble was that unity could only be achieved on the basis of consensus; and as there was no underlying consensus, the TUC's capacity to advance was limited.

The organisation put on a good show to disguise its failings of substance. Its headquarters, on Great Russell Street with a fine Jacob Epstein statue, made an instantly recognisable backdrop for television interviewers. There was indeed a whole class of journalists, the industrial correspondents, whose sole job was to cover trade union matters and who thus spent a great part of their lives at Congress House. The reality of TUC power, however, fell some way short of the promise – though it was still a long way ahead of the impotent organisation the TUC was later to become.

It was not, I think, any perception of the TUC's weakness that led me to refuse their offer. Rather, the General and Municipal Workers' Union (GMWU) came up with a better one. Whereas the lights at Congress House stayed on far into the night, the hours at the GMWU were 9.30 am to 4.30 pm. At £1,274 a year, the salary offered was £74 higher.

The union was based at a folly called Ruxley Towers in Claygate, Surrey, where the officers were the only Labour voters within miles. There was a pitch-and-putt golf course in the grounds. 'Nothing too good', as we used to say, 'for the representatives of the working class.'

However, the same did not apply to their genuinely working-class shop stewards. The splendour of Ruxley Towers was exploited by the creation, alongside the union's office, of a little country club for local residents. One day, shop stewards on a training course made use of the bar facilities and, things having turned a little exuberant, complaints were made to the union. There shortly followed an edict, banning rank-and-file union members from the bar.

The Research Department was the pride and joy of the union's general secretary, Jack Cooper. He believed sincerely that trade unions and their members should have the best brains at their disposal. A GMWU pay claim would be splendidly articulated, with the right conclusions drawn from a meticulous analysis of price and earnings data, of company profitability, of wages movements in comparable industries and so on.

Nothing more appropriately summed up Cooper's philosophy than his choice to head the department. Giles Radice was a Winchester and Oxford graduate, at the time conspicuous for his plum accent and worn cuffs, who defeated all efforts by his elegant and devoted wife Lisanne to tidy him up. Perhaps precisely because he was not from the same class, Radice was a trusted adviser to Cooper and his senior officers, and a figure of some weight in the Labour movement.

I nearly failed to get the GMWU job. At the time of my interview the union had just gone through a trauma. It represented the workforce at Pilkington's, a glass-making firm based at St Helens, Lancashire. Relations between the union and the company were, to say the least, cosy. There was no evidence that the union had done badly by its members but it certainly had not communicated with them. When a large-scale unofficial strike broke out, spearheaded by the GMWU's own shop stewards, the union regionally and nationally struggled to cope.

However, when Radice asked me to offer my thoughts on the matter, I had a problem. I had in fact been out of the country for the period of the unofficial strikes, or at least that is my excuse. At any rate, Pilkington, and the crisis of modern trade unionism, had escaped my attention.

The passage of time has brought a merciful curtain down on how I coped. Somehow, the subject turned to areas in which I was more proficient – economic policy for example – and I survived. Helped by a favourable reference from Bill McCarthy, for which I shall always be grateful, the job offer came through.

Jack Cooper's office was only a few yards from ours and among my tasks was to brief him for meetings of the TUC economic committee. It says something of the awesome power at the time of the general secretary of the third-largest trade union that I did not seem to have been introduced to him, still less to have discussed policy with him, when I took on this task.

I looked forward keenly to the annual staff outing, Dover to Boulogne, where we minions travelled with the great man and his acolytes. Some beers into the trip I found myself one-on-one with Cooper. My idealistic young ears looked forward to his reflections on politics, the unions and the sunny uplands ahead. Instead, Cooper proceeded to talk to me for thirty minutes about his investment policy for the union's money and the very satisfactory outcome. It is easy to mock, but Cooper's stash lasted the union for many years until finally his less financially astute successors managed to reduce it to near-penury.

The Research Department attracted able young people, some but not all bent on a political career. My successor when I left was the brilliant Rupert Pennant-Rea, later editor of *The Economist* and deputy governor of the Bank of England. I have not checked lately to see if he retains a Labour membership card! Other researchers included Dianne Hayter, later general secretary of the Fabian Society and now a fellow Labour peer. Radice, also now a peer, was succeeded by Larry Whitty, later general secretary of the Labour Party and then a government minister in the Lords. So, four former members of the Research Department are now members of the House of Lords. I think Jack Cooper would have been proud of that.

Thanks to Radice's inclusive leadership, morale in the Research Department was high. Nevertheless, certain tensions were apparent. A group of middle-class intellectuals had chosen to work for what was still then essentially a working-class institution.

We continually played a game among ourselves called 'Keeper of the Cloth Cap'. This consisted of finding plausible ways of linking ourselves with the working class. Xx's father had been an electrician, Yy's a boilermaker and Zz's grandfather had been down the pits. This was not a competition in which I did well. The fact that my maternal great-great-grandfather had not been able to sign his name impressed me more than the rest of the team. The unchallenged champion for many months was one David Williamson, a large Scot with a sharp mind and an enviable hit-rate with girls. He and I were best mates. I could nearly match him at snooker and beat him round the pitch-and-putt, but I had no chance in Keeper of the Cloth Cap. For David Williamson's father was, as he told us, a policeman.

We were thus in awe of him, until one day, he arrived in the office wearing, believe it or not, full morning dress.

'What's this then, Scotsman?' we asked.

'Going to the Palace,' he murmured almost inaudibly.

'Why are you going to the Palace, David?'

'With me dad.'

'Oh yes, David, and why is your dad going to the Palace?'

'Ta … ta … ta pick up his honour.'

His father would doubtless have appreciated our interrogative technique. He was indeed going to the Palace to pick up the gong he had earned as Chief Constable of Renfrewshire. Somehow, Keeper of the Cloth Cap was a game that thereafter became less popular with David Williamson.

Not all the union's officers were as keen on the Research Department as Cooper. Some were less than impressed by our cloth-cap credentials. They thought it was airy-fairy stuff. Pay negotiations depended entirely on industrial muscle, the threat to strike and its power, not logic. Sir Fred Hayday, the heavyweight official in charge of the gas industry for whom I nominally worked, made little call on my services.

However, two officials took me, wet behind the ears though I was, on board. One was Derek Gladwin. Gladwin was then a vigorous man of forty, who had an important section of the union as his remit. Local government workers, the 'municipal' in 'General and Municipal', were the largest tranche of members. Ours were of course essentially the blue-collar workers as they were then called, in contrast to the white-collar workers organised by the National Association of Local Government Officers (NALGO). Our members featured a disproportionately large number of low-paid workers. However, their industrial muscle was somewhat limited. A few bags of rubbish uncollected were not going to do much to fatten the wage packets. Moreover, they were not experienced trade unionists; unlike, say, the miners, with a long tradition of solidarity in industrial action, they had never had a major strike.

At the time I joined the GMWU, unrest among the local government workers was widespread. Inflation was starting to increase, the government favoured private sector over public sector employees and pay negotiations were tough. It perhaps did not help that they took place in an entirely national framework, conducted for the employers by LACSAB, the Local Authority Conditions of Service Advisory Board; nor that the negotiations took place in the full spotlight of national publicity.

There was also the complication, common enough in those days, that they involved more than one union. As well as the GMWU, NUPE (the National Union of Public Employees) and the T&G ('Transport and General Workers' Union) were also heavily represented. No individual union dared let it be seen that it was less militant over pay than the other unions. If it did, its members might defect.

When I joined the GMWU in late summer 1970, industrial action (as strikes were euphemistically called) was getting under way in local government. However, this was not industrial action as it is generally thought of. The council workers were not miners or dockers or steelworkers. They were not attuned to the notion of trade union discipline.

It happened like this: a group of workers in a given area would suddenly decide to go on strike. Very often, they would soon decide they did not much like this. Union strike pay was not as high as the working wage and they would decide to stop the strike. Meanwhile, however, another group would walk out and so the process went on.

This made the dispute difficult to run from a national point of view. In particular, it was difficult to persuade the press that this was a determined group of workers out to assert their God-given right to a decent wage, before whom resistance was futile.

I gained Derek Gladwin's faith by a bumper ruse. I acquired a large map of Britain and a few sets of coloured drawing pins. We proceeded as follows. From time to time a phone call would come through telling us that a certain group of workers had walked out. We would then put out a press release saying we had called that group out as part of our programme of rolling strikes and I would insert a red pin into the appropriate place on the map. Then, from time to time, another phone call would come telling that a certain group of workers had returned to work. I would withdraw the red pin, substitute a blue pin with the rubric 'ordered back' and put out a press release accordingly. Those few industrial correspond-ents who made the journey to Ruxley Towers – it meant a couple of hours away from the favoured watering holes in Fleet Street – would be permitted to inspect the map, get a drink in the bar and return to Waterloo mightily impressed.

The dispute eventually ended, as disputes in those days invari-ably ended, in a draw. Derek Gladwin's status had gone up as a result and, in 1972, he contested the union's general secretaryship against the towering figure of David Basnett, who was to trade unionism what Joe Bugner was to boxing. He was brilliant at strik-ing poses but the punches never came. The general secretary of the GMWU's large Scottish region, Alex Donnet, ran too. Gladwin came a respectable third, and then decamped to run the union's Southern region. I am biased, but had the contest come a little later, and had Gladwin then won it, the trade union movement might have avoided some of the calamities that later engulfed it.

Gladwin was succeeded as national officer for local government by Alex Donnet's brother, Charlie. He and the officer for electricity,

Jack Biggin, for whom I also worked, represented a different school of trade unionism, and one for which I often shed a tear. These were not militant men nor were they in any sense ideological. You would have taken Biggin, with his West Country burr, to be, say, an agricultural salesman. Yet they had imbibed trade unionism at its best with their mothers' milk.

They had a strong sense of injustice. They were no longer working class but they related to the working class. They saw their job as a vocation. No effort was too much to solve the problem of a single member. They played by the rules – literally: the style of the time was one which involved immensely detailed national agreements between employers and trade unions, setting out pay, principles and procedures for the resolution of difficulties. They were not in truth very political, though Donnet played his full part in the Labour Party.

Ask either of them which was more important to working people and their families, the Labour Party or the union, and they would have unhesitatingly plumped for the latter. This was not mere affectation. As we wags had it, those who failed to become general secretary of their union would want to be members of its ruling executive committee. Those who failed to get on the executive wanted to be members of the TUC General Council and its committees. Those who failed to get onto the TUC would try for the Labour Party national executive. The left-overs, the dregs, would be found Labour parliamentary seats to console them.

Sadly, the development of trade unionism did not go well for either man. They were disgusted by the left-wing militancy of the rising generation of trade unionists, shop stewards and officers. They became worn down, and eventually disillusioned, by the demands of the membership. Donnet in particular found himself in an alien habitat and yearned for his native Scotland. Neither survived long into retirement.

It was with Biggin that I was able to observe national trade union negotiations most closely. They were conducted on Mondays at Millbank Tower, later the headquarters of the Labour Party but at that time a prestigious office building housing the Central

Electricity Generating Board and its related companies. Electricity was then of course a nationalised industry, and it was perhaps significant that its headquarters was a few hundred yards from Whitehall and Westminster.

Workers in the electricity industry had potentially enormous strength, even beyond that of the miners. They could halt the nation with the throwing of a switch. For that reason, the far left concentrated its efforts on trying to infiltrate the electricity unions and urge them to industrial action – which, by their effects alone, could prove revolutionary.

However, there was a difficulty. This was not an industry whose bosses were bent on grinding the workers into the ground so as to feather their own nests. The managers were better rewarded than their workers, but they were no plutocrats. Rather they were technocrats, trying their best to produce power reliably at the least cost. They had their faults of course, a certain *insouciance* towards their private customers being among them. There was also a good deal of overmanning on the distribution side, overmanning which it finally took privatisation to deal with. What they could not be painted as was the class enemy.

This dilemma was mirrored in the make-up of the trade union side of the national council which determined terms and conditions. The trade union side was led by the largest union, the Electrical Trades Union (ETU), later EEPTU after amalgamating with the plumbers. Their lead negotiator was their general secretary, Frank Chapple, veteran of the moderate struggle to break the communist hold over the ETU. He was a militant anti-communist and a democrat. However, the long struggle had left a deep impression. Chapple's negotiating style was one any good communist would envy. He would inveigh against the employers and their evils, picking his arguments here, there and everywhere with scant regard to logic.

Biggin hated this. He was brought up to a gentler way of doing business in which courtesy and respect were important. But he hated the other side of the council, the Amalgamated Union of Engineering Workers (AUEW) and the T&G more.

The T&G was represented by a real-life communist, John Foster. In my experience, it has to be said, members of the Communist Party are not always the ogres that they are represented as being. It would be hard to get the children to shiver at the thought of John Foster. Bob Wright of the Engineers was a different matter. He was not a member of the Communist Party, but that might well have been because he was so far to the left of them. Wright was an iron-hard northerner, without a trace of humour. He spoke in a habitual sneer but was bright, and he could see the holes in his enemies' case – the chief enemy, of course, being not the employers but Chapple.

This was a singular cast list for negotiations that took a singular form. The trade union side would assemble at around 10.00 am for an initial inconclusive chin-wagging. Once or twice during the morning, Chapple would pop out for an informal word with the employers' leader. There might even be a brief meeting between the two sides.

Then it would be time for lunch. And what a lunch! There were drinks before, and white burgundy and claret. There was smoked salmon and beef and puddings. The sweet wine preceded the port and the brandy – with, in those days, a box of cigarettes and a box of cigars. Around 3.00 pm, we would break up, not to put it mildly, pissed.

I cannot give so clear an account of what then transpired. There was dozing. There were corridor chats. There were more corridor chats and then reports of the corridor chats. There was tea and cakes. Wright denounced the latest offer and then denounced Chapple for discussing it. There were more drinks. We might pop out from time to time to observe the handful of left-wing electricity workers demonstrating outside.

Late afternoon there might be a briefing for the industrial correspondents, who would be told that negotiations were difficult and the nation might soon be blacked out. At perhaps 10.00 pm, the coast would be reckoned clear. Chapple would then tell the union side where he had got to with Roberts. Wright would denounce him again. However, the two bigger unions were on one side and the two smaller on the other, so the deal was always safe. That, for another year, was that. Except one year, when Eric Hammond, later himself to become general secretary, tore up the rule book and voted against Chapple. He was exiled from the union's counsels for several years. Chapple, himself a communist in his youth, had learned a thing or two about discipline.

Two postscripts. The first is that, by the time we were done, the industrial correspondents had long since melted into the night. There was, however, invariably one exception. Donald Macintyre was still there, still looking for a story. And this was the more remarkable since anything that transpired at that hour would be far too late to appear when the paper was published. Donald was to become a good friend and colleague, most notably on the *Sunday Correspondent*. I have always appreciated people who go the extra mile.

The second relates to the year the process didn't work. Quite simply, the unions wanted more than the industry was prepared to give; and compromise did not emerge.

There was a good deal of messing around with industrial action, though no national strike. In the end a committee of inquiry was set up, chaired by Richard Wilberforce, a senior judge and peer. The sittings took place in the somewhat incongruous setting of Church House, in rooms generally occupied by Anglican bishops. The union representative on the inquiry was Derek Robinson, an economist with an interest in labour markets who had taught me at Oxford and whom I had suggested.

This is all worth recalling since such ways of settling industrial disputes have gone out of fashion. Undoubtedly it worked. The committee patiently listened to the arguments on both sides. Frank Chapple put up a *tour de force*, a detailed analysis of the financial position of the electricity supply industry and the various ways in which it had wasted money, lacking only one ingredient – any relevance to the issues under consideration. I prepared more conventional evidence on behalf of my union and worked closely with Hammond to create a case that would bear scrutiny. In the end we got something but not everything.

As a postscript to a postscript, I was back in the office when the telephone rang. It was Barbara Castle, then Labour's employment spokesperson, and she was in a panic. 'I've just read the report,' she said, 'and I can't make head nor tail of it. There's a statement in the House this afternoon. What am I to say?'

I took her through the deal, and she rang off profoundly grateful. That afternoon, in the House, she proclaimed the unions' victory. The only trouble was that she had totally misunderstood everything I had told her. Fortunately, in the roseate glow of peace, no one noticed.

The decline of the unions is one of the most striking changes in the British society of my adult years. Membership, which peaked at 13.2 million in 1979, was down to 7.1 million in 2009. If industrial militancy is a measure of power, it too is down – on average, sixteen million days were lost to industrial action between 1970 and 1972 when I was at the GMWU, but only 750,000 on average between 2007and 2009. The unions have been forced into a series of mergers – not those often urged by their supporters to increase their industrial success but in a desperate attempt to keep their heads financially above water.

Less remarked is a change in its nature. Trade unionism was traditionally a blue-collar activity, with the unions representing skilled working people – 'the aristocracy of labour' pre-eminent. At the time I worked in the movement the growth of white-collar trade unionism was remarked on with the rise of the Association of Scientific, Technical and Managerial Staff (ASTMS), led in its pomp by the wily Welshman Clive Jenkins. Even ASTMS, though, concentrated its efforts on the place where the old working class and the middle class overlapped with a strong membership in a job that is now scarce remembered: the draftsmen. As power looms did for hand weavers, computers did for the draftsmen.

Today, trade unionism is concentrated in two places. One is former nationalised industries where the new owners have not (or not yet) disposed of the centralised industrial relations regime of the past. And so Bob Crow of the railwaymen and the leaders of the British Airways cabin crew remain (to the frequent inconvenience of the firms' customers) powers in the land.

The second is in the public sector. Teachers remain heavily unionised, as do town hall staff. So do civil servants, particularly the more routine kind. As we enter a decade which is going to be dominated by public expenditure cuts we are already seeing bursts of defensive militancy especially from the public service unions – over pensions, over pay, over job losses and over 'efficiency savings'.

What we shall not again see is powerful unions in private companies using the strength of collective negotiation to force up wages. Unionisation rates are too low. Management has become more sophisticated in its communications with the workforce, while at the same time much more prepared to adopt openly anti-union stances. Moreover there has been a problem with trade union communications.

The old shop stewards, the workplace representatives of the unions, were adapted to the culture of their time. They were skilled at exploiting grievances. They also managed a sort-of radical conservatism peculiarly in tune with the temper of their members. The system was fundamentally rotten, they argued, so tinkering could achieve nothing. It followed (for them) that all change in the organisation had to be resisted. The shop stewards, therefore, as represented by the Peter Sellers character in the 1959 comedy movie *I'm All Right Jack* may have been loathsome, but it was an effective kind of loathsomeness. Today's workplace representatives – though thanks to their unions better trained for the job – lack that strong sense of who and why they are.

The appeal today is less on the button. Most workers just want to get on with their jobs and take home their pay. They do not share a set of ideological precepts with their representatives. They have learned, through hard experience, that too much militancy leads not to fatter pay packets but to company bankruptcy and the loss of their jobs. In these circumstances, private sector trade unionism struggles to gain a purchase.

It is not only Tories who rejoice in the decline of trade unionism. Social democrats too, who once were linked arm in arm with the unions, also approve of what has happened. Strong trade unionism proved incompatible with the social democratic ideal of non-inflationary growth in a regulated market economy. Militant trade unionism pushed up wages, and with wages, prices, and with prices, instability in the financial system. It made countries in which it was rife uncompetitive and prone to repeated devaluations of the currency. It could lead to political instability – even, at the extreme, political collapse and the rise of fascism.

I share this perspective. Yet, and call me an old sentimentalist if you will, there is much in the disappeared trade unionism which I – and I think the mass of our people – miss.

My father-in-law, George Fazakerley, was a local union branch secretary in the Electricians' Union, and a stalwart of the struggle to win it back from communist control. But most of his life was not lived fighting battles on such a stage.

Margaret, my wife, recalls members cycling to their home after work. He (and the members) had no phone so they could not be sure if he would be in. They were seeking advice, not on grand pay claims or strikes, but on the niggles of day-to-day shop floor existence, the bullying foreman, the few bob docked, the sick member.

Sometimes he could offer practical support. The unions after all began as funeral societies which enabled members to save for a decent burial. Sometimes, he could offer advice as to how things might be resolved. But even if nothing could be done, he represented a symbol of solidarity, of mankind's common rights and desires and the responsibility of his fellow man to work together to obtain them. When the Tories lecture us today about the evils of the unions, I like to think of George.

The years between 1970 and 1974, the period of this chapter and the next, was the only time in my life when I could lay any serious claim to be an active rank-and-file member of the Labour Party.

Streatham Hill, part of the Streatham constituency, was where I set up home. My first wife Liz was a Gloucestershire girl with whom I had been an item throughout my university years. It was pure chance that we ended up there, after answering an ad for an unfurnished flat to rent in the *Evening Standard*.

Nowadays, Streatham is a safe-ish Labour seat. This is partly the result of redrawing the boundaries but more as a result of social change. In 1945, when Churchill's nephew Duncan Sandys won the seat, it was literally the safest Tory seat in the country. It was the epitome of middle-class London, and, besides, had a substantial conservative Jewish population. By the time we arrived, however, the Tory majority of Bill Sheldon was eroding. Indeed, I can remember projecting that the seat would turn Labour before the turn of the century, as indeed it did.

The Lambeth Labour parties were generally left-wing bordering on barking. Lambeth Norwood, next door, was a nest of Trots kept on board only by a sensibly flexible MP, John Fraser. But Streatham was an exception, as most of its members were politically sane.

The words 'moderate' and 'New Labour' are often used as if they were interchangeable. They certainly weren't then. Streatham was 'moderate', that is to say the members on the whole believed in democracy, the rule of law and change through Parliament. However, they would also have embraced a set of policies which would have set Tony Blair's teeth on edge.

The local party was energetic and outward-looking. Unlike many modern local parties, it was mixed in class terms. The comrades – we still used the word with only a trace of irony – were Joy and Daniel Dahl, who ran Thornton Ward; Margaret Robson (later my second wife); Keith Cuthbertson, later a prominent academic economist; and a subsequent head of press for the Labour Party, Nick Grant. We were all middle class though not particularly affluent. But we had in membership a train driver, Bill Turner, who represented the traditional skilled working class. The core of the party was a group of long-standing council activists, including Laurie Drake, who became a mayor of Lambeth, and Minnie Kidd. There were trade union activists too such as Joan Parine, our good friend who was an official of the Greater London Council Staff Association.

This Labour Party in any event was not a group motivated wholly by politics, though we were serious about our politics. The Labour Party provided the social framework of our lives too. That remains one of its greatest strengths, though whether the class and cultural pluralism of those days remains is more moot.

I was soon made secretary of the party. This was not too demanding a task as we had a separate election agent in Alan Virgo. It required a degree of organisational skill and, being the most senior officer other than the chairman, a willingness to work to keep people on side.

Patience was a virtue. One half of the party, let us call it the working-class half, had one view of protocol. They felt that the best time to ring the secretary would be after he had finished his breakfast at, say, six in the morning. The other half, the younger middle-class supporters, were equally considerate. They waited until most of the secretary's daily tasks were done before coming through at, say, one in the morning.

Two substantial political tasks fell to me during my period in office. The first was to choose a candidate to fight the seat in the coming general election. This was an interesting experience. There were a number of enthusiastic candidates, mostly local councillors. They knew Streatham could not be won. They wished, however, to put down a marker as willing and effective candidates, in the hope of getting a safe seat at a later date. Each attributed to the other impossible machinations to get the seat. As the secretary, however, I was uniquely placed to observe what was really going on – and the truth was pretty much nothing was. Wards, women's sections and trade unions nominated. Then the general committee of the party would meet to choose.

I did have a preferred candidate. Margaret Jackson (as she then was) was a member of the party's national staff and a formidably energetic young woman. She can't have been as left-wing as she later – as Margaret Beckett – purported to be, making her name for a coruscating attack on Neil Kinnock for not voting for Tony Benn at the 1981 party conference. Indeed, her views may have been little different than those she later espoused as the temporary leader of the party after Mr Kinnock's resignation in 1992, and then as a senior and competent member of Tony Blair's Cabinets.

Margaret Jackson was short-listed but not chosen. Indeed, she came last. Nor did any of the local councillors succeed. The nomination went to the outsider in my book (and, being an enthusiastic punter, I did indeed run a book).

Jean Gaffin was relatively local. She had achieved an LSE degree after leaving school at a young age to be a secretary. She and her husband Alec lived modestly, and she worked all the hours God gave, most of them for the Labour Party. She knew all about health and education. She became a lifelong friend, and is evidence for the proposition that it is possible to combine fervour for causes with common sense. She never won a seat in Parliament, and the Labour Party is the worse for it.

The second important political task was a different one, and much harder. It is a tale that will seem incredible nearly forty years on, but at the time, it had a scary reality.

It concerned the Tory government's Housing Finance Act of 1972. That Act mandated increases in council house rents – councils at the time owned nearly a third of the nation's stock of homes – of 50p a week per year. That now seems incredibly modest, but it was portrayed at the time as a class attack on working-class people.

That gave it tremendous appeal to the party's Trotskyist entryists. They saw in this a chance to precipitate the revolutionary confrontation which would bring down capitalism. Of course, in retrospect, it is perfectly clear that this was political fantasy. But the fantasy managed to intrude rather far into reality before it was revealed for what it was.

Lambeth council included a core of far-left councillors, including Ken Livingstone and Ted Knight, later, unbelievably, its leader. The far-left stance was to support what was called 'non-implementation' of the Act. That is, the council was to refuse to put up the rents, thus breaking the law. This would render the councillors liable to disqualification and enormous fines, provoking a confrontation of revolutionary proportions.

I am not sure if they expected to seize control of Britain immediately or whether this was what in Trotskyist jargon was known as an 'impossibilist' strategy. An impossibilist strategy was one which was bound to fail but which in the process demonstrated the impossibility of ameliorative change, 'heightening the contradictions of capitalism' and thus bringing about true socialism.

The extreme left was far from controlling the council. However, there was a more promising candidate locked away in Labour's constitution. The local government committee was an assembly of representatives of local parties with the general aim of facilitating communication between the Labour Party and the council. The far left perceived that it could control this body and use it to put pressure on the councillors to adopt the non-implementation policy.

There was an atmosphere of physical menace about meetings of the local government committee. You could almost hear the guillotine's swishing. That drove good people to stay away and left the floor to the baddies. And of course such a problem was to become a national problem which nearly destroyed Labour in the early 1980s. I have never been able to vote for Ken Livingstone for anything ever since.

In the end, the council did implement the Housing Finance Act. Tenants, to the disappointment of the far left, did not rise up in protest. Indeed protest came later as the council moved from a reasonably competent traditional outfit to one where the provision of services came a poor second to the provision of politics. Knight is no longer heard of, though Livingstone is.

The parochial battles of the Lambeth local government committee were not exactly enjoyable, but they were exciting and, on the
whole, my side won.

An unexpected side-effect of my local party involvement was
that, for the first time, it occurred to me that I did not want to
become a Labour MP after all.

It is true that in 1974, I made an appearance before a selection
conference. The Regents' Park ward of the Marylebone Labour
Party asked me and I appeared. It is perhaps significant that I
cannot even remember whether I got nominated for what was a
hopeless seat. There is also evidence in my papers that I was asked
to appear before the Molesey ward of the Esher Labour Party but
this episode, if indeed it occurred, has been wholly expunged from
my memory. By then, my doubts as to whether I wanted to get into
Parliament were mounting.

This was nothing to do with ideological disaffection from the
Labour Party. I had none. I also loved it socially. It played a large
and enjoyable part in my life and I was proud to make a modest
contribution.

The reason was much feebler. I realised, quite early on, that I
loathed canvassing. Knocking on people's doors, asking them
their most intimate political opinions, noting down their preferences so, where appropriate, we could badger them to the
polling station on election day – I simply could not bear it. Being a
candidate, being an MP, was about campaigning. That was not an
optional extra.

There are MPs who feel the same. Gerald Kaufman, who fought
his eleventh contest in his Manchester Gorton constituency in
2010, once confided in me that he hated elections. Still I wonder
if he had the sick feeling in his stomach on walking up the path
to an elector's front door. In my case this was exacerbated in that I
have had a lifelong tendency to irritable bowel syndrome, a condition made infinitely worse by the thought, let alone the reality,
of canvassing.

Being an MP is hard work. You have to love the job. I began to intuit that here was a part of the job I would always hate. I had many of the skills that counted in politics but lacked two *sine qua nons*: temperament and commitment. So thereafter I made no attempt, at any point, to find a seat; nor did I feel jealous as friends and colleagues did find seats. To say I have no regrets is an exaggeration; I mostly feel a sense of relief, especially since I have ended up with the not inconsiderable consolation prize of a canvassing-free seat in the House of Lords.

CHAPTER 3

TONY CROSLAND'S
CHOCOLATE SOLDIER 1972–74

I might have stayed at the General and Municipal Workers' Union (GMWU) for the happy 1970s, and even for the unhappy 1980s, when Margaret Thatcher castrated the unions. But my eye was one day caught by a classified ad in *Tribune*, the newspaper of Labour's Bevanite left. Researchers were required, it said, for members of the shadow Cabinet. A young man on the political make did not require a second bidding.

The ads were the result of an imaginative move by the (then) Joseph Rowntree Social Services Trust. The Trust had been formed in 1904 by the eponymous Mr Rowntree to give money to progressive causes, and to do so, moreover, outside the constraints of charity law. This meant it was able to back ventures which more orthodox charities had to eschew. The trust gave part of its money to keep the (then) Liberal Party going but thanks to the British insatiable appetite for sickly milk chocolate – an appetite which I share – it was left with cash in the bank.

Sadly, this affluence was to be reduced later. The trustees, liberals to the man and woman, sold their shares in Rowntree in protest against its doing business with apartheid South Africa. Soon after, the company was subject to a large and lucrative takeover bid from Suchard. It is tempting to speculate how much better left-wing causes might have done for years afterwards if it had not been for the tenderness of the trustees' consciences – an example of the radical dilemma as to how far principles should be pushed in practice.

In 1972, Rowntree was at the peak of its puissance. It perceived a glaring defect in the British political system. Parties in opposition were expected to play their constitutional role with absolutely no help with their work. Members of the shadow Cabinet, wrestling with large and complex portfolios, were expected to be their own researchers, press officers and speech writers.

The trustees, an imaginative and creative lot, decided to mount an experiment to fill this gap. They paid for assistants to be appointed to a few leading shadow Cabinet members – on this occasion, Roy Jenkins, the shadow Home Secretary; Tony Crosland, the shadow Environment Secretary; and Jim Callaghan and Merlyn Rees, to help with Northern Ireland. Inevitably, given the ultimate source of our salaries, we became known as the 'chocolate soldiers'.

With an Oxford degree and a trade union background, I hit the spots ambitious Labour spokesmen wanted to hit, so I approached the selection process with confidence. I was summoned one morning to the House of Commons for interview. I forget the full list of the interview panel but among those present were Douglas Houghton, the formidable chairman of the Parliamentary Labour Party; Pratap (later Lord) Chitnis, who ran Rowntree; and Roy Jenkins himself. Mr Jenkins led in giving me a standard (though not unfriendly) grilling, during which he asked me a number of questions about my life at Oxford.

Five minutes before the interview was due to end, the door burst open and in walked the extraordinary figure of Tony Crosland. Crosland had been a man to swoon over in his youth. Time had reaped its ravages but he was still very large and very compelling. That morning, however, not to put too fine a point on it, he was evidently the worse for wear. He explained he had been up all night opposing the Housing Finance Bill in committee, a task which had evidently required liberal refreshment. He then sat, eyes hooded, jowls in hand, puffing on a small cigar without speaking until proceedings were complete.

Next day, nervously sitting at home, I received a call from Mr Jenkins. He was, he frankly admitted, torn between my candidature and that of Matthew Oakeshott, a near-contemporary of mine at Oxford. Would I perhaps be free to come to lunch at his cottage in East Hendred in Berkshire that Sunday? My fellow guests – a Roy-like touch if ever there was one – would be the 'Noel Annans' (the distinguished and grand Provost of University College, London and his wife).

Shaking with nerves, I eventually found East Hendred in my little Fiat. Lunch went swimmingly. I did not drink too much and didn't feel I was too stupid. I subsequently learned that Lady Annan later rang Roy to say how much she hoped he would appoint me.

However, pride came before a fall. After lunch, our host suggested croquet. Being no mean player himself, Jenkins recklessly volunteered to partner Lady Annan, who was less practised, against me and her husband. Jenkins was not to know that croquet had figured large in my mis-spent youth and I had yet to learn the art of losing deliberately. Shortly after, I despatched Jenkins's ball to a far flower bed.

A *froideur* settled over the party. After the game, Roy drew me aside to have a discussion about the job. I was well qualified, he said, and he congratulated me on being honest about my Euroscepticism. However, given his position, that could prove a difficulty. I left in genuine doubt as to my employment prospects, certain only that my prowess with the mallet had not helped.

Next day, I received a handwritten note from Houghton inviting me to start work, at my earliest convenience, for Tony Crosland. I was astonished, but glad. Though I was no lefty, I was not then as right-wing as Jenkins. Moreover the central pillar of his thinking was a passionate Europeanism, associating as he did Europe with everything that contributed most to civilisation. I did not share this, and the European difference between us was a worry for me as it was for him.

Crosland had already impacted on my life. I had read his great work *The Future of Socialism* in 1968, cutting short my brief sixties flirtation with Marxism and converting me into an egalitarian democratic socialist.

The Future of Socialism is generally reckoned to be the most important British post-war book on its subject; but I doubt it is now much read. Even the shortened version produced by Jonathan Cape, his publishers, in 1963, which tried to omit all redundant material, runs to 368 pages.

Nowadays Crosland tends to be thought of as a sort of John the Baptist to Tony Blair and New Labour. In one sense this is right: Crosland started the job of ditching Labour baggage that Blair, Peter Mandelson and Gordon Brown were to complete forty years later. Crosland was against many of the things that they were against: against nationalisation, against *dirigiste* economic planning, against crude anti-capitalism, and against militant labourism.

He believed these things because he believed that capitalism had changed radically. It had evolved from the crude exploitative beast of Victorian times to the shareholder capitalism of the 1950s, where civilised companies worked in civilised ways. It would be interesting to have his take on the new and rawer capitalism which emerged between the election of Margaret Thatcher and the financial crash of 2008. Crosland saw no reason why capitalism, properly managed by a Keynesian state, could not generate ever-increasing levels of national income. This in turn could be used to increase the effective incomes of the least well off, without undertaking the politically perilous task of actually reducing those of the wealthier.

But he was only half a Mandelson or a Blair; Crosland was in favour of much that the New Labourites were to ditch. He was a radical egalitarian, an educational egalitarian wanting the comprehensive school to be the norm. Indeed, Tories have pilloried him since for saying that he wanted to 'get rid of every fucking grammar school in the country if it is the last thing I ever do'. He reviled Britain's class system, and loathed social snobbery of all kinds. He was not 'intensely relaxed', to use Peter Mandelson's later tongue-in-cheek phrase, about letting people get 'filthy rich'.

He set out his view on equality in his book of essays *Socialism Now*, published in 1974.

> Socialism, in our view, was basically about equality. By equality, we meant more than a meritocratic society of equal opportunities in which the greatest rewards would go to those with the most fortunate genetic endowment and family background; we adopted the 'strong' definition of equality – what Rawls subsequently called

the 'democratic' as opposed to the 'liberal' conception. We also meant more than a simple (not that it has proved simple in practice) redistribution of income. We wanted a wider social equality embracing also the distribution of property, the educational system, social-class relationships, power and privilege in industry – indeed all that was enshrined in the age-old socialist dream of a more 'classless society'.

At the same time, his egalitarianism was never intended to lead to the authoritarianism typical of the eastern European communist states, whose system was erroneously seen by many on the left as a rival to capitalism. As did Americans, most particularly the American liberal left, he abhorred communism even more than he abhorred the inequalities of contemporary Britain. Indeed, he went so far as to reject even traditional Fabianism (though remaining for years a member of its executive committee) and its addiction to bureaucratic remedies for society's ills. Our attention in due course could turn to 'personal freedom, happiness and cultural endeavour; the cultivation of leisure, beauty, grace, gaiety, excitement and of all the proper pursuits, whether elevated, vulgar or eccentric which contribute to the varied fabric of a full private and family life ... Total abstinence and a good filing system are not now the right sign-posts to the socialist Utopia, or at least, if they are, some of us will fall by the wayside.'

Crosland believed in the highest sustainable level of public expenditure. However he was not in favour of public expenditure *per se*. Rather he favoured public expenditure so constructed as to do most to help the poor and least to benefit the middle and upper classes. This, for him, was what Labour governments were chiefly for.

A burning desire for change was an essential of Croslandism. It had drawn me to his book and now it drew me to the man. Crosland was a close friend of Bill and Margaret McCarthy, my Oxford Labour Club mentors, and people more concerned with what worked in practice than what was right in practice. Even more important, Derek Gladwin, a political organiser of energetic capacity, had begun his career in Grimsby, to which, like Tony, he was devoted. I have little doubt that it was a quiet word from

Gladwin (who typically never mentioned it to me) that secured me the job I so wanted; I am grateful to him.

Tony had a reputation for being somewhat difficult to work with. His complex character is brought out in the late Susan Crosland's wonderful *Tony Crosland*, published in 1982 and still the best book in the English language on what it is like to be a leading politician. In what follows, I have kept my account of Tony and his life to a minimum, simply because I could not, even in my wildest dreams, hope to come anywhere near the quality of Susan's account.

He was most comfortable in the company of clever men and exotic women. However, contrary to the conventional wisdom – and despite his plummy accent – he was neither a snob nor class conscious. In his constituency he embraced people of a wide range of intellect and backgrounds, hobnobbing with the fish dockers as readily as with the Fabian intellectuals. He talked football long before that became an essential qualification for advancement in the Labour Party.

What Tony could not bear were people who thought they were cleverer than they actually were. He was wound up by knee-jerk liberals, misty-eyed Eurofanatics, middle-class moaners and anyone who could not get the point of his beloved Labour Party. He did not go to much trouble to disguise his distaste of such people, whom he avoided. This was as well for, if trapped in their presence, his behaviour was not generally such as to endear himself to them, or to enhance his reputation for common politeness.

Because of my first-class degree I counted as clever. Whether for that reason or for other reasons, I practically never had any difficulty working with Tony. We soon settled to a pattern of existence. Typically I would repair from my home in south London to his grand and elegant house in Lansdowne Road, Holland Park. He would have a list of tasks to discuss. I always brought a numbered agenda, a device to which, throughout his life, he was partial. We would work for an hour or so, then he would get out two large tumblers liberally filled with whisky or gin for him, more sensibly for me.

'Any chance of a sandwich for D Lip?' he would call down to his devoted wife. 'Seems a bit cruel to send him home hungry.' A delicious sandwich would duly materialise and the three of us gossiped over lunch. In summer there might be a few overs of cricket on the television. Then he would settle back in his leather Eames chair and footstool, surrounded by piles of neatly filed paper and books, returning to work a short snooze later.

Tony was shadow Secretary of State for the environment. The Environment Department had begun at the end of the 1964–70 Labour government. In the early 1970s, it had become one of Ted Heath's super-departments, a huge empire embracing local government, housing, transport, planning and even sport.

These were important subjects, but clearly less prominent was the environment as we understand it today: combating global warming, promoting organic farming, saving the whale.

This suited Tony Crosland. Tony, remember, was an egalitarian. He cared passionately about the environment, but not the environment as we know it now. He cared about the environment in which his working-class constituents brought up their kids, the homes they lived in, the air they breathed, their journey to work. I think if he had known how much we now fuss over the survival of the last species of beetle, he would have thought us quite mad.

As it happens, when I joined Crosland he was dealing with the first flowering of the movement that we now think of as environmentalism. The immediate cause was a publication by a group of quasi-scientists called the Club of Rome.

The Club of Rome thought that mankind was about to destroy the race by its excessive consumption of raw materials. It stuffed giant computers – they were giant at that time – with data showing that in fifteen to twenty years the world would have exhausted its oil, its coal, its aluminium and just about everything else man needed to prosper. Its solution was to end economic growth.

Crosland would not – *could* not – have that. Growth was the lubricant that made his project for social and political amelioration run. And so he turned his formidable intellect to destroying the Club of Rome's argument. Passionate environmentalist though he was, Crosland had nothing in common with Club of Rome environmentalism. He hated them and they hated him.

He pointed out that there were never more than a few years' supplies of key raw materials, simply because there was no profit in discovering new supplies until the old ones were running short. He explained that the problems could be dealt with by technical change, for example recycling. However, it would require economic growth to finance the cost of this if it was to be politically afford-able. 'This obsessive conservationist attitude is a) morally wrong when we still have so many pressing social needs that can only be met if we have economic growth; b) self-defeating since, without growth, we shall never find the huge sums of money which we desperately need to cure pollution and improve the environment.'

On this subject he was not merely logical but compelling. Thus he wrote of one of the club, Professor Mishan, who wanted a ban on international air travel: 'The rich would proceed in leisurely fashion across Europe to the Mediterranean beauty spots where they would park their Rolls-Royces and take to a boat or horse-drawn vehicle. As for my constituents, who have only a fortnight's holiday, let them eat cake and go back to Blackpool.'

The implementation of his campaign against the club was perhaps less impressive. One night he was invited onto a late night discussion programme of the subject with a panel of liberals. The programme started with the showing of a propaganda film setting out the horrors to come, a 1970s precursor of Al Gore's later *succès d'estime*. When the film ended, a participant rounded on Crosland. The dialogue went something like this:

'I watched you. You slept through every moment of the film.'

'That, madam, is the only sensible posture that someone faced with such meretricious rubbish could adopt.'

Fairly soon, the fashion for Rome subsided. The economic crisis of 1973 gave people a taste of low growth, and they did not like it. It was a full quarter of a century before the same mode of thinking emerged in the climate-change movement of today.

I am often asked what Tony Crosland would think of this or that. I generally reply, as politely as I can, that, as he has been dead for more than thirty years, I cannot ask him. However, having lived through that experience, I am prepared to hazard a few thoughts about Crosland and climate change. As it happens, and without claiming to have gone into it in as much depth as he would have done, they also reflect my own views.

He would be highly suspicious of it. Like the Club of Rome, it has to it a millenarian quality which would clash with his generally optimistic outlook. As with the Club of Rome, he would suspect that its policies would impact adversely mostly on the less well off – forced for example, to give up their dreams of cars while the rich sped around in their gas-guzzlers. Climate change is yet another excuse for the rich of this world to pull the ladder up behind them.

However, I don't believe he would have been an all-out climate-change sceptic – a 'denier' in the offensive phrase used by the climate fanatics. He was a man for evidence. He would I suspect have found the evidence that something untoward is going on compelling. And he would have been fairly confident, because most informed scientists are fairly confident, that man's activities are part or all of the cause.

Where I feel sure he would have differed from the fanatics is in the kind of response that was required. What is needed, he would argue, is not some shuddering halt to growth or radical restriction of our way of life. What is needed is a prolonged adaptation, using a mixture of price mechanisms, of taxes on warming activities and subsidies for anti-warming activities, of technical changes encouraged by those price mechanisms, and so on. The idea that our generation should make major sacrifices now so future, much richer generations had to make much lesser adjustments later in life, would have seemed to him absurd. And so it does to me.

Less cerebral and equally heady was the political side of the work. The aim was the promotion of Tony Crosland as a major Labour figure who – should Harold Wilson fall under a bus – would be a natural choice as his successor.

Becoming leader was not an obsession with Tony. The contrast with Gordon Brown years later was stark. Tony never felt he had been diddled out of the leadership by Wilson nor that it was Wilson's duty to grant him a chance at the job. Indeed, by Brownite standards, Tony was an exemplar of loyalty.

Wilson, like most senior politicians, had a good side and a bad side. A good side was his lack of pomp and his good humour, his genuine affection for his party, his wily ability to avoid doing anything that would split it, and underneath all that, an underlying old-fashioned patriotism. His bad side was cronyism, paranoia and a lack of any real seriously thought-through philosophy.

This combination affected different people in different ways. Crosland was no natural Wilsonite. Crosland, remember, had been the right-hand man of Hugh Gaitskell, being offensively described once in the *New Statesman* as 'Mr Gaitskell's Ganymede' with the clear if not quite libellous implication of homoerotic tendencies.

Gaitskell was a radical but a radical of the right. It was he who by introducing prescription charges forced Aneurin Bevan (and with him the young Harold Wilson) to resign from the 1951 government. When Gaitskell died, Crosland voted first for Callaghan, and when he was eliminated for George Brown. 'We have to choose between a crook [Wilson] and a drunk [Brown],' he said. So Wilson and Crosland had the embers of a distant feud to dampen.

Dampened they were. Crosland could see that Wilson was a popular politician, who was the most likely of the Labour crew to lead them back into government. Wilson, in any case, was not a direct rival – if that proverbial bus had come along, Crosland would have had no chance of the job in the early 1970s. The enemy was not Wilson. It was the next generation, Crosland's generation. Among them, Denis Healey and more especially Roy Jenkins were the competition for the eventual succession – *Friends and Rivals* in the apt title of Giles Radice's definitive book on the subject.

Indeed, working for Tony, it often seemed that he defined himself overtly to magnify the differences between himself and Roy.

There were three popularity contests that were features of the opposition years for Tony. In two of them, his participation directly fits the thesis that it was Jenkins who he wished to ditch.

The first was the deputy leadership of the party in 1972. The vacancy occurred because Jenkins, who held the post, resigned over Wilson's decision to promise a referendum on Britain's membership of the Common Market (as the European Union was then invariably called).

For Jenkins, membership of the Common Market was a core article of faith. It was what he and his supporters in the party above all stood for. Not surprisingly therefore, Crosland decided that it was not core to his faith. Though a long-standing pro-European, he declared membership to be a relatively minor matter. It was of secondary importance, so he would declare, to his constituents in Grimsby. When Jenkins led sixty-nine Labour MPs into the Tory lobby to back Ted Heath for joining, Crosland, ingloriously but consistently, abstained.

Perhaps he felt that his loyalty to party ahead of loyalty to the European ideal was insufficiently appreciated. When Jenkins resigned, Crosland saw an opportunity to put matters right.

The leading candidate was Ted Short, a middle-of-the-road former headmaster, who had few enemies. Crosland determined to take him on. The campaign was orchestrated by Dick Leonard, Crosland's chief parliamentary supporter, who unfortunately (for British politics) lost his seat through re-warding at the February 1974 general election. It was neither a success nor a failure. He was eliminated on the first ballot, third behind Michael Foot and Short, with a respectable sixty-three votes. What was achieved, however, was a visible separation of himself from Jenkins and his supporters. His candidature was never forgiven by true Jenkinsites.

The second was the contest for the National Executive Committee of the Labour Party. The NEC was described by journalists as Labour's 'ruling' NEC. It is doubtful if it was ever that. But it was an important body, bringing together representatives of the unions and of the constituency parties.

Crosland stood annually for the constituency section, chosen by local Labour parties. 'I may seem patrician and aloof,' he was saying, 'but I love our party and sympathise with your aims for it.'

Standing consumed a good deal of emotional energy. Before the results were announced, Crosland required fortification and, where possible, the quiet of his own hotel room. He never looked like capturing one of the seven seats at stake, but he achieved near-ish misses in good years. A few thousand extra votes and he was in ecstasy; a few thousand votes down and in despair. During the 1970s he gradually slipped from a promising eighth place to a dispiriting twelfth.

The final regular contest was one where his participation owed nothing to Jenkins. The parliamentary committee of the Labour Party (more colloquially, the shadow Cabinet) was elected by Labour MPs.

It was significant in substance. It is true that it was for the leader to draw on its number in choosing his shadow spokespeople. A position at the top of the poll did not guarantee a top shadow portfolio. However, the more votes you got, the higher your standing with your fellow MPs. No wise leader would ignore that. And if you weren't in the shadow Cabinet you weren't much.

It would be tedious to rehearse Tony's parliamentary committee ups and downs. Unlike the other two contests, he consistently did well. His capacities in opposition were appreciated by the connoisseurs of the Parliamentary Labour Party. They liked a good speaker. They liked a hard worker. They cared less for ideological soundness than for results. So Crosland was their man, and they were a base that served him well.

I don't remember any tremendous campaign activities ahead of the vote. Dick Leonard would urge the candidate to spend more time talking to backbenchers in the tea room, where they filled their spare hours. The tea room, however, was not his natural habitat.

In addition, we would try to build things up with the press. For example, an extract from a speech would be circulated each Saturday in the hope of coverage in the Sunday papers – usually involving some would-be clever jibe at the government. Sadly, and to Crosland's disappointment and surprise, the Sunday papers, though they in those days ran short summaries of weekend speeches, rarely rewarded these efforts with the craved coverage.

In preparing these offerings, I was no doubt acting as what a later generation would call 'a spin doctor'. 'Spin doctor' is an American phrase of uncertain origin to describe someone whose main job is to manipulate the press. If this was indeed my job, I was not very good at it. Certainly I would not have survived five minutes in the Mandelson/Campbell world of 24-hour media and instant rebuttal.

As a consequence of my policy work, it is true, journalists would sometimes consult me. In those days, policy mattered and newspapers employed specialist correspondents to cover the main topics of the day. Thus *The Guardian* had, believe it or not, a full-time housing correspondent, Judy Hillman, who got a good show with her copy. I would help her so far as I could with her pieces and she in return would help us with useful advice. But the idea I could somehow manipulate her to produce stories modulated to fit our political agenda would have seemed absurd.

On rare occasions, I met the grander political types – the political editors and columnists of their day. I remember to this day – and so does he as he reminds me every time we meet – my first lunch with Michael White, now the senior political writer on *The Guardian*. I managed the *faux pas* of asking for a cigar after our meal at *The Guardian*'s expense. *The Guardian*, it emerged, did not do cigars.

David Watt of the *Financial Times* and Peter Jenkins of *The Guardian* were perhaps the doyens of the journalistic class at the time. They would lunch with the Croslands, at home as well as in restaurants, on terms of perfectly free debate. No politicians feared that if they used a good phrase it would appear credited to journalists in their next column. The commentators were part of the political class and had shared interests with it as well as conflicts.

Perhaps things were too cosy, I don't know. Certainly friendships developed; mine particularly with Peter Jenkins, who combined deep seriousness with a certain raffish lifestyle. Never mind my cigar, Peter's appetite for champagne must have made serious holes in the paper's editorial budget but he was too big an asset to be challenged.

With Peter I did make it into print, or at least into script as a political adviser in his underrated play *Illuminations*. The play was not successful but he caught my dishevelled febrility rather well. Alas, Peter died far too young, though I have remained good friends with his partner, Polly Toynbee, who is as good a journalist as any now writing, and the nearest to a Croslandite.

If 'spin' took up 5 per cent of my time working for Tony, I should be surprised. It is true that this may reflect my own lack of appetite for the game. Susan Crosland, herself a leading journalist, found this frustrating. When Tony was away on a trip, she would ring me up with suggestions as to how favourable coverage might be got in the diary columns of the national newspapers. She didn't dare when Tony was around, and I am afraid that I was backward at acting on her ingenious ideas.

How different is today's world! Now shadow spokespeople command armies of advisers, researchers and assistants. These are partly paid for by 'Short money', named after the eponymous deputy Prime Minister who first provided state funding for opposition politicians. In 2010, some £700,000 was made available for this purpose.

As with so much in politics, what seems like a step forward turns out to have resulted in at least one step backwards. I was among the first of what has become a new political class. These are men and women who start off in politics wet behind the ears, get jobs with think tanks or backbench MPs, graduate to shadow spokespeople and then, if their party wins a general election, look to go into government as special advisers. They in turn are courted by interest groups, public affairs consultants and PR men, all eager to persuade the opposition to commit to policies which will suit in government. They have become powers in their own right, hitching their stars to that of their lords and masters, in the hope of one day getting seats themselves. We have created, for the first time in British history, a professional political class.

If this leads to better-considered policies, it is desirable. But does it? Shadow spokespeople these days have a policy on practically everything. They have only to turn to the team to order one. But this is not the same process as Tony Crosland was going through in his study. The policies are not carefully rounded on the basis of expert advice. They are, too often, policies designed to get through today's debate, tomorrow's speech, this Sunday's *Andrew Marr Show*.

The occupants, spokesmen, deputy spokesmen, deputy assistants to deputy spokesmen and so on, regard themselves as professional politicians. So in a sense they are, as they are frequently neither qualified nor experienced in anything else. However, professions in general require a qualification, training and a set of prescribed skills. The professional politicians we are spawning have no such pretensions. You have to be able to understand an opinion poll and know what a focus group is. You need to be able to read a newspaper and draft a press release. But there is no preparation for any of this. Still less is there preparation in the sense of training for the kind of management and decision-taking which goes with high office. The professional polity is in fact a hunting ground for amateurs. It would be impossible for shadow spokesmen today to do the job the way Tony Crosland did.

First, and this affects all MPs, today's politicians have also to deal with an ever-expanding constituency workload. When Tony Crosland was first selected to fight Grimsby in 1959, he was asked at his selection conference how often he planned to visit. Swallowing hard, he said 'about once a month'. The meeting responded ecstatically. 'That's marvellous, Mr Crosland,' said one delegate. 'You predecessor used to visit us once a year.' And indeed the distinguished Sir Kenneth Younger, a deputy to the Foreign Secretary during the Attlee government, had annually repaired to Grimsby each Boxing Day for his constituents to pay their respects before returning to metropolitan safety.

Now, an MP who visits only once a month is brave (or foolhardy). A weekly constituency surgery, a home in the place, involvement in endless openings is a *sine qua non*.

Tony used to receive perhaps thirty letters a week from Grimbarians seeking support. Now many MPs receive hundreds a day, requiring a full-time staff of caseworkers. They will not gain much electorally by their assiduity – psephologists reckon that incumbency is worth no more than one or two thousand votes and then only the first time a new MP stands for re-election. However, fail to put in the hours and your local party may disavow you. Ultimately, the electorate, though it shows little gratitude for a job well done, may exercise its prerogative in the case of a job not well done and throw you out on your ear.

The other huge change in a shadow spokesperson role comes from the growth of the media. When I worked for Crosland in opposition, if we broadcast once a month we were satisfied. Crosland would lunch well with a few trusted senior lobby correspondents – or send me at the last minute if he feared he would be bored. Coverage was more earnest and knowing your subject was as important as spinning your soundbite. Above all, what was important was how you performed in the House of Commons.

That has now changed. It is not uncommon for a politician to race through a dozen studios in a morning, delivering rehearsed soundbites in each. The 24-hour media is on your back the whole time, looking for contradictions between you and your party colleagues. Besides, the modern politician feels he is nothing if he is not in the newspapers. By contrast, speeches in the House, addressed generally to empty benches, go unremarked. The result of all this is a change in style. Today's shadow ministers are busy, busy, busy.

I can recall early on in my days with Tony going to the Labour conference in Blackpool. We returned to the Imperial, the conference hotel, for a drink after fringe meetings. As we walked in, down the stairs walked Harold Wilson, the leader of the party, and Barbara Castle. 'Doing anything for dinner, Tony?' said Harold, and soon we were all ensconced around a table gossiping. Today, security considerations alone would make such *ad hocery* unlikely. All is scheduled, planned, even calculated so that a young man is unlikely to get the opportunity to sit next to a British Prime Minister by chance.

What has been lost amid this change is time for reflection and serious thought. Instead, politics is dominated by presentation and image. The office infrastructure that the modern politician carries with him is needed to cope with that world.

What contribution precisely it makes to better governance is another matter. Perhaps it is no wonder that so many of today's politicians seem lightweight compared with their forebears. They are so busy rushing around that they have no time to acquire *gravitas*.

Just as my time at the GMWU saw my one period of deep involvement with party grassroots work, my time in opposition with Tony brought one perk if you can call it that – a brief period of membership of the Greater London Council's housing development committee.

The Greater London Council was a curious beast. On the one hand, it was a local authority of limited power. Education for inner London belonged with the separate Inner London Education Authority, and for outer London with the boroughs. Most council functions otherwise were also borough functions. The GLC was left with planning and (limited) transport powers; and (this accounted for my committee) supplementary powers to those of the boroughs to build and manage housing.

Its powers therefore were restricted. Indeed, Margaret Thatcher managed to abolish the GLC as an act of revenge against the left which then controlled it without undue disruption. Yet its grandeur in its pomp was considerable. It occupied imposing premises in County Hall (now a hotel) a stone's throw away from Parliament. It had not then been subject to the Livingstone takeover, so its leaders were serious people dedicated to public service. The then Labour leader, Sir Reg Goodwin, was a municipal grandee of an old school, and immensely respected.

Housing was divided into two bits: management and building. The committee in charge of the latter, housing development, was chaired by Gladys Dimson, an energetic and capable north London councillor. She was allowed to co-opt a few outsiders to supplement the skills of the councillors on the committee. She obviously thought there was benefit to getting alongside the shadow housing team, so I was brought on for that purpose. I remained a member until we went into government when I had to quit to avoid conflicts of interest.

The fault does not lie with Dimson, but I don't remember much of what we did for housing. The GLC had built many good estates in the past. Low-rise family housing such as the St Helier estate in Morden was much sought after. More recently, however, it and its architects had been tempted by modernism. There were many GLC 'streets in the skies' which failed to delight the residents as the lifts were jammed open by postmen and meter readers. There was a backlog of improving past estates to modern standards. The sums before the committee always seemed to have lots of zeroes on the end.

What I remember rather better is the politics of the GLC. The epitome of that was to come later when Londoners voted for Andrew McIntosh to lead the city, only for Ken Livingstone immediately to stage an internal coup to replace him. But even then, the GLC was a hotbed of plot and counterplot.

There was the Labour leadership of Sir Reg Goodwin. Then there was a right-wing faction, led by two exotic characters, Douglas Eden and Stephen Haseler. They accused the leadership essentially of incompetence, and concluded that more power should go to them and the committees they chaired. Both subsequently followed long-lasting failed political careers, including in the Owenite Social Democratic Party.

Then there was the classic left – not then Trotskyist but a

conventional Tribune left, the sons and daughters of Aneurin Bevan. What they did at the GLC, as in the wider Labour Party, was to rumble on in complaint, willing to wound but afraid to strike, and ineffective at everything except wrecking the collegiate approach to the group's work. However, Goodwin kept this broadly under control through his deputy leader, Illtyd Harrington, a delightful man if one who enjoyed a drink, who embodied the left's emotions while remaining essentially a loyalist.

Below this were a number of rivalries based on personal hatreds. It is a truism in politics that it is not those of opposing political views who hate you most. Those who hate you most are those who share your own views, for they are not for long your friends. They are your rivals. The Labour group at County Hall was littered with frustrated ambition which expressed itself in petty struggles.

As I was not an elected member of the committee, I avoided most of this conflict. From time to time, one or other of the factions would seek to recruit me (or rather to use me to recruit Crosland to their cause). Even then I was canny enough to ignore their blandishments. However, I did learn a lesson about the workings of politics in power. I was to be reminded of it many times in my subsequent career, in futile form as Tony fought Roy and later in the destructive war between Tony Blair and Gordon Brown.

CHAPTER 4

INTO POWER 1974–77

On the day of the first 1974 general election, I was lying on my sofa in my little house in Streatham surveying the final opinion polls. They made gloomy reading. A renewed majority for Ted Heath's Tories seemed inevitable.

I had good personal as well as political reasons to want a Labour victory. Victory would mean going into government with Crosland, with a chance to implement all those policies on which we had worked so hard in opposition. More basely, there was the little matter of employment. Rowntree's fellowships terminated with a general election and there was no guarantee of renewal. An unemployed assistant to a member of what was doomed for years to be a defeated party did not seem likely to be strongly placed in the jobs market. Penury seemed imminent.

Tony, too, was gloomy. He rang me to ask what I made of the polls. I told him. He sadly assented. He too would have wasted some years on policies that were going nowhere and perhaps even on a party in terminal decline. It might even be the end of his career too – he would be getting on for sixty by the time of the election after next. A life on the back benches, assuming he held Grimsby, was not one which would appeal to a man of his disposition.

Fortunately for us both, the British people decided otherwise. It was a cliff-hanger of an election with no one winning an overall majority but with Labour the largest party.

Ted Heath had called the election on the slogan 'Who governs Britain?' with the country in the middle of industrial action by the miners. A three-day week was in operation in industry to preserve coal supplies at the power stations. In people's homes there were rota cuts. Attitudes to the miners varied – a romantic streak in the British character convinced many that they deserved better pay. But cutting off the power – no television! – was going too far.

Heath expected to win and the polls suggested he was right. Indeed, even after he failed to gain the sought-after majority he tried to stay in office by cobbling up a deal with the Liberal leader, Jeremy Thorpe.

However, this was never really a runner. If there is one piece of advice third parties need always to heed, it is not to prop up governments that are losing ground. Harold Wilson, the Labour leader, calmly sat out the last rites, until Heath gave up and Labour was asked to form a government.

The election result incidentally casts doubt on the common thesis that the electorate, for all its faults and foibles, always delivers the right result. I am afraid the incoming Wilson government had not prepared well for victory. Its policy of appeasing the unions, though it had short-term attractions, did not prove viable in the long run and the country had to endure Thatcherism to rectify the mistake. If we were to change governments, voters might at least have delivered Labour a healthy majority. Instead we sneaked back in, polling fewer votes than the Tories, and liable to lose a parliamentary vote at any moment.

The Labour government that resulted was not a strong one. The party was divided. A majority in the Cabinet and the Parliamentary Party were pragmatists but had lost all sense of direction. There were few who were committed, as Crosland was committed, to democratic socialism.

Many, perhaps a majority, in the party outside Parliament were not democratic socialists either. They yearned for a complete trans-formation of society, a goal which they summed up as the end of capitalism. Quite how that was to be delivered by a government that never had a proper majority was never clear; but then the government had no inclination to try to deliver it anyway.

Wilson, as Tony expected, soon confirmed his appointment as Secretary of State for the Environment. Tony also confirmed that he wanted me there with him.

This threw the civil service into a considerable tizzy. It was not that they were fundamentally opposed to the notion. They were not, and besides civil servants do not get far in life by taking on unwinnable battles with determined ministers, especially new ministers. It was that they hadn't the faintest notion what I was supposed to do.

J. D. Jones, the senior permanent secretary at the department, proposed putting me in something called the Policy Unit of the department. I assume it existed, though I never saw nor heard of it during my time at the Department of Environment (DoE). Fortunately, Crosland had a clear idea of what he wanted.

He knew that there were tasks that I could fulfil; he wanted me with him as his political ears and eyes. I was installed in an office, close to his, and got on with it.

Special advisers then were controversial, as they marked a break with the tradition that ministers are served entirely by impartial civil servants. They became more so many years later as their power grew. In some departments, a kind of warfare raged between political advisers and civil servants. Frances Morrell and Francis Cripps, for example, a sort of Little and Large team who worked for Tony Benn, were used by their minister as a sort of alternative socialist civil service. Naturally relations with their non-socialist counterparts were not warm. But even moderate political advisers could fall out with their departments. Adrian Ham, a friend of mine who worked for Denis Healey at the Treasury, later wrote a book to get his revenge.

I must speak as I found, and no such problems ever beset me.

Our civil servants soon found out I could be useful to them. There were tasks within a department that did not fall readily to being discharged by officials. Suppose, for example, a member of the Labour Party wrote to the Secretary of State, or a Labour ward passed a resolution. Terms of address such as 'Dear Comrade' did not come appropriately from your average middle-ranking civil servant.

There were also tasks that were appropriate but at which the civil service was not good. Speechwriting was a classic example.

Civil servants come (or at least then came) from a written culture. They were not used to speeches and so what was dished up when the Secretary of State had a speaking engagement was a dull policy paper, preceded by unctuous courtesies to the audience. I have heard more of these vacuous effusions over the years than I care to remember.

So I was soon the speechwriter. On occasion I would be a little too political and would have to be set right. But more often I could find the words for what Tony wanted to say.

I brought other dishes to the feast. I knew Tony and Tony's thinking better than any of them did, so my guidance was much sought after. I could provide an informality which he allowed only reluctantly in his relations with them. I could provide a political element to his profile, for example, through briefing the press.

I quite soon became not just a close colleague of my civil service counterparts but a good friend too. Indeed, I would say that at no time in my life, before or since, have I enjoyed such good relations with the people I worked for. In particular, I got on well with Tony's private office: Andrew Semple, his urbane private secretary, and then Terry Heiser, his successor; David McDonald, his assistant private secretary; and the other members, Maggie Turner and Noreen Bovill. David Edmonds, who was private secretary to one of our junior ministers, has been my lifelong friend and golfing partner, rising to run the Housing Corporation, to chair OFTEL and then *inter alia* Wincanton Logistics. There were many others I could mention but won't as they have retired into the anonymity that they rightly cultivated as part of their working lives.

Those at DoE were not conventional bureaucrats as their public image might have implied but singular individuals of integrity and drive. They believed in what they were doing, yet they were utterly loyal to the civil service ideal of impartiality and to the notion that, ultimately, it was ministers who decided and not them. Ours was, I think, the last government to treat the civil service – most of the time at any rate – with the respect it deserved. Those that followed have in my view been less effective and the nation has lost out in consequence.

It helped that we all liked a drink. Once Tony had been packed off to the House for the evening to await votes, we would adjourn to the Marquis of Granby in nearby Smith Square to laugh and cry over the day's events.

When, two years later, Tony was moved to the Foreign Office, I was just settling in when I got a call from Sir Ian Bancroft, Jones's successor as permanent secretary, with whom I got on well.

'David,' he said. 'I need your help. The new Secretary of State has arrived and he says he doesn't want a political adviser. As you know, the department can't function without one. Would you come and talk to him?'

An appointment was made for me to see Peter Shore in Tony's old office at DoE. He did not seem keen to have the conversation. After I had made my case with some force, he asked me if I had a candidate in mind.

Fortunately, I did. Barbara Castle had as one of her special advisers Jack Straw, my old acquaintance from the Callaghan dinner. Castle had been (to her outrage) unceremoniously dumped by James Callaghan when he took over as Prime Minister and so Straw was out on his ear. I mentioned his name and he ticked the boxes – left-wing reputation, anti-European and high ability to boot. Somewhat reluctantly, Shore agreed to talk to him. The relationship gelled, and Straw's career continued on its well-merited trajectory.

Out of necessity my learning process as a new political adviser had to be fast. One immediate problem was caused by the weekly meeting of ministers which Tony decided to hold. John Silkin, a man of quite exceptional ego even for a politician, was minister for land and planning. Fred Mulley, a correspondingly modest man though of high ability, did transport. Reg Freeson, a former council leader from Brent, was in charge of housing. But there were juniors almost too numerous to count. I am still less than clear what they all did.

My particular problem was with Alma Birk, the department's minister in the Lords. Alma was a nice enough woman, and not devoid of ability. But she had from our point of view two defects.

She had ideas on policies above her station. And she had a voice that made a dentist's drill seem like Schubert.

The meetings were supposed to be informal. But, quite soon at each one, Lady Birk would start expounding on her latest policy wheeze.

Both voice and content had an instantaneous effect on the Secretary of State. He would rest his head in his hands, puff quietly on a cheroot and gently doze, nodding his head politely from time to time, until she was quite finished.

Unfortunately, that was not the end of the story. Following the meeting, Lady Birk would return to her private office and inform them that the Secretary of State had endorsed whatever it was she was spouting about – her interpretation of his dozy nod. Officials around the department would be briefed, spring into action. Getting the genie back in the bottle required disproportionate effort.

And so the informality had to go. I went straight from the meetings to my office, where I would prepare a note of the proceedings. The Secretary of State's endorsement of Lady Birk's suggestions did not feature.

This may seem an inconsequential story but, many years later, it did have consequences for me. When I was appointed to the House of Lords it would have been natural for me to seek ministerial office and for a few weeks I was quite ambitious. But then I remembered Alma Birk and the disdain – that puts it mildly – in which she was held. I took an early opportunity to write to Number 10, admitting that the letter might be entirely otiose, but requesting never to be asked to serve as a Lords' minister.

All that hard work in opposition, Tony's with a little help from me; did that stack up when we got into DoE!

His – our – first move was indisputably a blunder. The Rate Support Grant was the mechanism by which the government distributed central government funds to local authorities. In principle, this was a purely mechanical (though horrendously complicated) exercise. A regression analysis was conducted in which local authority spending – and thus, it was assumed, spending needs – was related to various factors measuring each council's need. A council gained extra credit if it housed a particularly high number of immigrants or if its population was sparsely distributed.

In fact, however, this presented much scope for creative adjustment. In particular, politicians could tweak the formula so it gave more help to local authorities of their political disposition, and less to the opposition.

Just such a tweaking had been done for the draft settlement prepared by Tony's DoE predecessors. Our dilemma was this: their distribution was undoubtedly unfair, hard on the deprived areas and generous to the richer ones. It should be changed. However, if we changed it, we would get the blame, not the Tories. And we should fall victim to the oldest rule in politics: those to whom you give grant you no credit while those from whom you take create a tremendous fuss.

We ignored the rule and reversed the Tory policy. This, Crosland remarked in his regular summer reflections on his year's activity, was 'morally and socially absolutely right, but politically definitely wrong'.

However, we were not the only ones who could bend a rate support grant settlement. I sat down in those early days with the doorstopper document which represented the submission to the Secretary of State on the subject from officials. From an early age I have cultivated a habit of always glancing first at the annexes, for it is in annexes that people hide the things they want to hide but dare not wholly exclude. It was a technique that served me well in my subsequent career as a journalist.

One annexe set out the assistance to councils in inner London. It more or less made sense except for one thing: the London (Councils Special Needs) Assistance Grant (or some such). The effect of this grant was to take a little money from every London borough and give it to Westminster.

I was naturally curious. My Secretary of State (and I, come to that) were not in the business of politics to give fat-cat boroughs such as Westminster an easy ride. I rang the official.

'Oh David, I am glad you asked,' he said. 'I had lunch with the treasurer of Westminster last week, and he was telling me what a terrible time they were having of it financially. I thought the Secretary of State would want to help.'

The Secretary of State did not want to help.

Local government and how to finance it was a perpetual problem for Tony Crosland, as it has been for every responsible minister, before and since. On the one hand, all pay lip service to the need for local autonomy. In Tony's case this was more than lip service as he had immense affection for the local authority leaders of the time, especially the Labour ones. Just as Grimsby stood for the real world in his book, so did they. They, like he, were engaged in the onerous task of making Britain a modestly better place.

On the other hand, however, and long before the IMF crisis of 1976–77, public spending in Britain was threatening to get out of control. Tony was, of course, generally in favour of high levels of public expenditure, carefully targeted to redistribute income. But he was an economist as well as a socialist, and he could perfectly well see there were bounds to how far this could be allowed to go. Besides, if he didn't control his expenditure the Treasury would.

It was this that led to what became known as the 'Party is Over' speech at a local government conference in Manchester Town Hall, Tony using the phrase to tell them to control spending.

We could perfectly well claim to have been quoted out of context. 'With [local government's] usual spirit of patriotism and its tradition of service to the community's needs, it is coming to realise that, for the time being at least, the party is over,' was what Tony actually said. That sounds rather different. But we were not so naïve as to expect every word to be repeated every time our phrase was reported.

More accidental was the birth of the phrase itself. I had written a routine speech without in truth letting the brain get much in the way of the flow of my words. The fact that in this phrase lurked an insulting suggestion that council leaders and officials had been irresponsibly boozing away did not consciously occur to me.

However, we were aware of what we were doing. The speech had been sent to Gerald Kaufman, then a junior minister at DoE though formerly Harold Wilson's press spokesman. It came back with a single question mark placed against the phrase.

Gerald, Tony and I talked it through. I was by then alert to what I was actually recommending the Secretary of State should say. I argued that we needed to issue a wake-up call to local government before the Treasury clamped down and it was too late. He agreed.

I still think that in the context we were right. Local government spending had risen, year on year in successive years, by 7 per cent, 7 per cent and 8 per cent. This could not continue. However, when we jumped off the train from Manchester, it was clear from the *Evening Standard* billboard that we had something bigger than we had expected on our hands. Indeed, 'the party's over' became more than a phrase to describe local government. It became a metaphor for our whole national situation – plunging on towards bankruptcy, apparently unable to adjust to a world which had suddenly become much harsher.

In politics, single phrases can have lasting and disproportionate results. Harold Wilson was never forgiven his 1968 statement that the 'pound in your pocket has not been devalued'. It sealed his reputation for dishonesty. Ted Heath had 'the unacceptable face of capitalism' hung round his neck and Margaret Thatcher suffered similarly for 'there is no such thing as society'. I therefore sometimes think that my whole contribution to political life over forty years amounts to three phrases which I inserted into public discourse.

'The party's over' was the first. The second occurred when I was briefing the Prime Minister at Number 10 in 1978–79, when I referred to the industrial troubles sweeping Britain as the 'winter of discontent'. This was a phrase which was very useful to our spin doctors, since, in Shakespeare's original, it gave way to glorious summer. So it was rapidly given wider currency. This characterisation took hold and remains standard. Indeed, in its way, I may have helped legitimise all Tory election campaigns ever since, all of which threaten that a Labour victory would mean a return to the 'winter of discontent'.

The third is my coining of the phrase 'New Labour' as a name for Labour under Blair – which is dealt with in Chapter 10.

Politics is ultimately about communication, not just policy. A good phrase is the Pegasus of your message.

But I am getting ahead of myself. How did our opposition policies work out in practice?

Cancelling Maplin, the new London airport, may or may not have been right. I cannot answer this question because it was not one which Tony ever asked me to address. Some of the reasons he came up with in opposition for thinking it unnecessary proved right. We do indeed have more wide-bodied aircraft, able to take more passengers. We have indeed expanded regional airports.

Some were not right. We do not have the vertical take-off aircraft he looked forward to which would make aircraft movements less noisy. We certainly did not settle for ever the airport arguments which continue to rage, now over the third runway proposed then unproposed then proposed again for Heathrow.

The Channel Tunnel was another cancellation to which we were committed. In fact, we had little choice politically. A new tunnel was not likely to be a priority for public spending under our government, which was struggling hard to keep up with pressing demands from education and health. However, due ceremony had to be gone through. An early meeting of the Secretary of State with officials was called to discuss the Channel Tunnel. I remember the contribution of the under-secretary responsible. She had spent years of her life getting the tunnel through, and now some minister was determined to destroy her work.

'Secretary of State,' she began. 'I quite understand your *political* [did I detect a slight sniff?] commitments. I just want to make one thing clear. There is no possibility – absolutely *no* possibility – that the Channel Tunnel will go over budget.' She cited the costs of a similar tunnel in, I think, Singapore, which had ended up to the penny on price.

By the time it was actually built it cost £9.5 billion, twice the estimate. If today I sometimes seem a trifle sceptical about cost estimates for major projects, it is that experience that makes me.

Another of our policies from opposition was the public owner-ship of development land. Now, at first blush, it may seem curious that Crosland, the dedicated opponent of Labour's nationalise-everything Clause 4, should want to undertake this huge piece of public ownership.

However, the case of land was singular. Allowing people to profit from enterprise was one thing. Allowing them to cash in on their ownership of land was quite another, especially since that land generally had special value for one reason only – a local authority had granted or might grant planning permission for its development.

There was thus a strong *a priori* argument why nationalisation might appropriately apply to land. There was also of course a political reason: it was the sort of policy which distinguished him sharply from Labour's pragmatists. For the party, it showed that if you got Crosland, you got something other than a conventional right-winger.

Land was an area into which I put particular effort in opposi-tion. Indeed I set out my views – by implication my boss's – in a Fabian pamphlet entitled *Labour and Land* published in April 1973.

It gave rise to the proudest moment of my life. Tony, naturally, wanted to read it before it went to the printers. He took a copy up to his study, leaving me to chat with Susan. A few minutes later, he emerged with a sort of smile on his face. 'Young man, you just might one day revise *The Future of Socialism*,' he said.

So I had written a pamphlet, consulted the experts, got the imprimatur of the boss. All it now needed was for the civil servants to draft the appropriate Bill and for John Silkin, as the minister in DoE responsible for land, to pilot it through Parliament. The land would again belong to the people.

Except it didn't turn out like that. Our discussions of land policy in the department were focused on a single issue: the danger of creating a dual market in land. And, if I am truthful, this dominant issue was one which simply had not occurred to me or anyone else when we were in opposition.

The problem, essentially, was this. Suppose we declared our intention to nationalise development land. Anyone who owned a piece of land worth developing but not yet able to be sold would hold onto it. They would calculate that one day a government might reverse the policy and allow them to cash in on their ill-gotten gains. This might not be patriotic but it was realistic.

The difficulty then was to find a way of proceeding with the policy without gumming up the whole development process. Strong advocates of public ownership though we were, we had no desire to see the housing programme, of which we were equally strong advocates, collapse while we worked things through.

John Rowcliffe, the official in charge, battled valiantly with this conceptual problem. John Silkin, who was directly responsible, would contribute ideas of his own, which appeared mostly to occur to him in his bath. He took the precaution of rarely committing such ideas to paper, so he and Tony were left in a state of mutual non-communication.

Frank Dobson, later Labour's Health Secretary and prominent in Camden politics, remembers meeting the two. Silkin, a lawyer, was explaining some arcane point of land law. 'That may be the law, John,' said Tony, drawing on his cheroot, 'but I'm talking politics.'

Things weren't helped by the fact we were in a terrible rush. Harold Wilson wanted a proper parliamentary majority. He thought the best way of winning this was for his ministers to proceed with purpose, setting in hand the policies his party had promised in their election manifesto. This included land (though whether it would have been popular had the public been privy to its full implication is a moot point). So we had to work up from scratch a policy as the basis for a government White Paper before the summer recess. With the innate difficulties, and the weaknesses of ministerial input, the miracle is not that it was done well but that it was done at all.

None of this mattered much. The policy did become law in the form of the Development Land Act but it was repealed by the Tories before it had a chance to do much harm or good. The moral is the betterment problem (how to stop people making huge fortunes out of land without at the same time drying up its supply). This is one of those problems not susceptible to partisan remedy. The secret of success is to find a solution which will endure. This is not the only instance of matters of controversy in British politics which would benefit from a less confrontational political culture.

The two biggest policy areas for DoE remained housing and transport.

Transport was a great success. For this was a policy process that was an exemplar of its kind. In opposition, Tony was not instinctively grabbed by transport because he could not see how it related to his socialist objectives of greater equality. It just seemed like a vast maw down which public money was poured. At one point he suggested to officials that they should adopt the French approach to worn-out roads and erect a *chaussée déformée* sign by every pothole.

However, the gap had to be filled so Tony persuaded *Socialist Commentary*, a Labour journal, to fund a study group to look into it. *Socialist Commentary* was not, as it sounds, one of those leftie newspapers flogged to conference delegates as they queue to take their seats but a serious and respectable journal of the Labour right.

A group was duly assembled with Chris Foster, a friend of Tony's who had also advised Barbara Castle, effectively in charge. Soon and surprisingly, it came up with a concept that did finally engage Crosland. Transport, it emerged, was important in terms of equality – but not the way the Labour Party had thought.

It was not cars bad, trains good. Cars of course were disproportionately used by better-off people and so too much spending on roads would benefit the middle classes. But Crosland never needed much reminding of the importance of the car to his constituents in Grimsby. It had immeasurably contributed to their practical freedom.

The villain of the piece was the railways. These were heavily subsidised and, partly in consequence, run with staggering inefficiency and insouciance towards their customers. Nevertheless, the middle classes and business classes used them intensively, to commute from their suburban fastnesses or to travel longer distances not quite requiring an aeroplane. The better off were onto a good thing.

However, this did not mean we had to neglect public transport. Public transport was vital to those who had no cars and to families where the husband took the car to work, leaving the wife without. Public transport was crucial to the elderly and to the very young; it could save on pollution and energy.

However, this public transport with all the virtues did not comprise railways. It comprised the humble bus.

Bus journeys were in decline. The decline was particularly severe in rural areas, where there was often no alternative. The industry had a poor image. It was often publicly owned and correspondingly inefficient. To turn it round was a major task, for which the *Socialist Commentary* group came up with a number of remedies. (I have never understood why one, converting railway lines into cheaper, more flexible bus routes, has never taken hold.)

Thus Tony had a well-worked-out socialist policy to take into office with him and to get officials to work on. He took some time to grasp transport – he could only ever handle well one priority at a time – but when he did, it was to some effect.

I remember a short memorandum he sent to Sir Idwal Pugh, the transport permanent secretary. It instructed him immediately to transfer £200m – no small sum in those days – from the road programme to buses. Sir Idwal was not invited to argue.

DoE meanwhile set about preparing a Green Paper on transport. I was given the specific task of taking that Green Paper and comparing it with the *Socialist Commentary* report. Not until every proposal of that original report had been discussed, accepted or with reason rejected, was the Green Paper pronounced fit for purpose.

Days before its eventual publication, Tony Crosland was moved from DoE. He made a desperate and despairing effort to persuade Mr Shore to allow the old Secretary of State to return to DoE to launch the Green Paper. Naturally and rightly, Mr Shore declined.

The Green Paper survived but alas the policy fared less well. Mr Shore took a more conventional attitude to the virtues of trains.

And then there was housing. There is no question that housing was close to Tony Crosland's heart. If you read Susan Crosland's book, you will find that in opposition, wherever he was, study, bath or bed, he is invariably referred to as having a housing file under his arm. No doubt Susan used housing as a symbol for a subject which Tony found fascinating and bored everyone else to tears. Yet when Tony said that housing was far more important than the Common Market, it was not just a case of *épater les bourgeois*, though bait the fanatical pro-Europeans it certainly did. He genuinely believed that getting the right housing at the right price was the single most important step we could take to being a happier, more just Britain.

In opposition, we collected the best of the advisers from academia, local government and so on. We took many of them into government too as the advisory committee on the major review of housing finance, which Tony launched. His formidable intellectual apparatus was focused on housing to the exclusion of practically everything else for long periods of time. He wanted housing to have priority for public spending by his department, and indeed by the government as a whole. So why did we make such a mess of it?

One answer is that Crosland's radicalism tended to be tempered by caution. Housing was so complicated that it was a constant temptation to give up.

We failed on the important subject of council house rents. It was pretty clear that council house rents were too low. They did not provide sufficient revenue to finance vital new housing construction programmes and they represented at best a rather random form of distribution. Many poor people were subsidised; however, so were many better-off council tenants. A better solution would have been for subsidy to take the form of rent rebates for the poor.

But what was the alternative? Tony was tempted in opposition by a paper written by Martin Wolf, a former chair of the Oxford Democratic Labour Club but who was on a move rightwards.

He wanted housing entirely reformed on a market basis. Owner-occupiers' subsidies would be dismantled; council house tenants would pay the full market rate; so would private tenants and so on. Wolf, now a world-leading commentator at the *Financial Times*, is a brilliant man, and I do not think that Tony ever found a hole in his argument. Eventually, with a sigh, he placed it in the capacious box marked 'too difficult politically'.

This did not leave us with much and what was left was not much good. For council rents, Tony eventually resorted to what was called 'historic cost rents'. Each council would total up the costs it incurred for its housing, including the interest on its construction. Any government subsidies would be added in. They would then charge in rent sufficient to cover these costs.

This policy had one advantage. It left rent-setting to local councils, who were duly grateful. But in every other regard, it was the most conservative and unsatisfactory system imaginable. For example, it favoured those councils (and those council tenants) which had built their houses in the distant past so that they no longer cost much. It penalised those councils with a big need to build, as they could do so only if they were prepared to burden their existing tenants with the cost.

It did not help that the context changed between our building the policy and coming into office. Crosland had had an immense success in opposition attacking the Conservative Housing Finance Act, which mandated annual increases in rents. The trouble was that, after the oil price explosion of 1973, council house rents under the Act were not going up too fast. They were falling far behind inflation, making financing the housing revenue account harder and harder.

So a central feature of the housing policy on which we were elected had made no sense; and having made no sense when it was adopted, it made even less sense by the time we came into office. That, however, was not the end of the story for as part of Labour's anti-inflationary strategy we had agreed to impose a national rent freeze if we won.

I do not know how many votes this won Labour. My own experience of electoral bribes is that they impress the politicians offering them more than they impress the electorate. I do know it left another bloody great hole in the housing revenue accounts and another drain on funds which were not then available for more building.

A second blunder was to provide security of tenure for inhabitants of furnished flats. This was designed to tackle a genuine problem. If you rented a flat without furniture from a private landlord, your rent was controlled. You could if discontented go to a tribunal which would set a mysterious thing called a 'fair rent' for the property. Of course this was a useless right if the landlord could then sling you out in favour of a tenant willing to pay more, so unfurnished tenants enjoyed security of tenure.

This was not the case for those who rented private accommodation with furniture in it. For them there was no rent control and no security. There were some ghastly cases of Rachmanism, the exploitation of the shortage of housing by unscrupulous landlords. Housing charities, led by Shelter, were up in arms.

The Labour Party nationally had its solution, which in its way was as rationally coherent as was Wolf's. All private rented property would be 'municipalised', that is to say be taken into public ownership by the local council. They would then allocate it according to need.

This had two defects. Firstly, it removed all flexibility from the system. Take a young couple, newly married perhaps, seeking to set up their own home but unable to aspire yet to home ownership. What were they to do? No council was going to give them priority over families with children in need. For councils to have had an effective monopoly over rented accommodation would have represented an intolerable erosion of individual freedom.

Secondly, it was unaffordable. Councils simply did not have the capital funds available. They needed their money to complete their programmes for building new council houses.

Something had to be done. It could not be municipalisation so we went for the soft option. Furnished tenants too were given security.

We cannot say we were not warned. Officials gave us grave papers warning of the housing market grinding to a halt. Eventually I was convinced by them, and wrote a short paper for Crosland arguing that our policy was a disaster. When we discussed it, he agreed. But, he said, 'that's party policy'. It took years and a tortuous gradual liberalisation before Britain began to have anything of the free market in rented accommodation which characterised most European countries, whether under governments of the right or of the left.

Perhaps the first seeds of my distrust of Britain's partisan and divided polity were sown by this.

That left the owner-occupied sector. Already something like half of Britons owned their own houses. They mostly seemed to like doing so though their mortgages could prove a burden. Certainly we had no objection to owner occupation. But what could we offer them?

Our vulnerability became apparent in the second 1974 general election. Our expected canter to victory was interrupted by a young upstart opposition spokesperson named Margaret Thatcher. She promised to reduce the mortgage rate from 11 per cent to 9.5 per cent, though she never exactly specified how this was to be achieved. We grumbled that she was bribing the electorate with its own money, and the election was nevertheless survived.

Yet we were in the curious position of offering nothing to one half of the country. To its credit, the Number 10 Downing Street Policy Unit understood this. Under its leader, Bernard Donoughue – a subsequent lifelong friend – it developed a policy by which councils would be obliged to offer their tenants their homes to buy at attractive rates. The money raised would be used to build new council housing. With the exception of the latter element, the policy had much in common with that eventually controversially implemented by the Tories, with positive effects on their party credentials with middle England.

We – Tony, me, our officials – weren't against selling council houses. We could see virtues to doing so, for example to end single-class council estates and introduce social diversity. Policies were quietly put in place to make this possible.

What we were against, however, was a grand initiative. Quite simply, we believed this would be unacceptable to the Labour Party.

Of course, the left would reject it. Their ideal was a system of 100 per cent council housing, which the state allocated on the basis of need.

If, however, it had simply been a matter of the left, it would have been overruled. The problem was much wider. Labour councils, including moderate councils, held municipal housing as their greatest achievement. Demand in most places far exceeded supply. New building was limited. So the way tenancies became available included families moving out – for example to buy a home elsewhere – leaving their vacant property for the council to fill.

Among many party members, this empirical consideration had turned into an article of faith. Just as they believed in the party's Clause 4, providing for the public ownership of all industry, so they believed in municipal housing. Having talked to Margaret McCarthy – no tool of the left, she – Tony and I were convinced that the Number 10 scheme would lead to an explosion in the party which could wreck his career and the government.

Probably both sides of this argument were right. The Policy Unit was right that the battle between the national parties required some dramatic initiative, without which the Tories would establish a lien on the home-owning vote for ever. We were right that this would be at the cost of an enormous and unpredictable party explosion, which might undo all the good the policy was meant to do with the electorate.

In the end, a departmental minister who wants to do nothing is surprisingly powerful in the face of a Number 10 that wants to do something. We hummed and hawed, met the Policy Unit for hours over the details of its scheme, pretended to be considering it with the utmost seriousness and so on. Eventually, the steam went out of the issue. When it came to a Cabinet committee, the Prime

Minister, by that time past wanting trouble, sided with Tony and the initiative was lost.

Meanwhile, the housing finance working party in the department continued its work. Huge piles of paper were discussed, annotated by the Secretary of State, reviewed and discussed again. Meetings of our experts and officials ploughed through this stuff. It may be a failure of memory, but I cannot recall anything important coming out of this time-eating process.

Comparing the transport and housing reviews, why was transport a success – at least in yielding a coherent policy – and housing a failure? There are many reasons, including the involvement of different individuals. But one stands out for me.

The trouble in housing is that we took a particularly pure version of the Crosland approach to policy-making. That is to say, we accumulated a whole lot of facts, examined them logically through the prism of his political values, and then sought to make that into a policy. This was flawed in two ways. Firstly, it took no account of those areas where, for reasons of party policy and ideology, we did not have effective freedom to determine our policy. Secondly, it represents a wrong picture of how policy-making is done.

Policy-making is like science. It is best done by formulating a hypothesis on the basis of instinct and sniff, then subjecting that hypothesis to detailed analytic assessment. That was effectively what we did with transport and its hypothesis of the importance of the bus. We didn't do it with housing and as a result what happened was pretty well a waste of time.

This was perhaps the last occasion on which a progressive Labour housing policy could have been put in place. Crosland continued to advocate its importance. When, in 1975, the Central Policy Review Staff initiated an exercise to establish some prioritisation and co-ordination between the government's social programmes, he advocated that housing should be the main priority. He was prepared to cut other DoE programmes to accommodate it, and thought that so too should other ministers.

But housing has one huge disadvantage as a government

spending programme. It yields its results only over a very long time. If you build one house, you provide a home for those in it for a hundred years. However, the expense all falls in year one. It follows that you get little political bang for big bucks. Smaller sums, spent on programmes with more immediate results, are more attractive.

Combine that with the inefficiency of local authorities in managing their stock. Combine it with their difficulty in allocating that stock, between the claims, say, of long-established locals and immigrants with large families. Combine it with the fact that council estates just looked run down, in a way private estates didn't. The great era of council building was drawing slowly to an end. We ought to have realised it but we didn't.

So far as housing was concerned, those hours of deep concentration in the Eames chair were largely wasted.

DoE was a huge department. Indeed in 1976 Wilson recognised the fact by splitting transport off from environment. However, in those days, a Secretary of State's responsibilities were not confined to their own departments. In addition, they were members of the Cabinet.

Walter Bagehot, the Victorian constitutionalist, distinguished between the 'efficient' and the 'dignified' parts of Britain's governance. The efficient parts were the bits that actually made it work. The dignified bits were there for show.

At that time, the Cabinet was part of the efficient side of the constitution. It was in the Cabinet or its committees that collective decisions were made. It then followed that ministers owed a collective responsibility to uphold those decisions. They had had their say. If their colleagues decided otherwise, they had a choice between accepting that and resigning. Most of the time, of course, disagreements were resolved by compromise, brokered by the then powerful Cabinet Office. Government therefore hung together.

Harold Wilson took Cabinet seriously. Under his premiership meetings lasted for up to four-and-a-half hours, until stomachs were grumbling for lunch. So did Jim Callaghan. His efforts to

achieve unity over the IMF cuts of 1976–77 lasted weeks. With
the exception, however, of a short-lived revival at the beginning of
John Major's premiership, the Cabinet has since become a dignified part of the constitution. Its meetings are perfunctory and are
usually occasions for the Prime Minister to lecture ministers on the
line they are to take.

Tony Crosland took Cabinet seriously too. His objection to the
1964–70 Labour government was its lack of strategy. He believed
that, if progress was to be made towards Labour's egalitarian objectives, policy had to be taken as a whole, with priorities carefully
delineated. So, for example, he established himself early as a critic
of the deflationary proclivities of the Treasury under Denis Healey.

Although government worked off collective Cabinet responsibility, it was not well equipped to brief ministers for this
responsibility. When a matter affecting the department came up,
especially if it threatened its spending, officials would clad their
minister in burnished armour. But when the minister took an
interest in a subject outside the department's remit it was a different matter. Humphrey Cole, the distinguished chief economist at
DoE and son of the great Fabian academic G. D. H. Cole, laboured
valiantly to fulfil Crosland's needs. But he faced a dilemma. On
these subjects, was his loyalty to his minister? Or was it to the collective view of the government, which meant (as ministers did not yet
have a collective view) the view of the Treasury, as promulgated
through the weekly meetings of Whitehall permanent secretaries?

This left something of a lacuna. Needs must and I endeavoured
to fill the vacuum.

Even now, the economic debate of the 1970s stirs strong feelings.
Was democratic socialism dead and therefore cuts and Thatcherism
inevitable? Or could it have been better managed so as to avoid that
nasty period in British life? That debate came to its climax after
Tony had left DoE in the IMF crisis of 1976–77.

The debate between the two schools – and thus essentially between
Healey and Crosland – raged. It has to be said, however, that the
two sides rarely touched. Crosland argued – quite rightly – that

deflation was unnecessary. It was simply creating holes in demand which would mean more unemployment, less production and less growth and (because of the impact on benefits and tax revenues) would not impact the budget deficit. Healey argued – quite rightly – that none of this mattered. International forces in the money markets with the full backing of international monetary institutions such as the IMF were demanding cuts in spending. One day, perhaps, Britain would have a strong balance of payments and a strongly growing economy, and then would come 'sod off day' when these forces could be ignored. In the meantime, reality required that they be heeded if economic destabilisation was to be avoided.

In Cabinet of course hearts were with Crosland, especially since his approach avoided cuts to individual ministers' budgets. Heads, however, generally ended up with the Chancellor, especially the head of the man who in the end took the rap, the Prime Minister. For a raw 26-year-old to be briefing a Cabinet minister against international capitalism might seem a little unwise. But no good alternative source of advice was available.

Crosland's stance did not much change the course of economic policy. But we did hope it might change the politics. At the beginning of the government Tony was behind a number of other ministers in any race to succeed Harold Wilson. Healey was the obvious choice; Roy Jenkins had not only a bunch of devoted acolytes but national stature; Callaghan was always first division; even Michael Foot had a large coterie of adherents. So the Crosland critique of Healey was not only putting down a marker as an alternative to the Chancellor, should his formidable will ever weaken or his Prime Minister get fed up with him. It was also, overtly or not, part of a long-term Croslandite leadership strategy.

I am unsure whether this was a good plan. In some ways, Tony might have advanced his cause more successfully as a more orthodox supporter of Wilson and Healey. His perceived competence as a departmental minister might have led to a gradual but discernible advance in his prospects as others – Healey himself, Jenkins – lost their gloss.

This may be so, but I don't remember us ever debating it. For Crosland's radical stance was a matter not just of intellect but of temperament. He was genuinely in the business of social and political change. He often wondered if Hugh Gaitskell, whose loyal disciple he had been, was sufficiently radical to be a successful leader of the Labour Party. He did want to be Prime Minister, but he wanted to be Prime Minister not just for the sake of it but for what he could do with it. So the middle road between Labour's left and right was the only one open to him. Alas in the end it led nowhere.

The test of how he was doing came with the Labour leadership contest of 1976.

Harold Wilson's decision to resign as Prime Minister caused widespread surprise because it seemed to be a job he relished. All sorts of weird theories have been floated to explain it, including plots by the security forces and blackmail.

Occam's Razor applies: the simplest explanation is the best. Wilson had been Prime Minister for eight years. It was a long hard slog, made much more arduous by his tempestuous relationship with his political secretary Marcia Williams (later Lady Falkender). Curiously, I have always found Marcia charm itself, both inside Number 10 and later, when despite being in a wheelchair she was a loyal Labour supporter in the Lords. Others report differently. But there is no doubt that she was a divisive figure in Number 10, earning the undying enmity of Harold's press secretary, Joe Haines, and the head of his Policy Unit, Bernard Donoughue. That made a hard job worse. Besides, Harold may have been feeling the early signs of Alzheimer's, which tragically struck him after he had left Downing Street. And certainly he drank brandy from morning to night.

If our intelligence had been better, we might have been aware of the bombshell about to explode. Jim Callaghan certainly knew, and that perhaps lent a certain serenity to his campaign for victory. Tony had to go on a conversation with Arnold Goodman, Harold's ubiquitous solicitor. Goodman had remarked to him at a party that he shouldn't make his dispositions on the assumption that Harold would not go – a sinuous formulation, but one on which we should have acted. For whatever reason, we didn't. So when Harold told the Cabinet that he was off, Crosland was as surprised as everyone else.

As luck would have it, he was suffering a streaming cold at the time. When I met him outside Downing Street, he was not his usual clear-thinking self as adrenalin and bugs fought it out. But from the first seconds, there was never any question that he would contest the leadership.

Susan Crosland says Tony was ambiguous about whether he wanted to be Prime Minister. I am sure she is right, but then so is practically every candidate for the job. It involves a frightful sacrifice of personal privacy – a particularly hard blow to someone like Crosland who was deeply private.

Success is not assured. I was later to have the privilege of spending a few days with Neil Kinnock immediately after his defeat in the 1992 general election. He showed courage and dignity, but his sense that his true powers would never now find full expression was inescapable. Besides, you cannot but wonder if you are up to the job. Even Tony Blair, shortly before the 1997 general election, had a moment when he suddenly realised that he was almost certainly going to win, and wondered what next.

But Crosland would have run even if he had understood that he was not going to win. There was one thing more important to his psyche than becoming Prime Minister: to come out ahead of Roy Jenkins, his friend and rival. He wanted to show that his loyalty to Labour, which went (he thought) much deeper than Jenkins's, would be rewarded.

As with most elections, if you want to understand what happened, it pays first to master the rules. The election for the leadership of the Labour Party (and in this case for the Queen's summons to form a government) was decided at that time wholly and exclusively by Labour MPs. It was only later that the unions and constituency parties got a direct say.

Moreover it was decided by an exhaustive ballot of those MPs. A round of voting was held and the bottom candidate was eliminated. So was any candidate who could not overtake their next rival even if all those who had voted for the bottom candidate switched to them. The process continued until a final two-horse race.

To win, you needed two things. The first was wide support among Labour MPs or at least wide acceptance that you could do the job. The second was that you had enough MPs who would plump for you in the first ballot, so you were still in the race for the later rounds. Tony was confident, rightly or wrongly, that he would meet the first test. The second test was trickier.

Tony had done his duty talking to his Labour fellows around the House. He never, however, established a dedicated fan club, who would work for him and his advancement. He was a one-man band.

A few Labour MPs volunteered their services. Perhaps the classic Croslandite was Bruce Douglas-Mann, who had been the MP for Kensington North, loved locally for his campaigning mostly on housing, and who was of a Croslandite disposition. But no one could call him a worldly man. Years later, not only did he defect from Labour to the newly formed Social Democratic Party, he insisted that honour required him to resign his seat and fight a by-election in his Mitcham and Morden constituency. This showed up his colleagues, none of whom had the faintest intention of similarly giving up their own seats. He went down, gallantly, to defeat, a defeat which secretly delighted his fellow Social Democrats.

The only person who could effectively canvass for our campaign was Tony himself. I remember a long Sunday afternoon in his study at Lansdowne Road. Tony sat with a list of Labour MPs on a board with as many phone numbers as we could find. He began to ring round his colleagues.

We could hear both ends of the conversation. Tony would begin brightly soliciting support. We would hear the voice at the other end: 'Don't know yet', 'Haven't thought it through', 'Of course I am a great admirer of yours', 'Several strong candidates'. Tony would put down the phone. 'I think we can mark him as a probable, don't you?'

There were comic moments. One was when Labour MP John Stonehouse showed Tony his ballot paper, marked with a cross against his name. Stonehouse was a rum character, who later faked his own death in an attempt to avoid a political scandal. It turned out that he had photocopied his ballot paper and showed it with a cross in the appropriate place to all six candidates.

Within a day or two, it was clear we had practically no support. Dick Leonard, not in the House but advising, strongly recommended that Tony step down from the contest in favour of Callaghan. This was good politics, but misunderstood the man's psyche. He would rather lose than give up.

Tony himself thought that fifteen to twenty votes would be a 'v. bad result'. A v. bad result was what he got: seventeen. Roy Jenkins did less well than he must have hoped to, ending up with fifty-six votes. Nevertheless that was three times what Tony got. Jim Callaghan moved more or less serenely to victory and we prepared once more to do battle with housing at the Department of Environment.

CHAPTER 5

A FOREIGN EXPERIENCE
1976–77

It should not have been a shock when Jim Callaghan appointed
Tony as Foreign Secretary.

There were two other obvious contenders: Roy Jenkins and
Denis Healey. Jim could have appointed Roy or moved Denis to
the FCO and made Tony Chancellor.

The former, though expected by the Jenkins clique, would not
have been a wise move. Roy Jenkins's pro-European position,
widely admired in the press, was not then so well thought of in the
Parliamentary Labour Party (PLP). PLP opinion covered a wide
spectrum, from fanatical pros to fanatical antis. The referendum
in 1975 had settled the matter of British membership, but it had
hardly been an enthusiastic pro-Market verdict. Rather, the British
people looked at who was in favour of staying in and looked at
those who wanted to come out. The opponents, not to put too
fine a point on it, looked like a bunch of nutters, so they decided
to side with the sane. But, despite that, the public wanted a robust
British stance in pursuit of our national interests in Europe.
Certainly, that was what the majority of the Parliamentary Labour
Party favoured.

The trouble with Roy Jenkins was not that he would actually act
too pro-European. Parliament would not support him if he did.
The trouble rather was that, because of his views, people would
suspect him of being too pro-European. He would then have to
compensate by affecting a less positive approach than he in fact
favoured. The prospect of this pro-European pretending to be a
sceptic to please the crowd was not a recipe for success.

The Healey/Crosland switch was much more plausible. Healey,
like Crosland, was mildly pro-Market, essentially on political
grounds. But he did not care much about it. In 1972, he had

indeed announced his conversion to the anti-Market camp. For some reason, the Jenkinsites forgave Healey as they never forgave Crosland, perhaps because they had never thought Healey was a man of principle in the first place.

Healey was a former international secretary of the Labour Party and had been gripped by international affairs all his life. This may have been one reason why Callaghan hesitated to give him the job, for Healey would, from day one, have been his own man as Foreign Secretary. Callaghan as Prime Minister would have struggled to assert his will. As he had just been doing the Foreign Secretary's job, conflict would have more than likely lain ahead.

In any case, Britain was only just getting to grips with the economic problems which were to convulse it for the next couple of years. Callaghan was essentially an economic conservative, as he had proved when Chancellor in the 1964–70 Labour government. Crosland was a radical and a Keynesian. There was every danger that he would flirt with policies which seemed to Callaghan to be dangerous. Better to leave Healey in place at the Exchequer to do the heavy lifting. Crosland could always be shifted there later, once the economy had weathered its crisis.

Crosland, it was true, did not know much about international affairs. This was because they did not directly impact on his political objective: greater equality. Aid to developing countries was of course an exception, and arguably the most important egalitarian policy of all. He dutifully added it to his regular lists of ten (or six or whatever) priorities for a Labour government, though he had no particular expertise in it.

International issues could also occasionally impinge on egalitarian policies in other ways. One such was the zero-growth movement of the early 1970s, discussed in Chapter 3. Tony indeed was at an international conference in Tokyo on precisely this when the deputy leadership fell vacant in 1972, leading to an eye-watering telephone bill.

He did have an international reputation as a philosopher of democratic socialism. Even before we went to the Foreign Office,

I had gone with him on one international expedition as a result of this.

Óscar Arias was then a promising young student at the London School of Economics. He invited Tony to Costa Rica to deliver a lecture on social democracy in Europe. Costa Rica was that rarity, a democracy in Latin America, of which Arias later rose to be President.

To make the trip worthwhile, it was combined with an official visit to Venezuela. The Foreign Office at that time was keen on cultivating relations with Venezuela. It was an oil-rich country and therefore expected to prosper. Nigeria was similarly targeted. It was only many years later that economists came to understand the 'tragedy of the commons' or 'resource curse'. Nothing is worse for a country's prosperity than to be well endowed with natural resources. For in countries so endowed, the ruling elite invariably spend their time struggling to appropriate these natural resources to its bank accounts, rather than actually doing anything to enhance their country's productive wealth. At the time, however, oil wealth seemed to represent tomorrow's export markets, and so we spent several days in Caracas.

In Costa Rica, David McDonald (also accompanying Crosland) and I had striking evidence that he had at least one of the qualities required of a Foreign Secretary: stamina.

After the lecture, the Costa Ricans laid on a banquet. They had a promising student who they wanted to get onto a course in Britain and, as she was also exceedingly voluptuous, they conceived a cunning plan. She was sat at the dinner next to Crosland, on whom she lavished attention, while he was plied with industrial quantities of alcohol.

The party broke up in the wee small hours. Britain's ambassador to Costa Rica was on home leave – drying out, we were told – so the residence was occupied only by junior staff. With the greatest of difficulty did David and I – both little men – bear the slumped figure of the Secretary of State for the Environment into the residence and onto his bed.

It was 3.00 am and we left for the airport at 5.30. David and I did not sleep, as we despaired over how we were ever to get our man home.

At 5.29 precisely, the door of Crosland's room opened. There he stood, immaculately clad. 'Right, gentlemen, are we off?' We drove to the airport.

'Would you like a drink, Mr Crosland?' said one of the farewell party, no doubt thinking of a cup of Costa Rica's excellent coffee. 'Yes, I'll have a large whisky,' replied the Secretary of State. A large whisky he got.

Crosland was no Little Englander. However, it was possible in those days, when globalisation was in its relative infancy, to conduct yourself as a serious domestic politician without ever becoming involved in international politics.

Whole aspects of big power politics had passed him by. I never recall him expressing an opinion on the Cold War or on Vietnam or on the rise of Japan. I don't think he ever considered whether Britain needed a bomb or not (his instinct would be 'yes' just because 'no' was a cause of the party's anti-Gaitskell wing). I don't think he had considered the role of armed forces or the importance of human rights.

If Crosland was less than fully equipped for the new job he had been given, the same was true in spades for me. I had a shaky knowledge of geography. My history largely stopped at 1939. I had no great international acquaintanceship. The Foreign Office must have wondered why on earth I had washed up with them. This was particularly so because my predecessor, Callaghan's special adviser Tom McNally, later Lib Dem leader in the Lords, was a former international secretary of the Labour Party and a considerable expert.

It was not just Crosland's (and my) ignorance that made for initial difficulties. There was the little matter of class prejudice – ours.

Not all members of the Foreign Office were toffs – indeed not all of them were even Conservatives – but many of them seemed that way.

Crosland had had particularly bad experiences with ambassadors' wives. He would tell the story of one who had greeted him on a foreign tour when he was Secretary of State for Education. 'Now Mr Crosland, you know *everything* about education,' she said. 'Tell me, which would you recommend for Joanna, Roedean or Cheltenham Ladies?'

The main topic of conversation of the Venezuelan ambassador's wife was the wholly inadequate size of her swimming pool and the deplorable failure of the office to do anything about it.

There was also the matter of social styles. Tony was capable of laying on the charm, but he needed to be persuaded that it was necessary. Foreign Office receptions did not appeal. Meetings with ambassadors from countries of which he knew nothing to discuss nothing of importance (to him) seemed a total waste of time. This was not a popular stance with the diplomats.

One particular incident stands out. Tony was to attend a European meeting in Luxembourg. He had sent instructions to the ambassador that what he required on arrival was a briefing meeting over sandwiches.

Unfortunately, Sir Antony Acland, later a distinguished head of the office, had not believed him. He laid on a banquet. To make matters worse, there was a long delay while the food was being prepared.

I could see the steam rising from the Foreign Secretary's head. Finally, he could bear it no longer. 'David,' he said, 'I believe I saw a ping-pong table by the front door as we walked in. Would you care for a game?'

My life flashed before my eyes. If I said 'Don't be ridiculous, you rude man', I should have won lifelong friends in the Foreign Office. However, those friends would not include the man for whom I worked and to whom I owed my allegiance. I rose. We played. He won. (I had learned something from that croquet match with Jenkins.) Fifteen minutes later, Tony returned, equilibrium restored, and the evening went off without further incident.

There were also issues of policy. The Foreign Office generally took a conservative line on everything. This was partly a matter of background and temperament. However, it was also the case that diplomats tended to put a high priority on the relationship with America, and American politicians tended to be to the right of British ones. There was an exception to this, however, on two items. One was the budget of the FCO itself, where such items as free public schooling for their children and sumptuous residences were not negotiable. The other was defence. They therefore found it hard to adjust to a Secretary of State who was for public spending, against private education and sceptical about defence expenditure.

Foreign Office officials had an extraordinary knowledge of culture, of history and of the variety of human societies. They were, however, relatively ignorant of and indifferent to the ideological side of Britain's domestic policies.

In so far as they had a doctrine it was three-fold. The office was passionate for free trade. I was then a pragmatist on that subject, verging (probably wrongly) at times into a sceptic. I remember a magisterial memorandum by a senior official, John Fretwell, explaining to the Secretary of State why I was wrong.

They were also, by now and almost to a man, committed pro-Europeans. This was not always so. After the war, many hankered for Empire, and even those who didn't were slow to be prepared to give up a wholly independent British foreign policy. The conversion by the time we arrived was complete. It was indeed personified by Michael Palliser, the ultimate European, married to the Belgian statesman Paul-Henri Spaak's daughter, Marie. Palliser was an old Brussels hand with a deep personal commitment to Europe. Because of this Margaret Thatcher later denied him the peerage he deserved.

By then I had learned largely to keep my mouth shut about the subject. The referendum had not gone my way. I nevertheless remember one exchange with Sir Roy Denman, the senior Cabinet Office official with responsibility for Europe and a fanatical pro-European. Tony wanted some work done on the economic effects of community membership. Denman was not convinced. 'The Secretary of State's question reminds me of the man who jumped off the Empire State Building,' he said. 'On passing the 24th floor, he said, "Not much seems to have happened yet."' I pointed out that Denman's exceptionally deficient skyscraper jumper had presumably ended up in a bloody mess on the sidewalk.

The truth was that the FCO's pro-European disposition was not about economics at all. It was about wispy propositions about keeping the peace in Europe – as if by the mid-1970s there was any possibility of anything else. It was about a hope that, somehow, Britain could lead in Europe and in that way regain the strength it had lost.

Finally, the office was viscerally anti-communist. There was nothing wrong with that in principle, and it was a view shared by the Secretary of State. However, it could lead to serious distortions. For example, the FCO found it difficult to take Eurocommunism as other than a ruse. Enrico Berlinguer had risen to lead the Italian Communist Party (PCI) on a ticket which incorporated independence from the Soviet Union. The FCO would not take this at face value. Indeed, I was despatched by the Secretary of State to Italy to take a view. I found our embassy adamant in its scepticism. 'In Northern Italy,' I was told, 'they talk only of "the man with the moustache" – Stalin.'

When it became clear that the Foreign Secretary was not entirely convinced, officials were unabashed. 'Well, we may think the PCI is all right,' they would argue, 'but the Americans don't.' If an avowedly communist government took over a European state, then the Americans would rethink their security commitments, went the line. I think also it was tinged by the fact that some prominent Foreign Office officials were Catholics and shared their faith's opposition to the PCI.

They may have been right. We shall never know for Berlinguer never won power in Italy. Like most European left parties, it hit a vote ceiling some way below a majority, stuck and faded. I regret however that, as democratic socialists, Crosland (and I) never spoke out more firmly in support of Berlinguer. His shift sowed the seeds for the collapse of old-style communism in Europe.

A hilarious example of the office's anti-communism lay in the work of the Information Research Department (IRD). The ostensible purpose of this outfit was to produce briefings for unattributable use by journalists and others in support of Britain's foreign policies. It was headed by Ray Whitney, later a Conservative MP. Under him, it had turned itself into a sort of mini-CIA, a propaganda machine campaigning everywhere against communist policies. Its material, for example, exposed the links between liberation movements and Moscow.

We did not object to this work, crude though some of it was. What we objected to was the underlying assumption that there was only one force opposing Britain's foreign policy interests in the globe, and that was communism.

Exasperated, we turned on Whitney. The liberation struggle in South Africa was then raging, with the white regime floundering in its search for international legitimacy. 'Why', we asked, 'don't you do one of your briefings on South Africa?'

Some weeks later, they proudly presented their handiwork. I think it was called 'The ANC: the Communist Bid for Power'. That was not what the Foreign Secretary had had in mind.

IRD was a relatively open bit of the otherwise closed intelligence network. At that time, however, I am not sure that the intelligence services were bringing us much that was useful.

I was cleared to see some intelligence. It would arrive in locked boxes with ferocious instructions – eat before reading. I found it disappointing. Most of what I read I had already seen earlier in the *Financial Times* and *The Economist*. Never having been handy with locks and keys, I soon abandoned the unequal struggle.

The intelligence services came back into their own in later years, helping us to keep on top of the ongoing threat of terrorism. They also helped lead us into the Iraq war when politicians overinterpreted their cautious judgements on weapons of mass destruction. Like salt, we need them, but in modest quantities.

Foreign Office officials, who were gifted analysts of every country's politics, for some reason made an exception of their own. They had a respect for Parliament, but had neither time for nor understanding of British party politics.

So a right-wing Tory MP would put down some parliamentary question in some way critical of the government. Such happenings were quite rare, compared with the parliamentary and political tumult than engulfed DoE day in, day out. It seemed to Crosland and me that they drew quite disproportionate concern in the office.

However, they found it hard to accommodate Labour views. It is true that the Labour Party was already quasi-Marxist on foreign policy issues. The international secretary, Jenny Little, was more a naïve liberal than a Marxist. She was heavily under the influence of Alex Kitson, a trade unionist who chaired the party's international committee, who may or may not have been a secret communist. Certainly, the party trod perilously close to the Soviet line, besides being essentially unilateralist on deterrence.

We had no time for the substance of these views. But we felt we had to be willing to debate them openly, and to receive the endless party delegations urging support for this or that liberationist movement. Tony's reputation as a party man benefited from this, though it had little impact on the government's foreign policy.

On a visit to New York, Tony arranged to brief the press on what he had been doing. Ham Whyte, then the much-loved consul general there, arranged a cocktail party for this purpose. Among those he invited was a visiting Conservative MP, Jill Knight.

Tony was livid. How was he to brief in the presence of opposition spies? Whyte was bewildered. What possible objection could there be to British parliamentarians together flying the nation's flag? The difference between the two men hung round like a bad smell. Crosland thought little of Ham's efforts later, as the FCO's chief press spokesman. He came within an inch of firing him. Whyte, who wanted to like Crosland, was deeply hurt. Diplomats tried to heal the rift and I was even recruited to this noble cause, but wholly without success.

Given my ignorance of foreign affairs, a chief role was to keep Crosland as central as possible on the domestic stage. The Foreign Office resented any time this pinched off their tasks for their Foreign Secretary. On the other hand, they could see I was doing the Secretary of State's will, and furthermore that they collectively were incapable of what I did for him domestically. I was not perhaps indispensable at the Foreign Office, as I was at DoE, but officials could see I had my uses.

Seeing party delegations was one example. I remember in particular the visit of Nicu Ceauşescu, the odious son of the odious Romanian dictator. The Labour Party had invited him to London, no doubt to explore common ground between it and them. Mike Gapes, the national student organiser, who later became a moderate Labour MP, reported that Ceauşescu's first question to his party hosts was 'Where is this Soho?'

John Tomlinson, our junior Foreign Office minister, and I cooked up a good plot to deal with Ceauşescu. He would not be allowed to see a minister, but he could see me. I temporarily moved out of my rabbit hutch into Tomlinson's enormous and opulent office, where I sat behind his grand desk, looking down my nose at the baby dictator. I proceeded to berate him and his policies for a full half-hour before inviting him to depart. I don't suppose he had ever been so unceremoniously treated. Later, of course, he endured worse when he died of cirrhosis after years in prison.

I could therefore be useful to the Foreign Office. But it would be wrong to ascribe simply to self-interest the generally warm reception I received. Indeed, I made many friends there, some of whom remain so.

They were led by the – literally – towering figure of Euan Fergusson, the Secretary of State's private secretary. Fergusson was a Renaissance man, both hugely cultured and a former Scotland rugby player. He had enormous *joie de vivre* and a sparkling sense of humour.

Strangely, he rather looked up to me – not physically, where I barely reached his knees, but intellectually. Fergusson, good brain though he had, had taken a second at university. For some atavistic reason, he thought this made him much inferior to me with my first. At any rate, this corrected the balance between us and we got on.

My other special chum was John Kerr, later head of the Foreign Office and a crossbench peer. Kerr at the time was private secretary to Palliser. Crosland and Palliser were not naturally bosom pals for reasons of inverse snobbery on the latter's part. Kerr and I therefore had to work hard to smooth relations. Besides, we were temperamentally of a kind, quick minded, aware of human motivations and not too given to theorising. Unfortunately, Kerr's later headship of the office was marred by his poor relations with the Foreign Secretary, Robin Cook, who, he thought, tried to pressure him to say things were the case that were not.

Alongside me as Crosland's official speechwriter worked Chris Meyer, later ambassador in Washington and press spokesman at Number 10. Meyer shocked many in the Foreign Office by producing an indiscreet book of memoirs after he left. This was rightly felt to transgress the boundary which meant that officials never dumped on their ministers. With his fancy plumage and taste for the champagne lifestyle, Meyer was a character. I don't think he was a good speechwriter. To be that you have to put yourself into the character of the person for whom you are writing, and Meyer was not a natural empathiser with Crosland – or anyone much else come to that. Still, that left room for me.

One particular difficulty that goes with being Foreign Secretary is that your duties and ambitions as a domestic politician don't go away. Tony still had his Grimsby constituency to look after. He even insisted that urgent talks with Henry Kissinger, the US Secretary, could only take place if Kissinger flew to Grimsby for the purpose. He did, to a local American air base, and the two formed a lasting if strange friendship. But of course there is also the foreign travel – onerous even then but now even more so given the huge weight of European Union meetings the Foreign Secretary is expected to attend.

I am a poor traveller, always losing my passport or my luggage and not keen on being outside my natural environment. However, the currency in which I traded was my knowledge of the Foreign Secretary and that required that I went with him sometimes to top up my account.

The two main trips I did were to Yugoslavia and to China. Of these, Yugoslavia was the more enjoyable, and not simply because the endless slivovitz there was a good deal more palatable than the disgusting Mao Tai, which was all there was to drink in China. I ended up that trip with the worst stomach of my life, which traditional Chinese medicine failed to cure.

Yugoslavia is mostly fascinating because of subsequent events. All the talk was what would happen when Marshal Tito, the strongman who had bought the republics together, had gone. History records the dreadful answer.

China was my first adventure to a communist country. It was at the height of the revolutionary fervour which accompanied the Cultural Revolution and the bid for power of Madam Mao. This led to some comic incidents. After one long lecture at a school on the iniquities of the 'capitalist roader' Deng Xiaoping, Crosland asked the speaker to explain the meaning of 'capitalist roader'. He was not able (or at least the translator was not able) to help.

The Chinese had also evidently been told that Westerners could not tell them apart. As the corpus of politically reliable interlocutors was limited, therefore, they fielded the same person in different roles. In the morning, a personable young man would appear as the head of urban development. In the afternoon, I spotted the same man parading as a leader of a collective farm. I expect they thought we would not notice.

I was particularly struck by the complete lack of any attention, under communism, to health and safety. Steel was made in tiny open furnaces with no protection at all for the operatives.

When we finally flew from China to Japan, I felt an almost physical feeling of relief at escaping totalitarianism.

'When I pop off,' Tony told Susan at one point, 'and they open my heart, on it will be engraved "Fish" and "Rhodesia".'

I kept out of fish. The so-called 'Cod War' between Britain and Iceland was not a war, though the Royal Navy was sent to protect British fishing boats. Indeed, the issue – what, if any, fishing rights Britain should have in waters claimed by Iceland – was not of front-rank importance. It mattered to Tony, however, for his beloved fishermen in Grimsby were the ones who would lose from an extension of Iceland's rights.

It was impossible to be in the FCO and keep out of Rhodesia. Ever since Ian Smith, the white premier, had declared Rhodesia unilaterally independent of Britain in 1965 successive governments had sought to bring about a return to legality which required a transition to majority rule. As is common in diplomacy, this was a multifaceted problem. To progress needed Britain's support, but also, crucially, that of the African 'front-line' states, those bordering Rhodesia. At a crucial stage, Henry Kissinger, the American Secretary of State, decided to swing his weight behind settlement endeavours.

I was not an optimist. The presidents of the front-line states were not easy to deal with. The Rhodesian blacks were split between followers of Bishop Muzorewa, of Joshua Nkomo and of Robert Mugabe. The bishop was much courted by British diplomats because he was the most tractable. That meant weak.

Nkomo was a pantomime African leader, vastly overweight, surrounded by minions and courtiers, bullying, noisy and nasty. Nevertheless the Foreign Office was keener on him than it was on Mugabe. This was because Mugabe was an avowed Marxist. Personally, I thought Mugabe was the least bad of the bunch. That judgement does not today look one of my more sensible ones, though I doubt if either the fat man or the feeble bishop would have turned out much better.

My wider view was that this was a buggers' muddle with no hope of a peaceful settlement. Britain had failed when it allowed Smith to break away without the use of arms. We were *persona non grata* all round – with the white Rhodesians, for failing to back our kith and kin, with the black Rhodesian leaders, for backing them in imperialist fashion, and at times with Kissinger and the Americans, for an unwillingness to contribute enough by way of peacekeeping forces if ever a deal was done. We should just wash our hands of Rhodesia and let them find their own solution.

Tony let me put my view at a meeting of officials. To my surprise one senior official, and a top Africanist at that, sided with me. Sir Anthony Duff, the immensely distinguished Foreign Office supremo on Africa, disagreed and so, reluctantly, did Tony. It was put to him as a matter of duty; and he did not flinch. He was supported by an energetic junior minister with a fertile mind, Ted Rowlands.

One advantage of this was that it finally changed the way Tony viewed his job. He had been unhappy at the FCO early on. It was so different from domestic policy. Domestically, you had at any rate a strong illusion of being in charge. You had the money; you had the ability to legislate; you could call the shots. In foreign affairs, you did not have much of these things, nor could you painlessly turn to the old remedy, military force.

Over Rhodesia, Tony came to work closely with Henry Kissinger. It was Kissinger who taught him to enjoy this, for the very limitations added to the intellectual interest. And it turned out that foreign affairs involved some interesting dilemmas – national interest versus international interests, democracy and its relationship to prosperity, human rights and their selective implementation. It was not about equality, it was about other things which also mattered.

Eventually, talks to resolve Rhodesia began in Geneva. Tony sensibly held himself back to await the right time to make an intervention. Ivor Richard, a Labour-supporting QC who later became the party's leader in the Lords, was sent to lead our team.

At one point, I was sent on an advance expedition to advise Tony if he should attend. For those used to the propaganda of imperial splendour, it was a singular experience. The Africans were established in the plushest Geneva hotels, with fleets of cars and plenty to occupy them between negotiating sessions. The British expenses allowances extended to a room not much bigger than a decent closet, from which Ivor and his team were supposed to conduct business. Ivor did not have room to swing a cat, but he had at least acquired a decent supply of Her Majesty's whisky.

We got nowhere. Had Tony ever gone, I doubt if he would have got anywhere either. And the thought of Tony, with his strong preference for the swift despatch of business, in enervated Geneva – well, let us say, it would have created man-management problems.

My belief that Britain should have stayed out looked perfectly supportable then. However, in 1979, it certainly didn't. At the Lancaster House talks Mrs Thatcher and her Foreign Secretary Peter Carrington managed a deal.

My preference for Mugabe for a while looked unsustainable. Once majority rule was achieved, he wiped out large numbers of his tribal rivals. Then for a while it looked like it might succeed: Marxism took second place to pragmatism and it did not seem wholly ridiculous to dream of a peaceful, prosperous Zimbabwe. But then the long descent into the hell that is Mugabe's Zimbabwe today began.

The last weeks of Tony's Foreign Secretaryship were dominated by an issue that nearly destroyed the Callaghan government.

The markets were jittery about the pound. This was not surprising as Britain had a weak economy, threatening inflation and a government dangerously in hock to the trade unions. A package of cuts – opposed by Crosland – had been made in July 1976. They bought little time. By the end of that year, it was apparent that Britain would require more structured international support if a stabilisation crisis was to be avoided. Talks were therefore begun with the International Monetary Fund. It could itself lend to Britain. More important, its imprimatur on a country's policies in itself restored confidence, and opened the way to an inflow of private capital.

The sensible strategy for the Foreign Secretary would have been to sit on the sidelines. It was not his job to negotiate the loans. That was for the Prime Minister and his Chancellor. Britain's interests, as perceived by the Foreign Office, lay in stability, no matter what the domestic cost. So long as defence spending was not cut by too much, and so long as there was no question of us selling off our magnificent worldwide collection of embassies, the Foreign Secretary should have supported the Chancellor.

However, Tony was not able to separate himself as Foreign Secretary from being a domestic politician, nor indeed an economist. He believed there was no objective need for the cuts and that cuts would shred desirable social programmes; and he believed that they would lead to higher unemployment.

Tony was heavily occupied elsewhere – as indeed was I. He urgently needed a professional economist to help him. He chose Michael Stewart, an unrepentant Keynesian, for this role. Too late, for the IMF was done and dusted and Tony dead before Stewart could get into his stride.

The tale of how Jim Callaghan manoeuvred his Cabinet into accepting the cuts has been widely told. It was a classic case of divide-and-rule. A majority of the Cabinet was not initially behind the Chancellor so it had to be split. And fortunately for Callaghan, it was. The traditional Keynesian right wanted less deflationary policies, but within the context of the British economy as it was run. The Bennite left wanted less deflationary policies but within the context of a siege economy, directly cutting imports, increasing the role of the state and generally moving to something like a planned economy.

The period of the IMF negotiations was the most stressful I experienced in government. I shared Crosland's views. Though I did not have his years of experience with the ups and downs of government, the cuts seemed to me to be the end of that Labour government as a purposeful force for change. Years later, many felt the same way about Tony Blair's policy on Iraq.

Naturally, the Foreign Office could not be expected to brief the

Foreign Secretary to oppose cuts, so, until Stewart's arrival I had to do it. At first, we seemed to be doing well but gradually the wheels fell off.

Harold Lever, Chancellor of the Duchy of Lancaster and the government's unofficial minister for financial markets, was not an orthodox financier but neither was he an orthodox defender of public spending. He was soon ploughing his own furrow. Shirley Williams, though perhaps on our side, made things so complicated that she was hardly a worthwhile ally. Roy Hattersley was a supporter, though Tony knew he kept a foot firmly in the Prime Minister's camp. Our majority was soon fraying.

I myself was distraught. I even managed to come quite near to getting myself sacked. During the negotiations, a party was held at the Foreign Office. I was chatting with my friend Peter Jenkins of *The Guardian* about the cuts. I may have started off relatively discreet, I don't know, but I didn't finish up that way. I didn't actually tell him anything, but when he described to me what he took the state of negotiations to be, I nodded or shook my head with unwise frequency.

Next morning, he had taken the unusual step for a columnist of writing up the state of negotiations as an exclusive lead for the paper. It did not help that, when summoned by Crosland, I had not yet got round to reading *The Guardian*, and so had no idea what I had done. Crosland was rightly cross. If he had been 99 per cent of Cabinet ministers, I would have been out the door. But he was not and his loyalty saved me.

In the end, Crosland faced a stark decision. He could continue to oppose the cuts, perhaps even to the point of resignation, a move that would shake the government and play into the hands of the left opposition. Or he could swallow the cuts and keep his counsel. On the eve of the crucial Cabinet, that is what he decided to do.

When Cabinet met on 2 December 1976, the minutes record – and unusually ascribe to Crosland – the following. He 'remained absolutely unconvinced by the arguments which have been used in terms of merit. But his totally clear political judgement was that, given the position the PM had taken, it would not be right to press the issue.'

The IMF deal was often subsequently said to represent the end of social democracy, on the Croslandite model. This is nonsense. Firstly, the cuts it imposed were not that severe. They were no harsher certainly than the cuts of the previous year. And they were in turn outdistanced in their deflationary effect by the cuts which arose out of a new system of 'cash limits' for departmental spending, by which the Treasury re-established its control. With the benefit of hindsight, cuts probably were needed, if only because of the period of incontinent spending which followed Labour's election in 1974. We even subsidised food!

Secondly, it wasn't the level of public expenditure that brought us to the tricky hole we were in. It is true that the first Thatcherite murmurings about the size of the state were being heard. Roy Jenkins joined the club claiming that state spending of 60 per cent of GDP – he somehow persuaded himself that this was the true figure – was a threat to liberty and democracy. In fact, it is doubtful, extremes apart, if there is any level of public spending which is an absolute limit under social democracy. The Swedes and Norwegians cope with much higher levels than we do. It all depends on social mores and political structures.

There was a crisis in classical social democracy. It was not about public spending, which was never more than a symbol. The incompatibility which brought social democracy low was that between strong unions, practising free collective bargaining, and the need for non-inflationary growth. The traditional way in which these were reconciled was through incomes policies, designed to keep wages to what could be afforded. However, these were becoming harder and harder to enforce, and gummed up the workings of the labour market. Union support went up and down, with Jack Jones and Hugh Scanlon, the leaders of the TGWU and AEUW respectively, being prepared to lend their weight when the crisis was at its height. But this was a short-term fix with no long-term exit.

The dilemma was resolved in the end by a sharp deflation under

Thatcher, accompanied by wave after wave of legislation designed to curb the trade unions. As a result, it was again possible to conceive of a stable social democracy. New Labour provided that sort of government, or rather it did to the extent that Tony Blair believed in it.

Fish, Rhodesia, IMF – the strain on the Foreign Secretary was immense as 1976 ended and 1977 began.

I was lecturing to a group of civil servants when a note was brought in asking me to speak to Euan Fergusson immediately. I could tell it was serious, and hurried out to the groans of the audience, which was looking forward to ripping me apart.

He gave me the news that Crosland had been struck down by a massive stroke and was in the Radcliffe Infirmary in Oxford. I was to tell his stepdaughter, Ellen Craig, and bring her to meet Susan at the hospital. Of course, this was all top secret and I left my meeting without explanation.

The thought that Tony might get ill had never much occurred to me. He was only fifty-nine and of exceptional vigour. But there was no disguising the dangers of his lifestyle. Unlike Roy Jenkins, who rose early in the mornings to walk rapidly around his tennis court, Crosland took little discernible exercise. His cigars, adopted because the research showed cigarettes were dangerous, were ever present. Though he was no longer as keen on alcohol as he had been earlier in his career, these things are relative. Three large gins were his usual before taking parliamentary questions. He was overweight and he wheezed.

I don't much like to remember the week Tony lay stricken. The Radcliffe, bless them, provided a blanket of peace, so we were almost entirely isolated as we began to mourn.

There Tony lay like a fallen Colossus, breath coming in deep gusts, followed often by alarming silences. And yet he looked entirely normal, as if at any moment he could wake up and get back to work. Susan and the family sat with him except for short stints when I did duty so they could snatch a little sleep. There were tears.

At one point, it occurred to me that the country was without a Foreign Secretary. I raised the matter with Susan, and we agreed I would talk to the Prime Minister. He preferred to wait.

From time to time, I would take a call from a national newspaper. They offered fabulous sums for an interview with Susan.

Eventually the breathing stopped. In the small hours, at Susan's request, I made a short televised broadcast to the world from the Radcliffe. My years with Tony Crosland were over.

Had Tony kept health and strength, would he have become Prime Minister? At first blush, this is as pointless a question as to ask what his views might be on x, y or z. We cannot know.

Nevertheless, it makes for an interesting speculation. The question breaks down into three. Would his career as a Cabinet minister have continued to prosper? If it did, would he have succeeded Jim Callaghan as Labour leader in opposition in 1980? And if he did so succeed, would he have won the 1983 general election?

There is some reason to doubt where his career might have gone. He might have succeeded Healey in 1978, he might have grabbed credit for the recovery that got under way and he might therefore have been in good shape after Labour's loss in the 1979 general election.

However, he had made a bloody nuisance of himself over the IMF cuts. Callaghan, having promoted him, might have expected more support from him earlier. He might have been punished.

Moreover, those close to Callaghan at the time claim to have detected in Tony some slowing up, a loss of edge. That was not apparent during the IMF debates themselves but the fact of ageing could not be disputed even without special health factors. Thirty-odd years ago, people got ill a few years earlier than they do today. He had a 50:50 chance of his career prospering.

The leadership election that did take place was between Denis Healey and Michael Foot. This was the last Labour leadership contest in which votes were confined to Labour MPs.

There is no doubt that Denis Healey's views were closer to those of the majority of the PLP. Moreover, Michael Foot, dear man, was never going to be the people's choice for Prime Minister. Healey, however, had put little effort into cultivating backbenchers and had gone out of his way to insult the left, describing them in a speech shortly before the leadership as 'out of their tiny Chinese minds'. The left was beginning to assert its control of the Labour Party in the country. By electing Michael Foot, the PLP elected to pay a form of Danegeld to the left, in the hope of a quiet life.

How would Tony have fared? He would have been less unacceptable to the left than Healey, and more acceptable to the public than Foot. However, one problem would have raised its ugly head again: the first ballot problem. Foot and Healey represented left and right respectively, and therefore had core votes. Tony, in a right-of-centre but philosophically distinctive position, did not. We could have made a case – competence, sense of direction, vigour, strong character, unifier. Much would have depended on the dynamics of the leadership contest as it evolved. As a betting man, I should have had Crosland as around a 9/2 shot, behind Healey and Foot as co-favourites.

Finally, would he have won the 1983 general election? He would have been up against a formidable character in Thatcher. Moreover, not only was the economy by then starting to recover, she had just won the Falklands War. Crosland's military credentials were unquestioned, but he would not have been the victor of Stanley.

The worst obstacle would have been the Labour Party. The election manifesto was described by Gerald Kaufman, a shadow minister, as the 'longest suicide note in history'. It was not just that the party had a Trotskyite wing; it was that it had as a whole moved in a fundamentalist direction, towards state planning and state power. It must be doubtful if even Tony Crosland as leader would have been able to stand out against this shift, though at least he would have avoided the shambles over which Foot presided.

As things were, the party split. The breakaway of the Social Democratic Party is dealt with later but the split meant Labour lost many of its most publicly appealing figures, such as Shirley Williams. It lost men of weight, like Jenkins, and it lost the energetic, like David Owen. Now, if Crosland had been leader not Foot, it would have been harder for these people to break away. For all the rivalries, Crosland clearly had common ground with them. My own view is that the split would probably have happened anyway. It would have been at least as difficult for the Jenkinsites to rally behind Crosland as leader as it was for them to back Foot.

Even under Crosland's leadership, therefore, the chances of Labour winning the 1983 general election were slight – perhaps 7/1 against. He, like Foot, would have had only one go.

I should like to believe he would have become leader and would have ushered in a marvellous decade of social democratic government. But I am a betting man. Even money, 9/2 against, 7/1 against – that represents cumulative odds against a Crosland premiership had he lived of just shy of 90/1. And although this is a speculative exercise, it does perhaps illustrate just what a gamble political life is for an ambitious man.

Of one thing I am absolutely certain: Tony would have hated being leader. He would have loathed being constantly in the public eye. He was a good speaker but never a great orator, in the House or outside. There can be no guarantee he would have bested Thatcher. He was not naturally ruthless, nor selfish, and he didn't like sacking people. He might have proved popular in the country, but he was a singular taste. Eccentricity, even mild eccentricity, is something we tolerate less and less in our political leaders.

The state of the Labour Party would have been a sore in his side. He had no sympathy with the left, whom he had fought all his life. He would also have been frustrated by the right – both the Healeyites, lacking as he thought a philosophical basis for their socialism, and the Jenkinsites, lacking gut party loyalty. He would no doubt have set out a plausible stall, genuflecting here to the left while drawing lines there for the right. I doubt if he would have been comfortable with it. And in those circumstances I doubt if the British people would have been comfortable with him.

At the time, his death was a terrible blow. But at least he died at the peak of his powers, still able to dream that he might yet lead the Labour Party, still a leading politician in Britain and a growing figure in the world.

CHAPTER 6

THE DOWNING STREET
YEARS 1977–79

Many people lose their best friends young. Many people lose their jobs. Not so many, I think, lose both at the same instant. I did, and Tony's death left me utterly bereft.

He was my chum, my mentor and my idol. My views, professionally, were his views, but so were they in fact. We thought the same way and we usually reached the same conclusions. Even while he lived after the IMF cuts – a matter of weeks – I was in political despair. We had a Labour government to fulfil certain purposes. Following the cuts, we would not be fulfilling those purposes. So what were we for? My faith in my politics was severely shaken even before Tony died. After his death, what was I for?

I was unemployed. Special advisers cut grand figures today, much grander than they did then, but one fact has not changed: they are a heartbeat from unemployment. Indeed, I had already lost my job three times since 1974: when the February election was called, when another was called in October and when Harold Wilson resigned. Tony's death was a fourth. I did not have any assurance of a new job, and matters were not helped by the fact I was in the throes of the break-up of my first marriage to Elizabeth.

Liz and I – thank God! – had no children. Though in retrospect it had not been a well-advised marriage, breaking up was both painful and demanding. I am pleased to say that she later married Brian McHenry, a delightful friend of ours from the Streatham Labour Party days who followed a distinguished civil service career by becoming a vicar. She was a great deal happier with him than she ever could have been with me, as I was, wondrously, with my second wife Margaret.

Today, special advisers who leave government usually walk into well-paid jobs in public affairs. Then, there were practically no such jobs. We simply did not know whether our skills were going to be in demand, or whether we had walked into a dead end. So the future outside government looked bleak.

Fortunately, I had a reasonable reputation as a special adviser and Labour in those days looked after its own. David Owen, the new Foreign Secretary, generously offered to let me stay as long as I liked. Owen's appointment was controversial since he was only thirty-eight. He had been Crosland's deputy at the Foreign Office, so his appointment signalled continuity. Owen's career, it turned out, reached an early peak with his appointment, and he was a casualty of the politics of the breakaway SDP.

Owen could not have been more supportive to me following Tony's death, which he too felt deeply. His reputation was not pleasant, largely because he was reported to have said to his wife, Deborah, that he would plug her into the mains if she suffered post-natal depression. In fact, I could have done with being plugged into the FCO mains, but instead he held my hankie as I cried.

We agreed I would give it a go as his adviser, and while I was principally engaged in tidying up after Tony's death, answering the thousands of letters which poured in and so on, all went well. But, no fault of his, it began to emerge we were not well suited for each other.

Tony had an enormous orderly mind. David too had an enormous mind, but his greatest fan would not call it orderly. He proceeded in great leaps and then, when they turned out to be in the wrong direction, he leaped back again.

Almost as soon as I started with him, an episode occurred that decided we should not remain together. The issue was elections to the European Parliament and, in particular, what electoral system should be used.

Owen had a natural predisposition in favour of more proportional systems, such as those used in every other European country. I was sent off to write a Cabinet paper, setting out the case.

Merlyn Rees, the Home Secretary, popped in to see Owen. Owen expounded on the case with great eloquence. 'But Foreign Secretary,' said the saintly Merlyn. 'Don't you understand? The Labour Party is totally opposed to proportional representation. You'll never get it through the Commons.'

Owen paused, as if this was not a difficulty that had occurred to him. 'David,' he said. 'Please draft me a Cabinet paper setting out the case for first-past-the-post for European elections.'

Another of his Cabinet colleagues popped by. Owen warmed to his theme: the absolute superiority of first-past-the-post for European elections. 'But Foreign Secretary,' said the colleague. 'Don't you realise that the Liberals are adamant they must have proportional representation? Go for first-past-the-post and that is the end of their support for us' – support which was essential to our remaining in office.

Owen paused as before. 'David,' he said. 'Perhaps you would draft me a Cabinet paper setting out the case for proportional representation for Europe.'

I should emphasise that this seems to me, some thirty-five years later, a perfectly defensible way of working. You try a garment on and if it does not look good, you try another one. However, this was not how Tony had worked and it did not suit me. I wrote the paper, and then I wrote a letter of resignation. David Owen later recruited a political adviser, David Stephen, who was fit for purpose.

Once I declined Owen, I had two good offers open. One was to join Denis Healey as political adviser, a vacant position which he had been having some difficulty in filling. I was more than a little surprised to be asked, given I had been at Crosland's side as we sought to destroy his IMF package. But Denis, the Renaissance man of British politics, was too big to bear grudges.

I was tempted of course. The trouble was that I was also shattered. I had just lost my boss, with whom I had had a special relationship. The thought of serving someone else in the same way, particularly someone who had been Tony's opponent in recent controversy, seemed too demanding.

This, of course, is one of the great 'what ifs' of my life. I can sketch out a scenario where I managed to have some influence on Denis, dissuaded him from unnecessarily burning party boats, got him elected to the leadership after the loss of the 1979 general election, beat Thatcher in 1983, and entered Number 10 triumphant.

Fortunately, this cannot be disproved. Nor can the other scenario: that Denis paid relatively little heed to his pipsqueak adviser, went on his own doomed course, and took me with him into the backwater of the shadow Chancellorship in 1979 where I lingered looking up trade statistics for a few years before disappearing off the map into lifelong obscurity.

The final offer came from Number 10. It was more complex. There were two vacancies there, and I was asked to fill both of them.

Inside Number 10, Bernard Donoughue led a small group called the Policy Unit. Created by Harold Wilson, it was a dipping of toes into the water of creating a much stronger centre of government. Its members were Labour supporters, but also knowledgeable about their subjects, and, through Donoughue, they offered advice to the Prime Minister. When Wilson went, the Policy Unit's future was temporarily in doubt, but Donoughue's abilities, which are considerable, include an unequalled capacity for survival. His diaries and autobiography are required reading for anyone wanting to understand modern British government. His titanic struggles with Marcia Williams would be dubbed unbelievable were they the subject of a novel.

The Policy Unit was short of anyone who knew about housing and local government. Donoughue knew me and, despite our earlier disagreement over council house sales, we got on well. We have remained friends to this day, enjoying that most intimate of relationships, joint ownership of a racehorse.

Quite separately, Jim's oldest and most trusted adviser, Tom McNally, ran the political office. This had a number of formal functions, such as dealing with the Prime Minister's political engagements, preparing him for meetings of the Labour Party's ruling National Executive Committee, dealing with party conference and so on. It also dealt with his non-official correspondence. McNally was hard pressed, especially as he was also the person whom Jim relied on to write his political speeches. I was invited to help with the latter function.

Speechwriting was then a job in its infancy. It was peculiar since you were then supposed to pretend that you didn't exist and all your boss's words were his own. You also had to learn two voices: your own and his own.

I did a pretty good Crosland. Indeed when I see him quoted today, I am sometimes hard pressed to identify which words were his and which mine. I was much less good at Callaghan. I did not have the advantage of having listened to him for many years. He was more formal as a speaker than Crosland and more careful. Flashy phrases were not to his taste.

In retrospect, in accepting the job at Number 10 I was going to the wrong place at the wrong time.

Callaghan, after he had left office, was hard on his period at Number 10, 'I let the country down,' he used to say. In this, he is not fair on himself. For a start, he was dealt a difficult hand.

Every premiership has its crises – the Falklands for Margaret Thatcher, ERM exit for John Major, Iraq for Tony Blair and the credit crunch for Gordon Brown. But it is hard to think of a period with so many intractable difficulties as the period of Callaghan's premiership.

The economy was in trouble. A thin line had to be walked between further depression and unemployment, further inflation and unemployment, or the virulent combination of the two that was the curse of the seventies – stagflation.

The government was losing its majority. It relied on forbearance from the Liberal Party to remain in office. From March 1977 to July 1978, there was a formal pact between the two parties. Callaghan played the then youthful David Steel, the Liberal leader, with avuncular skill, getting him to commit to support the government in key Commons votes in return for minor concessions. The

Lib–Lab pact did not survive the travails of devolution but for sixteen months it brought relatively stable government.

Devolution itself was controversial. The Scots demanded it and if they were to have it, the Welsh had to have it too. However, there were genuine fears among Labour MPs that it was a slippery slope to the break-up of the United Kingdom. Two in particular opposed it to the limit. Tam Dalyell posed the (unanswerable) West Lothian question: why should Scottish MPs have votes on matters affecting England while English MPs had none on matters affecting Scotland? George Cunningham, a London MP though a Scot, in the end scuppered devolution by getting a requirement inserted in the Bill that at least 40 per cent of Scots eligible to vote backed it in a referendum. Our failure to achieve this led directly to the end of Callaghan's Labour government.

The international situation was also unstable. Weak American government followed the resignation of Richard Nixon in 1974 and his replacement by Gerald Ford. Ford was succeeded in 1977 by a tortured President in Jimmy Carter. Britain was struggling to come to terms with Europe, as the Conservative Party turned against Heath's decision to go in. Iran was a huge worry, as was oil generally, though at least in the North Sea we had some.

The Prime Minister had another cross to bear. Harold Wilson's victory in the European referendum of 1975 and the subsequent demotion of Tony Benn to the Energy Department immeasurably weakened the latter in government terms. But Benn was not daunted. He proceeded to build up his base in the Labour Party generally and on its National Executive Committee in particular.

If he was to be stopped, Number 10 had to give a lead. We eventually got organised with the help of John Golding, a trade union MP of impeccable loyalist credentials. Before each NEC meeting, John, briefed by us, would ring round the trade unionists on the NEC lining up the votes.[*]

---

[*] A full account is given in his *Hammer of the Left*, Politico's, 2003.

The trouble was that ministers on the NEC were busy with their departments, and running their departments was a much more congenial task than arguing with the Labour Party. The party machine, under its egregious general secretary Ron Hayward, was unambiguously on the side of the left opposition. It had no country to run. So we were fighting a continual rearguard action.

Among my tasks was briefing the Prime Minister for its meetings. Such was the suspicion of the government that Jim used to remove the tabs from the careful briefing notes I inserted in his papers lest it be thought that he was taking civil service advice.

Jim attended practically every meeting. I had the impression, however, that this was an unbearable penance for him. Here he was, as he saw it, trying to save a country, never mind the party, and there the left on the National Executive were, as he saw it, trying to destroy both.

Politics to Tony Benn did what an overactive thyroid does to others. This made him suspect plots whether or not they existed. He was backed by Eric Heffer, a man who rivalled John Silkin in the disproportion between his ego and his ability (and who was less effective because he thought he should be as famous as Benn). This was raw stuff, power politics, and it sapped the Prime Minister when he needed all his energies to run the country. Of all the changes under New Labour, getting the NEC back in its box is perhaps the one that most helped preserve Labour in power for so long.

This is not a burden that I or anyone could relieve Callaghan of. In truth, I never got near to having that kind of relationship with him anyway. I was a nervy type, sensitive to criticism. I was also in poor shape personally. Jim found my presence less than soothing and therefore the last thing he needed. He always had an ambiguous relationship with academic intelligence. Not having gone to university himself, he was inclined to underestimate his own intelligence while not entirely trusting those with degrees. He relied for support on McNally, and he got it.

Callaghan was widely known as 'Uncle Jim' for his allegedly

avuncular personality. This nickname was appropriate to a large part of his character but not to all of it. There was another side to Callaghan: a ruthlessly tough side born of a hard early life. He had risen from poverty, the orphaned son of a naval petty officer. His early training had been as a trade union official, not a world for the super-sensitive. Not surprisingly he did not take prisoners.

My relationship with him improved over the years, especially when I sat with him in the Lords. He went out of his way then to be supportive. But it was a shock to go from the kind of intimate relationship I had with Crosland to one with a man I greatly admired but struggled to love. Equally, in retrospect, he was patient in putting up with me. He could see there were things I could do for him and his government, and tolerated the frictions of personality between us.

I remember the first occasion when I went to his study, then on the first floor of Number 10, to take his instructions for a speech. We concluded our discussion, and I rose to leave. Unfortunately, I was faced with two identical doors, and could not remember through which I had entered.

I guessed and walked into the Prime Minister's lavatory.

'Ha ha, Prime Minister,' I said, trying to hide my humiliation. 'I bet lots of people do that.'

'No, David,' said Jim. 'You're the first.'

My career as a speechwriter was mixed. For his official speeches, Callaghan generally preferred to use Nigel Wicks, his economics private secretary. For his conference speeches, several hands were involved, but with McNally supreme. On at least one occasion, I produced a draft so little to the Prime Minister's taste that he in effect told me that I had better produce a better one by 6.00 that evening or I would be fired. On another, when I congratulated him on his success with one of mine, he rather sourly said it was nothing to do with him. On another, when I suggested one wasn't his best, he angrily defended himself, though there was not much room for doubt that he had produced a flop. It was a great privilege to be speechwriter for Callaghan, but not a constant pleasure. From time to time since I have been invited to ply my old trade and I had a go at providing words for Blair. But it is not a satisfying role and I am glad that, today, the only speeches I write are my own.

As for the work of the Policy Unit, that too had its limitations. Callaghan was the last of the old-fashioned Prime Ministers. Included in his creed was that Secretaries of State were important people, who on the whole should be left to get on with the jobs to which they had been appointed.

Today, emissaries from the various Number 10 units are sent out to departments. They bear what seem to be messages from the Prime Minister – at least there is no way of telling whether they speak his words or ones of their own. They are given free range to canvass ideas. Ministers give them far more houseroom than they should, though they cannot be blamed. Ministers are appointed by the Prime Minister and sacked by him.

We were not allowed this much scope. Donoughue himself had close relations with many members of the Cabinet. But he thought it best to keep his staff on a fairly tight rein. He did not want Cabinet ministers complaining to the Prime Minister about interference from Number 10 as Jim would most likely side with the minister.

Moreover, we were limited in what we could do. Donoughue had taken a strategic decision to limit the number of fronts on which the Policy Unit got involved. This was sensible. We had limited knowledge. We had limited influence over the Prime Minister. We could easily make mistakes. So it made sense to stick to heavy hitting.

The Policy Unit was enormously influential in Callaghan's Ruskin speech. This was a call for a return to traditional values in education and has arguably conditioned government thinking ever since.

It also had an influential voice on economic policy. There was a vacuum here. Callaghan like all Prime Ministers wanted to influence the Chancellor. He, like most Prime Ministers, for example always wanted lower interest rates and lower taxes while his Chancellor, like most Chancellors, didn't. However, before the coming of the Policy Unit, the Prime Minister lacked any separate source of advice to that of the Treasury.

The Policy Unit filled that gap. This was largely because Donoughue had recruited a brilliant young economist called Gavyn Davies – my best friend then and for many years to come. Then in his twenties, he was faced with the whole weight of Treasury officialdom, which he handled with aplomb. He even built a model of the economy so he could run his own scenarios. Davies had a distinguished later career, chief economist at Goldman Sachs and then chairman of the BBC.

Prime Ministers and Chancellors have fallen out on a regular basis ever since: Thatcher and Howe, Thatcher and Lawson, Blair and Brown, Brown and Darling. Callaghan managed the relationship with great skill. He created a new institution, the seminar, at which economic policy could be discussed not only with the Chancellor but with the governor of the Bank of England. He supported his Chancellor but that did not stop him from nudging him. With Davies's help, and Donoughue's judgement, things worked well, and by 1978 the economy was through its worst.

There were some downsides to having an in-house forecasting capacity. In our last months, Davies ran a simulation of future unemployment. He showed it could not be prevented from rising to 2.5 million in 1981–82. That filled us with gloom. This was human misery on a terrible scale. We did not believe Britain's politics could survive such a level, still less the Labour Party. Thatcher's actual three million was beyond our worst nightmares.

The limited number of issues on which we were allowed to comment by Donoughue meant there was a big downside to Policy Unit life. Quite simply, we were bright young things with too little useful work to do. Davies and I were evenly matched over the chess board, which frequently emerged. We would ring down to the front door enquiring if the *Evening Standard* had yet been delivered, in the fantasy that the Prime Minister might at any minute demand a brief on it. And the devil makes work for idle hands.

We fought among ourselves. Elizabeth Hartley-Brewer was the beautiful and knowledgeable adviser on social security and related matters. Unfortunately, she was also married to Mike Hartley-Brewer. Mike was political adviser to David Ennals, the minister for that department, who rates among the most incompetent ministers I have come across in any government. Ennals did nothing much but bleat for more money. Mike of course amplified his bleating and we believed, fairly or unfairly, that Elizabeth listened too much to the pair of them.

Gavyn and I did not like this. We did not support the constant demand for higher benefits. We wanted money to go to the poor, but some benefits, for example child benefits, were tailored to the middle classes. We thought, ahead of our time, that it was important to incentivise people to work, rather than to claim. We did not believe that resources for social security should grow, exponentially, faster than the economy.

We were always going to win those arguments, which were not in any case likely to go before the Prime Minister. The Treasury was not likely to give priority to healing Ennals's bleeding heart. At the same time, we were more abrasive in pushing our points of view than was strictly necessary. Liz, quite naturally, tried to find a way round, and she had the strong support of Tom McCaffrey, the press secretary, who was among many who admired her looks as well as her brain.

Much today is written about the stresses of Gordon Brown's Number 10, the ins and outs, the internal politics, the alleged bullying from on high. I am not qualified to judge how much of this is true. What is undoubtedly true, from my experience, is that such rifts will always be part of Number 10. There are simply too many people, too driven, all seeking one person's ear. Moreover the structure of Number 10 is invariably loose. So, whereas in departments a tried-and-tested framework regulates relations, Number 10 practises a form of anarchy. In our day it was the private office which tried to keep order. The principal private secretary, Ken Stowe, was a strong figure whose authority few dared to question. But even so we were too often struggling for power with each other. And as the government's political plight worsened in the winter of 1978–79 – see Chapter 7 – the tensions rose. Only the Prime Minister's calm kept things in order, but the calm soon became paralysis.

CHAPTER 7

THE WAY OUT 1979

Helping to run the 1979 general election campaign was not part of my job description at Number 10. As nature abhors a vacuum, so does the centre of government. The conventional wisdom dictated that you did not leave general elections too late, for fear of getting boxed in. When I arrived at Number 10 therefore, an election was probable within the next eighteen months or so.

The job of preparing for that election fell to Tom McNally and the political office – except that, in terms of high-level staff, Tom McNally *was* the political office, and he had many other tasks on his plate.

Tom and I were complementary characters. He had wonderfully honed political instincts and good judgement. He also had an encyclopaedic understanding of the Labour Party. I brought to the team a systematic way of working and attention to detail. As time went by I spent less time on the two jobs to which I had been appointed, and more on getting things ready for the election.

That was not the end of the story. McNally was eager to get a Labour seat while he was still young. However, this was a frustrating task. The Labour Party was swinging to the left, and with that came anti-Callaghan feeling. Of course, the benefits of having a candidate close to Jim were pointed out, but they did not have the same emotional sway. Despite his qualities and his efforts, McNally was getting nowhere.

Then, with the election not far away he was selected for Stockport. He did not disappear altogether from our lives but he could not both be a candidate and run Callaghan's election campaign. I don't think anything was ever said, certainly not by the Prime Minister. Rather, I invented a job – a sort of organising secretary to the campaign – and carried it out as best I could.

From the time I arrived at Number 10, the timing of the general election was a live issue. It was complicated by the fact that we did not necessarily have control over it. We did not have a secure majority in the House of Commons. We relied on the Liberals, not in itself a secure foundation for government, and what the whips could cobble together.

We had to try to hang on. The IMF deal had been a considerable humiliation for the government – nearly equivalent to John Major's humiliation when the pound was forced out of the ERM in 1992. We were miles behind in the polls and lost the safe seat of Ashfield soon after the IMF deal. In a touching display of loyalty to Tony Crosland, Grimsby returned Austin Mitchell for Labour on the same day. He has held the seat ever since.

It was the spring of 1978 before we gave serious attention to when we should go to the country. If things looked good, we could go in the autumn of 1978; if they looked bad, we could hang on until 1979 and hope for the best.

As the summer went on, the poll gap closed. Labour was even in the lead in some.

In mid-August, the *Daily Mirror* led with a world exclusive: the general election was to be held in October. In those days, even popular newspapers did not do that kind of thing unless they were sure of their facts. A reference to Tom McNally's luncheon diary would have cleared up any question as to the source; and the source would not have been the source if he had not had the direct authority of the Prime Minister to say what he said.

Almost as that lunch was taking place, Callaghan was at his farm in Sussex talking to friends and allies. His doubts were growing. I cannot say when he made up his mind but by the time he addressed the TUC congress in September he had decided not to go to the country after all.

He did not want to say this directly to the unions. He felt the Cabinet should be told first and then the country in an address on TV to the nation. So he decided to hint rather than spell out. He used the words of a popular song (its origins much disputed ever since but said to have been performed by Marie Lloyd): 'There was I waiting at the church…'

By then though, the press 'knew' there was going to be a general election and thought that Jim was merely teasing. The Prime Minister was annoyed at this, but there was not much he could do without revealing the truth. That he was not yet ready to do. There were doubtless valid reasons for the delay, but it did not look like good management.

The TV broadcast itself was an embarrassment to me. When Jim decided not to go in October, he told Tom McNally. He also told Tom not to tell anyone else. Tom, however, knew that my work depended entirely on the date and he presumably trusted my discretion.

Early in the week of the announcement, I was giving him a lift home. We stopped, not unusually, at a pub in Dulwich. He told me the news, in the strictest confidence.

The dilemma this presented me was that I could not tell my other boss, Bernard Donoughue. Bernard was told only on the day of the announcement, so he could break to his friends on the *Mirror* the news that they had been sold a pup.

So we sat down to watch Jim's broadcast. If you read Donoughue's diaries he records the astonishment with which I listened to the broadcast. My thespian talents were evidently rather better than I had previously realised.

I (with McNally) was always a supporter of an October election. I thought we would probably win then, though not with any startling majority. A hung parliament was quite likely. We might win after the winter, but there were plenty of perils ahead that made it not worth taking the gamble.

Jim decided otherwise and has been much criticised for it. This is unfair. One of the lessons I have learned from my years in politics is that a decision that turns out badly is not *ipso facto* a bad decision. Arguably much the same applied, years later, to Tony Blair's fateful decision to back the American invasion of Iraq. Even Gordon Brown's fatal flunking of calling an election in 2007 can be defended since he can hardly have been expected to understand, when he made it, just how disastrous his premiership was to prove.

Political decisions are clouded with uncertainty. All the facts are often not known. All the known facts do not necessarily lead to a particular conclusion. There are layers of complexity to political decision-making, including national and party considerations, personalities, constitutional and legal issues and so on. Much of the time, all that can be asked is that you make the best shot of it you can.

The more I think about Jim Callaghan's decision in 1978 the less inclined I am to think it was a bad decision, disastrous though it turned out. Evaluating the position, Jim had plausible reasons to think he was acting in the interests of his party and indeed the country.

The economic recovery was in its infancy, as indeed was the accompanying political recovery. Both might bed in with time.

This was particularly important for Callaghan. He had got fed up with handling what was effectively a minority government. He didn't want to be negotiating deals with David Steel or be held hostage by his own left. He did not only want to win. He wanted to win big.

He accordingly laid great store on a private opinion poll by Market and Opinion Research International (MORI), carried out in the marginal seats in April–May 1978. This appeared to demonstrate that Labour was doing less well in the seats which it needed to win than it was in the country at large. MORI described it as a 'disturbing finding'.

This particular point is a sore one with me. Politicians are, in my experience, not at all professional in their use of opinion polling, rarely appreciating its strengths and limitations. In particular, they have two weaknesses. Firstly, they tend to ascribe greater significance to private polls, in preference to public polls. Secondly, they tend in particular to give special weight to polls carried out in marginals.

In fact, private polls are no more or less accurate than public polls.

They use precisely the same techniques to try to measure precisely the same things. However, they get surrounded by all kinds of rituals which increase their mystique. Bob (later Sir Bob) Worcester, Labour's pollster, refused during the 1979 campaign to let anyone but the Prime Minister see his daily measure of voting intentions.

As for polls in marginals, these are subject to a whole set of technical defects in addition to the technical defects of national polls. A further layer of sampling has to be undertaken to choose which marginal seats from within the constellation of marginal seats in general the polling is to concentrate on. Demographic data is often limited. When you start breaking the sample down – into for example Labour-held marginals with a larger majority, Labour-held marginals with a smaller majority and genuinely neck-and-neck seats, you start getting into small sample sizes and big margins of error.

The fact was – and I told the Prime Minister this at the time – that the apparent underperformance by Labour in the seats we needed to win was not statistically significant. It could be the product of pure chance. He had a saying by which he evaluated polling: 'Never believe the polls unless they are bad.' He preferred to believe what he was told. As the pollsters were professionals and I just an enthusiastic amateur, he took their message at face value.

He was also taking advice from colleagues, but I am not sure that he was taking advice from the right colleagues. Those closest to him were Rees and Foot. Rees was a shrewd man, but not perhaps an expert assessor of electoral facts. Foot was a romantic, whose own views were rarely attuned to those of the public. I think Callaghan would have got better advice from the harder-wired brains of Healey, Owen and Williams. As, arguably, he was getting from McNally, Donoughue and even myself!

He doubted his prospects of victory in an October election. I think, however, that there was a greater factor behind postponement, though it may seem surprising to those who are cynical about politics. I think he thought that not having an election was in the national interest.

The outlook for inflation was balanced in the summer of 1978.

Britain had come back from the brink, with the aid of Healey's tough fiscal stance at the Treasury. The unions were not on board, however, for a new bout of pay policy.

Callaghan was a hawk on this. That summer, McNally and I were summoned to his study.

'I've decided we will have a 5 per cent pay policy next pay round,' said Callaghan.

We were dumbstruck. Five per cent lagged behind prices. It would never be accepted by the trade unions.

Tom was braver than I was. He remonstrated mildly.

'What are you saying?' Jim retorted, angrily. 'That 5 per cent wouldn't be best for the country?'

Of course we were saying no such thing. It would be best. It just wasn't obtainable. And, shameful thought, it would lose Labour the general election if we tried for it.

My own view is that Callaghan understood that risk perfectly well. However, he saw an upside.

If he had an election in October and won, the unions could bank the gain of a Labour government. They could go for whatever pay increases they chose.

If, however, an election was still pending, Callaghan had something to hold over them. An election was coming. If they started striking, that could mean we lost, and they got Margaret Thatcher. So they had an incentive to play ball.

To be fair, it nearly worked. After initial skirmishing, the TUC only turned down a form of words on pay on the chairman's casting vote. Had there been a negotiated deal, we should not have had 5 per cent pay rises or anything like it. But we might have had a reasonably peaceful winter. Private companies that granted big pay rises might have suffered financially as a result. Inflation, while not decisively defeated, might have been checked. We might have found a way forward to a less inflationary economy without three million unemployed and the anti-union policies of Margaret Thatcher. At any rate it was a not wholly unrealistic prospect. I do not blame Jim for having tried.

But what actually happened was the 'winter of discontent'. Wages and wage deals were not keeping up with prices. There was an upsurge of trade union militancy. The leaders of the big unions mostly preferred to take on Labour rather than risk alienating their angry members. The result was widespread industrial action, particularly in the public sector.

There is a revisionist school among historians of the period which argues that the 'winter of discontent' never happened, or at any rate was much exaggerated. It was, these historians argue, got up by the press to discredit the Labour government.

It did not feel like that inside Number 10. I do not attempt here a history of that dreadful winter as I did not personally have much of a role in the policy-making. But there was no mistaking the atmosphere inside Number 10, nor was there much mistaking what was happening outside. In Liverpool, the dead lay unburied as the municipal workers struck. In Leicester Square, a few hundred yards from the centre of government, stinking rubbish was piled high in the streets. We felt we had lost control. Indeed we had lost control. And the British public is not charitably disposed to governments who lose control.

Callaghan did not help matters when he went off to sunny Guadeloupe for a summit of world leaders. No doubt the business they transacted was of supreme importance. But so far as the electorate was concerned, they remembered only that their Prime Minister was not at home where he was needed. They remembered the remarks he made on returning home. Though he never said 'Crisis, what crisis?', which was *The Sun*'s headline on the story, he said something uncomfortably near to it. From neck and neck in the polls in the autumn, we went twenty or so points behind.

The Policy Unit, like everyone else in Number 10, did its best to think up ways to deal with the crisis. For example, we wondered if pay policy might stick if we introduced much tougher controls over prices, and Gavyn Davies and I held discussions with Charles Williams, the urbane chair of the Prices Commission, to explore this. We sought to mobilise the moderate trade union leadership around restraint. But, really, this was a tragedy (for the Labour movement at any rate) that was impossible to stop once the curtain had risen. We were powerless but, then, so was the Prime Minister.

As the election constitutionally had to be held by the autumn of 1979, time in any case was running out. But we had no guarantee that we would last that long. Our parliamentary position was as perilous as was our political position in the country. In particular, the result of the referendum on Scottish devolution meant that it would not go ahead. That in turn meant that the Scottish Nationalists no longer had any incentive to keep Labour in power.

The end was not long in coming. On 28 March 1979, the government faced a vote of no confidence in the Commons. Callaghan, back to the wall, made a great fighting speech. He mocked the Liberals in particular, who looked sure to do badly in any election: 'Turkeys voting for an early Christmas.' But when the vote was taken, we lost by one.

Did we have to lose? Probably not. With or without Callaghan's permission, various attempts were made to get the minority parties in the Commons to support us. There was much talk, for example, of a gas pipeline under the North Sea to Ulster, to win us Ulster votes. In the event, no deal emerged. Frank Maguire, an independent Republican MP, made a rare trip to Westminster so he could 'abstain in person' in the vote. With his support, we would have survived.

But Callaghan was past wheeling and dealing. Tired by office, morally exhausted by the failings of the trade union movement, he had a kind of death wish about him that doomed the government.

After the result of the vote was announced, some from Number 10 attended on Callaghan in his office behind the Speaker's chair. They were disconcerted to find the Prime Minister, pen in hand, composing a letter. It was addressed to the wife of Sir Alfred Broughton, a Labour MP. Sir Alfred was mortally ill with heart disease. He was prepared to come to London for the vote, against his doctor's firm advice but Callaghan discouraged him from doing so. Callaghan's letter was to tell his wife she should in no way feel guilty for the fact he had not voted. Broughton died less than a month later.

So the election started, in the worst of all conceivable circumstances.

First we had to have a manifesto. This was not merely a question of drafting. Under Labour's constitution, the manifesto was a joint production of two bodies – the National Executive Committee and Labour's Parliamentary Committee, effectively the Cabinet. The NEC, however, was well into its descent into madness. The Cabinet was not, but its corresponding fault was that it was entirely absorbed in existing policies. Indeed, much of the time it could think of nothing beyond day-to-day survival.

So a manifesto had to be drafted to be agreed by two bodies, fundamentally at odds. It had to be sound enough to survive the rigours of a long election campaign, and indeed (for we were far from conceding defeat at that time) to provide a plausible basis for a Labour government. At the same time, we had to avoid a public split in the party on the eve of battle.

What happened? A mythology has grown based on Tony Benn's accounts. After the election defeat, he made a deadly speech to the party conference, accusing the Prime Minister of in effect sabotaging Labour's policies. Policies were 'vetoed secretly, late, quietly before the party could discover what had happened. That is wrong…'

In his old age, Benn has come to seem an almost saintly figure, much admired by those who never knew him in his earlier incarnation. He was not saintly then or indeed through the period running up to the election. He was a man bent on seizing control of the Labour Party, in the hope that it would win an election after he had done so and deliver him the power he craved. He had a motivated team of similarly dedicated people round him. He was not easy to stop.

Contrary to the myth, there was no Number 10 plot to impose a manifesto on the party. Leastways, there was no such plot until the last possible moment, when it became transparently clear that the Bennite forces were not prepared to compromise. Even then, every effort was made to ensure that the final manifesto had as broad a support as was obtainable.

To prepare the way, in 1977 a series of Cabinet/NEC working parties were set up to discuss manifesto policies. I can't remember why but Number 10 decided that I should act as secretary to them. It was a frustrating business.

On the Cabinet's side, the great problem was absenteeism. The groups invariably met to debate papers drawn up by the party's research staff and which accordingly bore little relation to the real world of ministers. Any excuse was good enough for ministers to send apologies for absence.

A stern prime ministerial note improved things a little, but the meetings could still be quite dreadful. I remember once enduring a long discussion between Shirley Williams, as minister responsible for the arts, and Renee Short, a member of the NEC. The NEC was then determined to ensure that the Arts Council, which handed out government grants, should be 'democratically accountable'. Short and Williams proceeded to wrangle for what seemed like hours as to whether this meant a majority of the Council should be elected or whether a minority would suffice. At no point in this argument did either appear to grasp that there was an important prior question. Was the election to be one in which everyone had a vote – a sort of general election of the arts? If not, who was to have a vote? Artists? People who liked looking at art? Both sides preferred to talk nonsense about nonsense.

Other Cabinet ministers had a different way of playing things. Their sole objective was to gum up the mechanism, leaving it to the Prime Minister to solve things later.

I remember attending one meeting with the then Home Secretary, Merlyn Rees. A delightful man, Rees did in fact have something of the Merlin about him. The meeting went on interminably with the NEC representatives proposing this, that and the other left-wing policy for the conduct of our national security. Rees sat with his head in his hand, mumbling incoherently about how difficult it all was. When we eventually reached pack-up time, I had no idea how to draft the minutes. I dared to ask what had been decided. Rees's mumbling recommenced until I gave up.

I shepherded Rees to the lift, still clutching his head as if it might fall off with the stress. We got in and the doors closed. Rees lifted his head, looked around him to check there was no one to hear, smiled broadly, and said: 'That went well, didn't it, David? We didn't agree anything, did we?' With hindsight that was indeed a triumph, though not one that made my job any easier.

As the election drew nearer we had a draft manifesto from the National Executive. This rivalled the manifesto of 1982 as a suicide note. It had the additional defect that it was also supposed to be the manifesto of a party in government, yet it involved a complete rejection of pretty well all of its policies.

We also had half a draft manifesto provided by McNally. This was a well-written defence of Labour's record. What it did not have, for he had not got that far, was a set of policies which we could promise in the election to come. Voters rarely thank parties for what they have done for them. They understandably want to know what they will do for them next. So the absence of policies was a not inconsiderable defect.

The Prime Minister's team met at Chequers, his country residence, only weeks before the election, to decide what to do. Callaghan was at first inclined to tough it out, produce a draft of his own and defy the party to do anything about it. However, he was persuaded that we should not go down that route unless it was absolutely unavoidable. One last attempt to find a draft acceptable to both sides should be mounted.

In retrospect, this was a doomed exercise. The NEC was not interested in a deal, still less a deal which might give us a chance of winning the election. It was interested in being able to show afterwards that it had fought for socialism, and had been blocked by the leadership. The betrayal myth has always been potent in the Labour Party, and it was to be used now to propel Tony Benn and his acolytes to total party power.

I still believe that it was right to try to agree. If we had simply gone ahead and steamrollered the party, Benn's loony left would have been in an even stronger position to take its revenge after we lost.

The effort got nowhere. The instruction came down from Callaghan that I should draft the manifesto for his approval. It was a good thing I had learned to touch-type early in life, as I had something under twelve hours in which to complete the job. I did my best. Indeed so far as I can remember there was only one proposal that Callaghan queried. It was the abolition of the House of Lords!

So we had a draft. How were we to show that it had support beyond Number 10? Here Callaghan's skills as a party manager reached their apogee.

Lena Jeger was a member of the National Executive Committee, and later of the House of Lords. She was by anyone's standards a leftie, but certainly not a Bennite. You could do business with Lena, and she and I always got on well. But that wasn't her main attribute for the job Jim had in mind. Her main attribute was her liking for a drink.

'What you do, David, is this,' said Jim. 'You tell Lena that I have asked her to look over the manifesto to give me her considered opinion. Invite her to Number 10 and put her in a small room with the draft manifesto, a pen, a bottle of whisky and a glass. Don't let her leave until she says she is satisfied with it.'

A couple of hours went by. Then, so did Lena. The bottle was empty. The pen was unused. The manifesto was, if in slurred terms, pronounced fit for purpose. A crucial ally had been recruited for the struggle ahead.

The manifesto had to be formally adopted at a joint meeting of Cabinet and NEC, but this was far too large for the effective conduct of business. So Jim summoned a smaller meeting of repre-sentatives of both sides one evening in Downing Street. I was to act jointly as secretary to the meeting with Geoff Bish, the head of the party's research department, who alas had fallen under the Benn spell.

An account of that meeting at Number 10 has subsequently been produced by Tony Benn. This is how it appears in his diaries. 'I raised every single point from our [the Party's] original draft ... At 3.15 am when we left Geoff said we'd given away a lot tonight.'

Without equivocation, this is not what happened at all. What happened was that Tony Benn turned up for the meeting, not saying a tremendous amount. He shortly announced that he had to catch the last train to his Bristol constituency and left.

Shorn of their leader, the NEC representatives had little idea what to say. Indeed, and quite inappropriately, they left it to poor Bish, officially no more than a bureaucrat, to stick up for the Benn policies. He took an ill-deserved hammering.

There was one moment of drama in the meeting. For there was one issue on which the government itself was divided. Michael Foot, Callaghan's loyal deputy, remained a convinced supporter of unilateral nuclear disarmament. Callaghan was just as convinced that the British deterrent was necessary, both militarily and politically. However, Callaghan needed Foot's support to keep the Labour Party together in the election.

In the small hours the issue arose. It immediately became clear that the two had fixed it. Foot read out the following:

In 1974, we renounced any intention of moving towards the production of a new generation of nuclear weapons or a successor to the Polaris nuclear force; we reiterate our belief that this is the best course for Britain. But many great issues affecting our allies and the world are involved, and a new round of strategic arms limitation negotiations will soon begin. We think it is essential that there must be a full and informed debate about these issues in the country before the necessary decision is taken.

Jim nodded. The deed was done, and the words appeared unchanged in the manifesto.

It just showed that agreement can be reached over even the most difficult issues when the will is there. Between Tony Benn and Jim

Callaghan in 1979, that could not happen, because Benn had not the least intention of allowing it to.

At least the delay in the date of the election from October 1978 to May 1979 gave us some time to get our election team sorted. In effect there were two groups. One was the Prime Minister's personal election team. To my delight, Derek Gladwin was brought in to run this. Gladwin was not only my former boss but a great friend. He was a legendary organiser. He was also superb with people, keeping morale up even when it should have been down.

Also imported into our team was Roger Carroll, the political editor of *The Sun*, who was to be the Prime Minister's speechwriter. Roger was much loved. He was not, however, quite attuned to the ways of government. He was master of the bright wheeze, the amazingly energetic policy proposal that would swing the election in our favour. His memos invariably started 'Why not...' In truth not all of his proposals were practical.

Separately, there was a group charged with communications, and specifically with making Labour's party political broadcasts. It was headed by Edward Booth-Clibborn, a veteran of the advertising world. Tim Delaney of BBDO was its most dynamic advertising practitioner.

We were therefore, to a degree, well organised. But the campaign arrangements were dogged by the same defect which dogged the making of the manifesto. There was one important player who neither wished to be nor could be allowed to be included in the inner circle.

The general secretary of the Labour Party, Ron Hayward, wanted us (or so I believe with hindsight) to lose. The National Executive of the Labour Party was divided but many of them wanted to lose, and even those who did not had a pretty rum idea of how we should go about not losing. Many of the party staff had minimal allegiance to the government though there were exceptions. Reg Underhill, the national agent, who had been defeated in his bid to become general secretary by a leftist plot, remained impeccably loyal throughout. Percy Clark, the press officer, was on our side as was Doreen Stainforth, his partner and colleague.

The relationship with Hayward was positively bizarre. The party had its own election committees. So far as I remember, we paid no attention to any of them. I was working out of Transport House, the party's headquarters, but with limited contact with them, and taking my orders only from the Prime Minister and his team. When I had no orders, I just did what I thought best.

The epitome of this bizarre way of conducting business came in the last week. Jim wanted a million-pound-plus last burst of campaign advertising. Hayward simply refused to confront this issue. He would not sign the authorisation forms. Nor would he refuse to sign them. Time was marching on so, in the end, on no authority whatsoever, I signed the forms and the campaign went ahead.

The party political broadcasts were made in similar conflict mode. Here it was not even clear where ultimate authority lay. The broadcasters provided producers, but they expected you to write the show. But who was 'you'? In the end, 'you' was our communications team and Delaney in particular. But the co-operation from the party that such a team would normally expect was not forthcoming. Advertising famously has its demanding clients, but I don't think our team could even in its worst nightmares have imagined the multifaceted dysfunctionality which was the Labour Party machine then.

You expect in an election campaign to be fighting the other parties. You do not expect to be fighting your own.

Callaghan had been gloomy most of the winter. However, the start of the campaign gave him a new lease of life. He was, after all and despite everything, one of the most popular politicians in Britain. He outpolled Margaret Thatcher by seven percentage points at the beginning of the campaign (and nineteen points at the end). If we could make this an election about Callaghan and Thatcher, rather than about Labour's record or the Labour Party, we might yet have a squeak.

One discussion in our team is relevant given the 2010 election debates. The broadcasters were asking if we were prepared to agree a debate between the party leaders. What should we say?

Tom McCaffrey, the Prime Minister's secretary, was strongly against a yes. As he saw it, the incumbent was at a disadvantage in such debates. He had to defend his record against specific criticism. The leader of the opposition could resort to airy gener-alisations which sounded good. McCaffrey made no bones about it. He thought in these circumstances that Thatcher would beat Callaghan. I dare say the same thought occurred to some members of Gordon Brown's team thirty years later.

Tom McNally, with my support and Donoughue's, put forward a contrary argument. We were by no means confident that Callaghan would win the debates. However, as things stood, he wasn't going to win the election anyway. We were a mile down. We needed a game changer. We foresaw, again perhaps thirty years before our time, that debates would dominate the campaign. If Jim did win, big 'if' though that was, the polls could swing our way.

Unfortunately, we were not the only ones to think that way. Margaret Thatcher, sailing serenely to victory, could see that debat-ing Jim was a high-risk strategy for her. Mrs Thatcher did not share McCaffrey's confidence that she would win. So she flunked the challenge and the debates were off.

Callaghan fought a traditional campaign, touring the country, meeting voters and delivering set speeches at night. He returned where possible to Downing Street each night, sometimes joining the team for a good cooked breakfast in the small dining room at Number 10 next morning. Funnily enough, I do not recall any thought being devoted to what would make a good picture opportunity.

Callaghan loathed Thatcher and all she stood for. It was not easy, however, to get him to unsheathe the knife. He was increasingly helped in the drafting of his speeches by Gavyn Davies and the Policy Unit but he had to be pushed.

I remember one battle. Callaghan, so Davies argued, should

claim in a speech that the Tories would double VAT. Callaghan was hostile. 'I can't do it,' he said. 'Of course they aren't going to double VAT. If I say they are, I will just lose all credibility.'

In the end he was persuaded to say it. And he turned out to be right: Margaret Thatcher raised VAT from 8 per cent to 15 per cent – a mite off doubling so that she could say she hadn't done what Callaghan said she would do – within weeks of taking power.

There is some advantage in fighting an election campaign where you are miles behind. You don't have expectations to disappoint. The polls were mixed. They always are. But there was some sign of headway. Indeed just before the last week of the campaign one NOP poll even had Labour a smidgin ahead. I made the mistake of allowing myself to hope.

It may have been a fluke. In any case, our campaign then hit a rock. Jim was confronted with a nurse complaining about health cuts.

Would-be public speakers are told the story of the expert on naval affairs who was delivering an eloquent lecture on the sinking of a battleship. From the back row a man piped up, 'I was there.' No one was then interested in the lecturer.

It is much the same with politicians and real voters. Real voters often have a view of the world that is limited, partial and often vacuous. Nevertheless, the politician confronts them at their peril. Phone-in election programmes have now virtually disappeared for this reason. Staff are expected to vet everyone the leader may meet to ensure they have nothing out of line to say.

This nurse was eloquent too. Jim was, sad to say, slightly testy. That was our election chances gone.

Winning ain't everything, but losing ain't anything. We had fought a decent campaign, got our arguments across, put some pressure on the Tories and occasionally rattled Maggie. The problem was not with our campaign. It was with the state of the country. We could use words. But they did not displace in people's minds the unburied bodies, the piles of rubbish.

Voters had held their noses at the relationship between Labour and the trade unions just so long as that relationship was delivering for them. Once it ceased to do so, the stink could not be kept out. That was what Callaghan meant when he told Bernard Donoughue:

> There are times, perhaps once every thirty years, when there is a sea-change in politics. It then does not matter what you say or what you do. There is a shift in what the public wants and what it approves of. I suspect there is now such a sea-change – and it is for Mrs Thatcher.*

We could have fought any campaign – even a campaign where we had the full weight of the Labour Party behind us rather than undermining us – and the result would have been the same. That did not mean that losing hurt any the less.

---

* Quoted from Kenneth O. Morgan, *Callaghan*, Oxford University Press, 1997.

CHAPTER 8

FROM POLITICS TO
JOURNALISM 1979–86

Why do politicians stop at nothing to win elections? Because losing is so frightful.

Until Thursday 3 May, we had run the country. On Friday 4 May, someone else did.

The guillotine falls. If you are the government, you lose your physical workplace. You lose your working relationships. You lose what you get up in the morning for. You lose your salary. You lose everything.

If you are Prime Minister, you will probably soon lose the leadership of your party. Harold Wilson went from government to opposition to government again, but he is the only premier since Churchill to achieve this.

Callaghan after 1979 made the disastrous decision to cling to party office. Weakened by defeat, demoralised by what he perceived to be his failure, he did no good. He thought he could use his links with the trade unions to restabilise his party. But this was not an available option as the unions were by now politically unstable themselves. Callaghan could not decide whether to confront the resurgent left or compromise with it; and whichever tack he took, it worked out wrong.

This disastrous period ended with the Bishop's Stortford agreement of 1982. There, the Parliamentary Party lost its exclusive right to choose the leader. Had it been replaced by a one member, one vote ballot of party members, this might have proved satisfactory. Instead, in future, Labour's leaders were to be chosen by an electoral college with union block votes and activist cabals sharing the majority of the vote, No longer was there a leader. There was a prisoner. Not surprisingly, the results were not good. The situation was made worse when Labour's subsequent conference voted to give a lion's 40 per cent share of the vote for leader to the trade unions.

But at least Callaghan had something to do. He was party leader and he was an MP. He moved into offices at the Commons where he could continue a life not so different from that which he had lived in opposition from 1970 to 1974.

Labour MPs who lost their seats as a result of the failure of our government were less happily placed. The loss of a seat in the Commons equates to a major bereavement. An intense relationship exists between the modern MP and his or her constituency. You are there every week, making love to it, ministering to those there with problems, in return enjoying their flattering attentions. Suddenly, they have run off with a total stranger, and one you do not like. You feel empty. Thinking of all you did for them, you feel angry. Unless you swiftly find a new lover – by getting adopted for another seat – the feeling does not go away. There are MPs who still hanker after getting back into Parliament ten and twenty years after they have lost.

No doubt, the fate of a political adviser seems a matter of little significance in this scheme of things. But political advisers too are jobless the day after an election. They get a three-month payoff, that is all. You also lose your job when it is most difficult to get another one because the party you belong to is out of favour.

Most of the advisers to the Callaghan government in fact found jobs quite quickly. Some were amazingly successful. Gavyn Davies swiftly became the dominant City economist of his day. Others found niches. Adrian Ham, Denis Healey's adviser, was chief economist to the British Waterways Board. No one that I can recall remained unemployed for long, but most fell a longish way.

Despite the near certainty we would lose, I had given little thought to what I would do next. The days were too full with the battle to survive. However, I thought I had a job to go to.

John Pinder was head of Political and Economic Planning (PEP). PEP was perhaps the first British think tank, dating back to the 1930s. It pursued a left-of-centre planning agenda, produced much decent policy work and was in the forefront (under its director) of pro-EU opinion. Pinder had approached me to do a project on the future of the trade unions. I sort of said 'yes'; he sort of said he would raise the money; and I said I would be in touch after I had taken a break.

I made two mistakes. The first was to go off on my own to France for a few weeks. I needed the rest, but being alone with failure, even in beautiful countryside, was not great fun. The second was to assume the money would materialise. Not for the last time, for PEP it turned out that money was an insuperable problem.

I returned from France to nothing. But there was a glimmer of hope. Paul Barker was the editor of *New Society*, a weekly magazine. I had met him with Crosland earlier in government and obviously had made some mark. A letter arrived from him asking me if I would like to write for *New Society*.

Barker was a shy man, with whom it was not easy to have straightforward relations. His offer was typically ambiguous. 'Write' – was he offering me a job or to carry a piece of mine?

At first, I placed the latter interpretation on the letter and submitted an article. 'Towards Fraternalism' was not much of a title for my analysis of what had gone wrong with our government, but the substance was better.

In the wake of that piece, Barker's ambiguity was resolved. Yes indeed, he did want me to work for him. He would like me to be his 'industrial correspondent' – even a little magazine had one of those at the time. And so, after some ducking and weaving over salary, it was to *New Society* I went.

Nearly a quarter of a century has elapsed since *New Society* died. But tribute is paid to its memory anywhere sociologists, social workers, policy thinkers and their ilk assemble.

New Society was the creation of Tim Raison, a Tory minister in his time, but a liberal one. Its initial inspiration was two-fold. Raison saw that an enormous expansion was taking place in the number of social workers and related professions. Their jobs would have to be advertised somewhere. A magazine which was in that place would have juicy revenues.

Moreover there was much interesting editorial matter which

such people would like to have available – sociological analysis of the nature of society, cries of disgust at the state of the poor, architecture and its impact on how people lived, and then, by extension from that, the place of the arts, and so on. *New Society* was later taken over by IPC, a large publishing corporation with a stable of dull specialised magazines, each with their own classified ad market. *New Society* became the jewel in its crown, not because of the profits it made but because of the kudos it brought to the company.

Barker, who had worked for *The Economist*, became its editor in 1968. All publications tend to reflect the character of their editor, and that was true of *New Society* under his editorship. Barker dreamed of becoming editor of *The Times*, turning it back into a paper of record, and he had a share of the qualities such an editor would require. I do not, however, think that he and Rupert Murdoch would have hit it off.

He had, truth to tell, a limited interest in the kinds of things social workers bought the magazine for. He functioned at a higher level altogether. He drew intellectuals and literary figures to the magazine like moths to a flame: for example Frederic Raphael and John Berger. He also gave space to writers who were on the verge of unemployment. I remember one who was in fact a virtual tramp in between contributions. He would get himself paid in advance so as to be able to afford the necessities of writing: pen, ink, food. The magazine attracted a fiercely loyal readership and an even more fiercely loyal bunch of supporters.

Barker produced a good magazine for an astonishingly long time. He was in many ways a great editor, with a refined and cultured mind. His many distinguished contributors generally revered him.

Barker had a principal defect. He was not a great man manager. He found conversation a strain. When he himself went out to write a piece from somewhere in Britain, it rather rarely contained quotes from people he had talked to, perhaps because he hadn't talked to anyone. This meant that he found it hard to praise his staff. Joy Melville, his production editor (who sadly died in 2011),

kept the place running. She used to say that his highest approba-
tion was 'I've sent your piece to the printers'. Journalists being
thin-skinned characters, this was not the most successful way to
run the show.

You can always get more journalists where the last ones came
from. But if you are not commercially successful, getting the money
to survive is harder. Competition for social worker advertising was
increasing. In particular, *The Guardian* spotted an opportunity,
and proved a rival to *New Society*. Competition came also from
Community Care, a magazine concentrating solely on this market
and containing the trade press articles that most social workers
wanted to read.

Social workers did not necessarily share the cultured tastes to
which Barker liked his magazine to cater. Tony Gould, for example,
himself a brilliant writer, produced a book review section that was
the equal of that in any publication in the land. However, it
was not necessarily one to which the social worker wished to turn
at the end of a hard week. So the readership included fewer and
fewer social workers; the response rate to the job ads declined; so
the ads declined in number, and became less lucrative.

Capitalism was becoming harsher at this time and IPC got fed
up. *New Society* continued in being and teamed up with the *New
Statesman*, a left-wing political magazine with a long and glorious
history but a rather less glorious present.

I left *New Society* in 1980 to go to the *Sunday Times* – of which
more below – but in 1986 Barker asked me back as his deputy
editor. I had quit the *Sunday Times* for a quieter life but it was not
to be. When I arrived at *New Society*, it was perfectly clear to me
that its financial position was unviable. Indeed, as things were, it
could not legally continue to trade. The staff moreover had lost
confidence in Barker.

After a short, sharp and nasty confrontation, the chairman of
the *New Statesman*, Phillip Whitehead, was persuaded that Barker
must go. Barker was like a mother whose baby had been stolen
from her. So far as I know, he never again talked to Whitehead,

formerly a friend, until Phillip died, tragically, in 2005. He has not talked to me to this day.

Of course, in getting rid of one editor with flaws, they got another, who also had flaws. I didn't have Barker's talent for nurturing good and great writers. Nor was the magazine my whole life as it was his. But I was good at things he was bad at. I was good as a commercial leader for example. By cutting spending viciously, I was able to eliminate for the moment the eye-watering losses which week by week we were accumulating. With the aid of an excellent commercial manager, Rob Hall, we just about washed our face.

I persuaded the Rowntree Trust, which had backed me as a chocolate soldier, to back me as an editor. They injected a life-saving investment for which I remain profoundly grateful.

I was quite good too at recruiting and motivating staff writers. I had a wonderful team around me, including Caroline St John Brooks, later editor of the *Times Educational Supplement* until she died in 2003; and Jeremy Laurance, later an outstanding health editor of *The Independent*. Recruits included Yasmin Alibhai-Brown, who emerged as one of the leading columnists of our times; Steve Platt, later editor of the *New Statesman*; and Amanda Mitchison, a great feature writer for us and later for several national newspapers. Under a different approach, they produced many more words that they had done before; and words produced in house were words that did not have to be produced – and so paid for – out of house. With the stalwarts Joy Melville and Tony Gould, we were a good team.

Finally, I reoriented the editorial content so it appealed to more readers and more advertisers. Circulation edged up. In the process, I offended some of Barker's most devoted fans. To the charge that we moved downmarket, I plead guilty. But we were also more readable, which is not a crime in journalism.

For a while, I thought we might succeed. The deficit, getting on for a third of revenue when I took over, was eliminated by painful cuts, including cuts in staff salaries.

But the hill was too steep. To compete with *The Guardian*

required a weekly act of levitation both by the journalists and by the ad sales team. When Rob Hall and I contemplated the future, we could see no route to sustained viability.

In the end, Whitehead and the *New Statesman* did the deed. I had in fact applied for the editorship of the *New Statesman*, but did not get it. Stuart Weir, a former deputy editor of *New Society*, was appointed. And this tipped off Whitehead and Rowntree to one possible way out. The *New Statesman* and *New Society* were merged. At first the new magazine was called *New Statesman and Society* but, predictably, the 'Society' bit was dropped off the masthead at the first opportunity.

At the time, many thought that the era of the weekly magazine was over. Not only did *New Society* die but so did *The Listener*, the upmarket BBC-run magazine edited by Anthony Howard, a distinguished political journalist. By rights, the *New Statesman* should have died too and it often nearly did. Eventually it was saved by Geoffrey Robinson, a rich Labour MP. Meanwhile, on the other side of the political spectrum, *The Spectator* became a great *succès d'estime*. Right-wing opinions, elegantly expressed, turned out to have a market. More recently an intellectual monthly *Prospect* has joined the scene, also proving a survivor. We are not all confined to the internet for our reading – yet.

I have spent roughly as many years in my career in journalism (1979–99) as in politics (1972–79 and 1999 on). Those years take up less space in this memoir. On the whole, the internal machinations of newspapers are less interesting, and less significant, than those of government. Great editors are certainly less important than Prime Ministers, and probably less important than senior Cabinet ministers.

My period in journalism was not without interest, however. For one thing, it covered what might be regarded as the 'transitional' period. First, in early transition, was the smashing of the power of the printers and their trade unions, which promised a new freedom and a new power to the authors of the printed word. Then came the growth of the internet, with consequent change in the newspaper and broadcasting world. That period was again changing to the present high gothic period, where basic structures are everywhere embellished with electronic decoration, but that only happened after I had left the trade.

Like every ex-journalist, I believe the trade is not what it used to be. When I joined the *Sunday Times* in 1980, it genuinely felt like a great institution with a great mission. That sense of mission still existed when I ended my career at *The Economist*, but by then, *The Economist* was an exception to the rule of decline. I now claim, not entirely truthfully, that the *Racing Post* is the only paper I ever read as it is the only one where the facts are still accurate.

The creation of daily and weekly newspapers is an extraordinary human achievement. Modern capitalism prides itself on the speed with which its products can be changed and distributed. Not many modern firms, however, are called upon to reinvent their product, from scratch, every day. Still fewer have to do so when the quality of that product requires a huge creative input from everyone: writers, photographers, picture editors, news editors, designers and cartoonists. Still fewer have to do it with a set of workers who, because of the creative qualities that this process requires, comprise mostly nervous, egoistical, neurotic and febrile individuals, many of whom would be unemployable anywhere else but on newspapers.

This unbelievable achievement is owed to a few basic rules. The first is that the editor's decision is final. You can argue with him or her for a little while, but in the end, you go and do what you have been told to do to the best of your abilities. Otherwise the damn thing would never appear.

The second of these is that deadlines are deadlines. On every paper there are one or two writers who daily test this rule to the limit, yet such is their genius that this is tolerated and accommodated. But for the bulk of journalists, the quality of what they write matters less than that they deliver the right number of words at the right time. And if things change, as they always change, that number of words can be cut, halved, decimated. They can moan but there is a tacit agreement that they put up with it.

We often – I often – complain that newspapers are not much good. Remember the story of the man in the railway carriage playing chess with a dog.

'What a remarkable dog!' says a fellow passenger.

'Tsch, he's not much good,' replies the man. 'I beat him the last three games.'

A few months after I arrived at *New Society*, I was approached by Don Berry. Berry was a senior editor at the *Sunday Times*, loved and revered by all who worked with him. The paper had a vacancy on their political staff, and reading my stuff, the editor wondered if I might be interested.

Harold Evans, the then editor, was a legend. His *Sunday Times* was regarded by many as the greatest investigative newspaper in the world. His campaign over the thalidomide scandal, in the face of official resistance, has never been bettered.

The *Sunday Times* would stop at nothing – or at least at nothing ethical – to get a story. Once, following the Moorgate tube disaster, it flew a huge piece of the braking system across the Atlantic, so it could prove its thesis that it incorporated a fatal engineering flaw. It later turned out that the real problem was the driver's behaviour.

To be granted an interview by Harry was an honour. However, it did not turn out to be quite the event I had hoped for. Evans, a true newsman, was most interested in whatever had happened most recently. Diary engagements took second place. I entered his office and shook him warmly by the hand; he explained courteously that he was otherwise engaged, and ushered me through to see his deputy, Frank Giles. Frank had not the faintest idea who I was or what I was doing in his office. Nevertheless we passed the time amiably enough. It was later confirmed that I had got the job.

My time working for Evans was pretty limited too. Rupert Murdoch took over *The Times* and the *Sunday Times* soon after I arrived. *The Times* was doing badly while the *Sunday Times* coined it in. It was decided that Evans should be moved to *The Times*, it was hoped, transferring success with him.

The story of the resulting disaster has been told from every perspective – by Evans himself, and by those on *The Times* who resisted him. What is clear with hindsight is that different qualities are required of a great Sunday newspaper editor than of a great daily newspaper editor. The new editor's ambitions of what *The Times* should do every day were not compatible with his team's ability to get the paper out.

I had been hired for the *Sunday Times* with a specific task, to help with the commissioning of opinion polls and a general task, to act as a dogsbody on the political staff. I could not have had better tutors. The political staff was overseen by the patrician Hugo Young, a distinguished columnist and soon deputy editor of the paper. The political editor, Michael Jones, was a different kind of character, old Fleet Street rather than new, beer not Perrier, and not a man to let his own opinions stand in the way of a good story.

They had to be patient. When I started, I was hopelessly slow. Things were not helped by the technology. Then, you wrote your story on an old-fashioned manual typewriter, providing several carbon copies for those who needed to read it. My problem was a psychological one. If I made a mistake, I had to rip the whole thing out of the machine and start the page again. So to be sure of making my Saturday morning deadline for a poll story, I had to start to write on Thursday evening.

I benefited hugely from the coming of word processing and the ability to delete. Indeed, having learned to touch-type at an early age, I reckon by the time I finished to be the Speedy Gonzales of journalism. I might not be good, but by God! I was quick.

The partnership of the streetwise Jones and the cerebral Lipsey ought not to have worked. But it did.

In those days, the paper's political staff was under a particular pressure which demanded creative teamwork, for the paper required, each week, a lead story to attract people to buy it from the news stand. The convention was that, if no one else on the paper had a real story to fill the gap, the political staff would provide.

Saturday morning followed a ritual pattern. On Friday night, we tended to hang around, and hanging around meant drinking. Michael would take the train to Orpington, I would return to Wandsworth. Though Michael had a head for drink, the motions of the train would often induce a visit to the land of Nod. He often ended up on the south coast, arriving at the office on Saturday either via or not via his home, where his devoted and long-suffering wife Sheila acted as base camp.

On a bad Saturday, slightly hungover, we would sit and contemplate the scraps of information at our disposal. Michael would puzzle over the notes of the briefing which Number 10 gave every Friday afternoon for the benefit of the Sunday lobby. I meanwhile would flick through the week's Green Papers, Treasury statistics and ministerial answers in Parliament.

I had also acquired information during the week. I benefited from an ability to read any document upside down – a skill I mastered in Whitehall. This allowed me to access confidential material on ministers' desks while chatting amiably to them about the weather.

Having served me well previously, I used one of my old Whitehall techniques and read government documents from the back. Governments had hit on the fact that, if they placed embarrassing facts in the annexes to their documents, it could be pretty well guaranteed that no journalist would read that far.

On all too many Saturdays, at around 11.00, Young would appear. 'Thinking caps on please, gentlemen,' he would say, and we knew the search for a splash, the lead story, was on. The team was expanded with the addition of George Jones, later political editor of the *Daily Telegraph*, Don Macintyre, later of *The Independent*, and Kim Fletcher, who later edited the *Independent on Sunday*. In my last days, we were joined by a young defence reporter called John Witherow, who has since edited the *Sunday Times* for more than a decade.

I am afraid that we were not entirely scrupulous as to whether the story we created was strictly true – could be 'stood up' as the phrase went. Our aim, certainly in bad weeks, was to create something that had not been shown to be false by, say, Sunday lunchtime. So I am perhaps less critical of some of the creations of today's political journalists – especially since I am not sure that modern editors use phrases as polite as 'thinking caps on'.

A more satisfying activity was contributing to the 'Focus'. This was the long account which appeared in the middle of the paper which tried to explain and add to a story that was running elsewhere, or spell out at length a scoop of the paper's own. The goal was an estimable one of combining intellectual rigour with readability. It sometimes degenerated into something less high. 'I don't want you to tell me what you talked about,' one desperate Focus journalist was heard asking a contact. 'Just tell me what wine you had with the pudding.' 'The delicious Rieussec 1961 sweetened the talk as the Prime Minister sat with the President,' the article could run, giving the reader a wholly spurious impression that we had been there. Credibility thus established, you could make up a plausible account of what transpired.

When Harold Evans went to *The Times*, Frank Giles took his place as editor. I liked his old-fashioned manners and he did the job perfectly well. I also flourished under his editorship. When Sarah Hogg, the economics editor, went to *The Times*, I applied for the job and got it.

Unfairly, most journalists did not think Giles was one of us. He had high society, even royal, connections. He was not neurotic. He did not hate authority, and he edited in an orderly manner. He was also clearly not Harold Evans, and he was not the first person to suffer from taking over from a charismatic predecessor.

Giles was eventually the victim of a mess that was not of his making. The purchase by the paper of Adolf Hitler's diaries was indeed a great scoop, perhaps even greater than thalidomide, or at least it would have been if they had been genuine. I can still remember the slightly sheepish look on Giles's face when he produced the volumes in front of his editorial conference, trying to look sure of them and not succeeding.

The diaries had been authenticated by Hugh Trevor-Roper, the leading historian of Nazism, and if anyone deserved to lose his job over the affair, it was he. It fairly soon emerged that he had done a rushed and therefore a botched job. A head was bound to roll, and in the end it was Giles's.

Giles, in turn, was succeeded by Andrew Neil – who later became a leading political television presenter with the BBC. Andrew Neil was then still in his thirties, and came from *The Economist* where he was the editor of the Britain section. This was an important and influential job, but not obviously training to edit a complex national newspaper. To the *Sunday Times* journalists, 'not one of us' was being succeeded by another 'not one of us'.

Neil's politics were of the right, of a particular *Economist* genre. That is to say he was economically fairly 'dry', viscerally pro-American and anti-union. At the same time, he was a liberal on social matters. I made my inquiries and rather welcomed his appointment. He clearly had a brain and, besides, I thought that complacency had crept into the *Sunday Times*, which could do with a good shake-up.

Neil has written his own account of the period in his book *Full Disclosure*. It does contain a reference to me which I should like to correct, not because it is of the faintest importance but because it illustrates the chip on Neil's shoulder which was part of his character. He was talking of the reaction to a tough leader he had written backing the American intervention in Grenada. 'The first sign of dissent came from David Lipsey, who glared at me angrily when I went down to the composing room that Saturday afternoon to check the front page.'

Now I have no direct recollection of this so-called event. But it is implausible to the point of impossible. Yes, I was close to Young. No, I never shared his views, being myself instinctively anti-European and pro-American. If I had any opinion on the invasion of Grenada therefore, it would have been the same as Neil's. Most likely, however, being an eccentric sort of chap, I was ruminating on the inadequacies of the pudding served at lunchtime, or the unexpected defeat of my fancy in the 2.25 at Newton Abbot.

Neil alienated the old guard of the *Sunday Times*. One by one they left, culminating finally in the departure of Young himself.

I was affected by this of course. I lost good friends and colleagues. But I also gained a more direct role as I had taken on a job at the paper which put me on the front line.

The phrase 'father of the chapel' probably means nothing to 99 per cent of people today. The quaint old phrase meant plenty to newspaper managements though, for it meant union boss of each group of workers on the paper. And in the days when the unions ran Fleet Street, fathers of chapels struck fear into management's boots.

To be father of the National Union of Journalists chapel, admittedly, was to be a copper in the gold and silver of fathers of the chapels. I could not stop the printing presses with a flicker of my eyebrows as the print union bosses could and often did.

Nevertheless most journalists were unionised. Indeed in theory it was hard to get a job without having served an apprenticeship on a provincial paper. (I had got round this rule when I was appointed under a special exception allowed for those with particular knowledge.) As was the way in middle-class unions at the time, they modelled themselves on what they took to be the language and militancy of blue-collar unions though I think I was the only one on the paper who had any direct experience of what real unions were like.

NUJ FoC was not a job that was heavily sought after. My predecessor Peter Wilby, later editor of the *New Statesman*, had performed miracles to keep the chapel together. But year after year when the pay claim came round, the chapel would walk him up to the top of the hill, threatening all sorts of industrial action, and then walk him down again, flunking it.

I decided on a different approach. I would not pretend that journalists were what they weren't. I would instead present reasonable cases reasonably. I would rarely issue threats to management.

However, if I did issue a threat, and if they chose to ignore me, I would demonstrate that I was not bluffing.

Sackings were a challenge. Typically, the editor would decide he had had enough of someone. Often, he would act on his impulse, without paying much regard to all the nuances of dismissal law. I would be confronted with a hurt journalist, demanding action.

The trouble is that action was not in the journalist's interests. They could of course go to an industrial tribunal. They would win. However, they would not be likely subsequently to be offered jobs on any other papers. Or we could strike. However, most of those sacked had weaknesses that were only too apparent to their colleagues. Solidarity would be unlikely to extend to a withdrawal of labour which stopped the paper.

I took an unheroic route. I would promise my aggrieved member that I would see what I could do. I would then go and have a chat with the managing editor, Peter Roberts, with whom I struck up a close friendship.

Editors are usually concerned to get rid of someone they don't want. The cost of doing so comes down their list of priorities. So Roberts – often as appalled by the way the deed had been done as I was – would agree a sum in compensation for the sacked journalist. This was usually appropriately generous. Invariably too the colleague concerned would be known on other papers for the by-lines he had accumulated rather than for the faults he exhibited. An ex-*Sunday Times* journalist was sought after. I therefore did well by my dismissed members, or at least so it seemed to me. When I was myself sacked from *The Times* some years later, Roberts, by then managing editor there, reached another fair settlement with me. The cash helped me buy my home in Wales.

I was not sacked from the *Sunday Times*. Neil did consider demoting me so as to be able to hire an economics commentator whose views accorded with his own, but I produced an above-quota number of stories of reasonable competence and survived. In any case, NUJ FoCs were unfireable since the members would not tolerate victimisation of their official representatives.

However, a conflict broke out between Murdoch's News International and the print unions about their stranglehold over production. Murdoch had had it to the back teeth with the print unions, who would disrupt production at the drop of a hat. Incredible as it may seem today, journalists then would input their copy through one keyboard, only for the copy to be completely retyped by members of the print union before being turned into type. He decided to break the unions once and for all by moving to a new print centre at Wapping, where such absurdities no longer applied – and sacked his existing printers in the process.

For journalists that gave rise to a dilemma. We were delighted to see the print unions weakened. For one thing, that meant we would no longer work all week on good stories which on Saturday night they refused to print. Yet we could also see that, without them, Murdoch would be in total power, and our ability to defend the rights and freedoms of journalists would be reduced.

The conflict led in due course to the long year when working at the paper involved crossing picket lines, the agony of good journalists torn in their loyalties between their paper and their hatred of management, and the eventual crushing of the printers. I saw this was coming and I had personal reasons for not fancying it.

This is not a book about my personal life, though. I fear that, even if it were, it would be rather lacking in material which would find it a home in *Hello!* magazine. But by the early 1980s, I was living with Margaret Robson, my fellow Streatham Labour Party member, and in 1982 we got married. To say we 'lived happily ever afterwards' would be an oversimplification, but I find it simply inconceivable that I could have led the life with all the happiness I have enjoyed without her.

In 1983, my daughter Becky had been born, the greatest joy of my life and wholly uncovenanted as my wife already had two children of her own. However, shortly afterwards Margaret developed breast cancer.

The health service was at the time under pressure to cut spending, including that on radiotherapy treatment. Margaret was entered into a programme where radiotherapy was delivered five times a fortnight, rather than the normal five times a week, in bigger doses. With a small baby, fewer hospital visits suited us well.

Arguably in consequence Margaret was one of a number of women – some 800 in all – who developed brachial plexus injury. She was relatively lucky in that she did not suffer permanent intolerable pain. She did, however, totally lose the use of an arm, a particularly severe impediment in a mother with a young child

She was, and is, uncomplaining, making minimal demands on me. However, I had a stressful home situation and I did not particularly want the stress of the coming work situation. When I saw that *New Society* was advertising for a deputy editor, I applied, though, as already reported, the job didn't turn out to be the low-stress one I had hoped for.

These domestic complications may go part way to excuse the compete mess-up I made as FoC on the road to Wapping. I kick myself for it particularly because it started with one of my best ideas.

As the Wapping move approached, I could side neither with the print unions nor with Murdoch.

So far as the print unions were concerned, not by any means all their leaders were the Luddites that they were painted as. I met the print union FoCs on several occasions. They knew that they were being lured into a trap; that they no longer had the power to stop the newspapers moving to new technology; and that their time was up. But where others saw Luddism, they saw the protection of old rights and traditions, as well as fat pay packets.

I cannot say the same for the journalists' union. Harry Conway, the general secretary of the NUJ, and his officials, behaved with incredible stupidity. His duty was to identify where their members' interests lay, and to stand up for them. Instead his officials came and delivered mock Marxist lectures about our duty to stand shoulder to shoulder with our print union brothers.

Brothers! But we *hated* them. These were the people, Saturday after Saturday, who deliberately went slowly to extract extra payments from the management. These were the people who imposed on us workers they chose. The PA to the political department was for some while a man who none of us ever dared ask to do anything for fear of the consequences. These were the ones who insisted when we had typed our stories that they retype them. These were the ones whose pay depredations on the company eroded the pay available for us. These were the people who openly despised us.

I saw an alternative route. At the time, a *Telegraph* journalist called Andreas Whittam Smith had conceived the idea which led to the *Independent* newspaper. He had seen that technological advances meant that newspapers could be created by direct input of copy by journalists and then printed at remote printing sites, removed from the influence of the East End print unions. He was raising the money to start a paper along those lines.

As the Wapping move came near, News International was threatening to sack any journalist who did not move there. My idea was simple. Let them sack us. We would set up a company to employ all the journalists and produce a paper – in content if not in name – just like the *Sunday Times*. We would control the product. We would enjoy the profits.

I still believe that this might have come to something. But by then I was committed to leaving the paper. It was clearly impossible for me both to lead a major initiative of that kind and to walk out on it. The flame burned, then sputtered, then went out. The hell that was Wapping inevitably followed. So did the victory for Murdoch and Neil. A great opportunity to diminish proprietor power and to enhance the professional role of journalists was lost. It was not my finest hour.

CHAPTER 9

HACKING ON 1986-99

The *Not-the-Sunday-Times* never happened, but that was by no means the end of that particular story.

The more I thought of the idea of an alternative quality Sunday newspaper, the more attractive it seemed. Everywhere you went you heard complaints about the ones that existed. They were too big but contained too little of interest.

As it happens, the same idea was occurring to David Blake, an old friend who was economics editor of *The Times*. He in turn had discussed it with Gavyn Davies, now a wealthy man.

The coming of *The Independent* was the talking point of journalists in London. If it would work for a daily, why should it not work for a Sunday?

Blake, Davies and I talked, together with Martin Knight, who ran a boutique financial company in St James's. The more we talked, the more excited we got.

Quite early on it was apparent to me that our success or failure could depend on our relationship with *The Independent* itself. If they helped us, we would be well down the road to success. If they launched against us, we faced an uphill task.

I knew Andreas Whittam Smith as a fellow economics commentator, and rang him up. He could not have been warmer.

He and his team had their hands full with launching the daily. They could not help us, for that would distract them from their main task. However, he was entirely encouraging of our enterprise. The conversation closed with him wishing me the best of luck.

This seemed a perfectly logical stand for *The Independent* to take. The arguments about distraction were valid. Moreover they were taking one big risk in launching a daily paper. Why should they take another by launching a Sunday? The latter could bring the former down. More sensible surely to let another group try a Sunday. They could always take it over if it proved a success.

It seemed an obvious judgement. It also proved a wrong one, in the end destroying not only our new Sunday paper, the *Sunday Correspondent*, but theirs – not 'independent' for very long!

To get our paper going we were going to need a lot of money. In the first instance, we needed first-round seed money, about £1m. This would enable us to hire the professional help we needed, and to pay a skeleton staff. In order to show we were serious we would ourselves have to inject substantial capital sums into the project.

We would meanwhile prepare a prospectus explaining and justifying our project. This was subject to the dreaded 'due diligence', a procedure whereby every fact and opinion in it had to be justified to the satisfaction of our lawyers so we could show that we were not deliberately misleading would-be investors. Off the back of that prospectus, we would seek to raise some £25m to get us launched and to cover initial losses.

This was all supposed to take a few months. In fact it took nearly two years. They were the most agonising of my professional career. Indeed, at one point, I said to my wife, 'Suppose we raise the money. Suppose we get the paper off the ground and it is a wild success. Suppose I make the £4m due to me if we fulfil our plans. Even if all that happens, it won't remotely have been worth it.'

Every step forward involved a step backward. We required a chairman to oversee the business and deal with the bits about which we knew nothing: production and distribution. Douglas Long, who had done this job for *The Independent* before parting from them, seemed an ideal candidate. Unfortunately, Douglas was well into his sixties; he did not in fact live long after the paper was created. Moreover, he and the *Independent* crew had fallen out and by hiring him we turned Whittam Smith's original support into deep enmity. As it happened, I could not stand Long any more than the *Independent* team had been able to stand him; and the feeling was mutual.

Then there was the question of who was to be editor of the new paper. We had two candidates among our little group of founders, David Blake and me. The trouble was that neither had the confidence of the other. My view of David was that he was a journalist of high talent and great brilliance. However, he lacked the organisational application which I felt an editor required. I am sure he had equally good reasons why I would not be up to the job.

Having two apparently qualified editors neither of whom was going to do the job was a curiosity in our set-up, and did not help us in recruiting a plausible alternative. A number of candidates were approached: I remember for example David Bell of the *Financial Times*, who would have been ideal. All politely said no. We got to a near-conclusion with David Dimbleby, who, besides being famous, had a family-owned chain of local newspapers. He dabbled with the proposition before deciding against.

In the end we got our man and a good one: Peter Cole. Cole was deputy editor of *The Guardian* but unlikely ever to become its editor due to the dominating presence in that job of Peter Preston and his heir apparent, Alan Rusbridger. We also succeeded in recruiting a plausible chief executive in Nick Shott, who had an advertising sales background. Nick had charm, inexhaustible energy and a persuasive tongue and was never discouraged. He has subsequently enjoyed a successful City career with Lazards.

Cole had one quality above all others. He believed in the project, and he could make others believe in it. Even while we were still fundraising, he was recruiting his editorial team. Some had to be persuaded to leave their existing jobs long before we had any guarantee of money to pay them. And yet, to the astonishment of Fleet Street, stellar name after stellar name was signed up. Henry Porter would edit the magazine; Mick Brown the review section; Phil Bassett, succeeded by Paul Vallely, home news; Jon Connell foreign; and Simon Kelner sports. The writers were stars. The photographers were stars. The cartoonist, Chris Riddell, was one of the contemporary greats. We gave Chris Hitchens his first-ever newspaper staff job as our American correspondent. Writers included Don Macintyre and his deputy Michael Prescott on politics; Robert Peston, who doubled as deputy business editor; great sports journalists such as Dudley Doust; others mentioned below… well, the trouble with the list is that it is virtually endless and I shall offend anyone I omit. The duds in our ranks could be numbered on the fingers of one hand.

I was asked to recruit two young graduates at small salaries. The two I chose were Ian Katz, now deputy editor of *The Guardian*, and Jonathan Freedland, its leading columnist. Both oozed talent.

If this lot could not produce a great newspaper no one could. Except of course that the money men did not know anything about the newspaper men (and vice versa), so they did not know that, in terms of product at any rate, they were backing a certainty.

Getting the money made getting the people seem a doddle. It would be boring to go over and over the investors who seemed likely to join and then backed out. A motley crew put money in for motley motives. *The Guardian* invested in order to distract and then screw *The Independent*. The Tribune Company of Chicago put money in to dip a toe in European waters. Robert Maxwell put money in so we would use his printing presses. Besides, Captain Bob always liked a gamble. And so it went, for month after month. Each success was matched by several failures. We were still short of target despite the high standing of some of the 'yeses', and the list of possibles was shrinking before our eyes.

Charlie Geffen of Ashurst's, our solicitors, was getting troubled: if we were not going to get the money, we were arguably trading illegally by spending what we had. Eventually, one afternoon he told us solemnly that in his judgement, if the money were not raised by 6.00 that evening, we would have to throw in the towel.

If anyone thinks City people don't earn their corn, they should have seen Martin Knight that day. 'I am not going to see this project fail,' he stormed. He made call after call, wheedling here, cajoling there. The rest of us watched the clock hands advance: 5.00 … 5.30 … 5.45 … 5.55. Unbelievable as it may seem, it was 5.59 precisely when Knight secured the last pledge. We were in business.

Then a big cloud appeared. Whittam Smith's original support

had more than disappeared. He was cross that we had aped his idea. He was furious that we had given a job to Long. He was enraged that we had modelled our prospectus on his prospectus. From a one-man encapsulation of the higher morality of journalism, he became a one-man encapsulation of the vices of capitalism, red in tooth and claw. *The Independent* announced they would launch their own Sunday newspaper, shortly after ours. We did not know if this was for real or merely a spoiling tactic. Either way, it hurt.

Before launch, one attempt was made to prevent the *Sunday Correspondent* and the *Independent on Sunday* from colliding. Its begetter was the ubiquitous Richard Branson, a friend to both enterprises and quite able to see what would happen if both proceeded. We were invited to his magnificent Notting Hill residence to see whether we could find a way forward together.

We could not. On our side, Cole and Long were at their truculent worst, snarling like caged lions at their would-be partners. On their side, Whittam Smith and Matthew Symonds, his deputy, conducted themselves like monarchs dealing with a peasants' revolt. The war between the two papers on the streets was growing ever nearer.

Somehow morale was maintained. We went through the tortuous process of producing dummy issues of the paper. They were filled with real stories filed by real journalists as if they were going into a real newspaper. As the dummies arrived, and the paper was refined, we began to think that perhaps this really was the business.

We did produce a newspaper. The newspaper critics could hardly find a bad word to say about it. Our team, though small, was dedicated. Under Cole's amiable leadership it was almost as if we had created an adventure playground for journalists. We had parties. We had a hungover full English in the Red Lion near our Clerkenwell offices each Saturday. We had rows and reconciliations. Much more important and tragically, we even lost a great journalist when David Blundy, a world-class foreign correspondent, was shot covering the conflict in El Salvador.

We had affairs, quite a lot of affairs, some of which survive to this day. Nowhere but on the *Sunday Correspondent* could Ben Macintyre, the son of a leading academic, have met Kate Muir, down from the *Scottish Daily Mirror* – two great journalists and a lovely family. If some television executive had been on the ball, we could have stopped bothering with a newspaper and instead have created a soap opera to trump all soap operas.

Unfortunately, we made two key errors. The first was to keep the paper small. We had market research which showed that people thought the upmarket Sundays had too much to read, so, as a consequence, we decided to produce just two sections and a magazine. The trouble was that the market research had not told us something else. Potential readers did indeed want a paper which was small but they also wanted one that gave them at least as much coverage of their favoured subject as its rivals. Sports fans wanted lots of sports. Politics addicts wanted lots of politics. There had to be a crossword, a chess column, bridge. They wanted in other words a quart in a pint pot.

The second error concerned our promotion. We had persuaded BBDO, one of Britain's biggest advertising agencies, to take on our account. They were clever and professional. However, there was an unfortunate misunderstanding between us.

They thought that the market gap we should be trying to fill was just above the middle of the middle market. We should be pitched somewhere below the *Sunday Times* and above the *Mail on Sunday*.

This was not what we had instructed our journalists to produce. We thought the existing quality Sundays had drifted downmarket and intended to position ourselves above them.

Our advertising campaign was an immense success in one sense. It persuaded some 800,000 people to buy our first edition. Unfortunately, they thought they were buying one paper, the one cleverly promoted by the ads BBDO produced. Then they found they had in their hands a quite different paper, and not one they wanted. The initial sales exceeded our expectations. The speed with which they then declined, week on week, alas exceeded our expectations too.

The *Independent on Sunday*, when it arrived, wasn't doing well either. Indeed, the losses it made were soon dragging *The Independent* down with it. No doubt we should have been saddened by the troubles of such a noble venture. That was not, as I recall it, the principal emotion expressed on the *Correspondent* editorial floor.

There is nothing as dead as an old newspaper. It would serve little purpose to trace the *Sunday Correspondent*'s progress through its year or so of existence. We tried everything. Cole went grey with effort, took no holidays, put his all in, and was thus naturally aggrieved when the board decided months before closure to give someone else a go. That someone was not me. Instead they recruited John Bryant, the deputy editor of *The Times*. He recreated the paper as a tabloid, somewhere downmarket as the advertising agency had wanted it to be. It gave away vintage cars as a promotion device. The circulation did not respond, not for long anyway, and the losses were horrendous. Its closure a few weeks after it launched was inevitable.

Twenty years later Robin Morgan, one of the *Correspondent* journalists, organised a reunion for the staff. Cole could not be there, but Blake and I were. Given a printing press, we could have created a great newspaper there and then. Those who were not famous when the *Correspondent* was in business had become famous since, the cream of journalism. And on one thing we were all agreed: it was the most enjoyable if demanding experience any of us had ever had during our journalistic careers.

Newspapers by their nature are transient affairs and their cultures similarly. Even so, and though the *Sunday Correspondent* has long died, it was hard not to feel that day that its soul survives. And my wife will still not let *The Independent* into our house.

As the *Correspondent* sank below the waves in 1989, I received a kind and comforting letter from Simon Jenkins, editor of *The Times*. 'Should your brave venture fail,' he said, 'a comfortable berth awaits you with us.'

I later learned that the berth Simon had in mind was that of economics editor, a job that eventually went to Anatole Kaletsky. It would indeed have been a comfortable berth and as Anatole has shown over the years, potentially of great influence.

With John Bryant's move to the *Correspondent*, things took a dramatic turn. Simon's deputy editor, Peter Stothard, was enjoying a spell writing from America. There were other strong internal candidates to be deputy in London, Michael Hamlyn, who ran the news desk, being one. However, Jenkins had apparently heard good reports of my doings at the *Correspondent*. A double-page spread of a map of Iraq, which all the writers on the *Correspondent* hated because it took away space for their stories, attracted his attention. So did a leader supporting the findings of the Calcut inquiry into press regulation, of which Jenkins had been a member.

So when Simon and I talked it was not about the economics editorship, but about being his deputy in London. The absent Stothard retained the title and consequently his claim to be Jenkins's eventual successor, but I did not care about this. I already knew that I was not cut out to be a Murdoch editor, so could not rise higher on *The Times*.

The new job came both as a relief – for the strain at the *Correspondent* was intense – and a thrill. *The Times* may not have had the reputation of its peak, but it still had its history and it was still a force to be reckoned with. It also had a well-honed machine, especially on the news side, and had many talents of its own.

Unfortunately, my move did not really work out, partly because I (like Harold Evans before me) did not find the transition to a daily newspaper easy. If *The Times* was to be on the street each morning, senior editors needed to resist the temptation to interfere. News editors and the back bench survived only by strenuously defending their territory against invasion.

There was also the Simon problem. Simon Jenkins, now Sir Simon and chair of the National Trust, is one of the finest writing journalists of his age. He had the social contacts to be a great editor of *The Times*, and radiated confidence in the job, as he had when he was first made an editor, of the *Evening Standard*, at the age of thirty-three.

It took a while for me to realise the faults that went with this genius. In the neat phrase adopted by the staff from one coined for Beaverbrook, Simon had a whim of iron. Typically, he would go into the morning news conference, demanding blanket coverage of this, that or the other story and the machine was set to work. When he came to the afternoon conference, he would express his astonishment that so minor a matter should be getting such extensive coverage. 'Whose idea was that?' he would mutter. No one dared to say, 'Yours, Simon.'

He had dogmatic views on layout, but they were not good ones. I never found out what he really wanted in his leaders. His judgement of public affairs was pretty good, but I was not so convinced by his judgement of style. And the fact was that, by and large, circulation was falling, month after month. Stothard showed when he came into his inheritance that this was not inevitable.

Some people came under his protection because they were friends of Murdoch. Jenkins would spend hours on the phone as Barbara Amiel, an extreme right-wing columnist married to Conrad Black, poured out her angst as to what she should write about what. Woodrow Wyatt, a renegade Labour MP who had become chairman of the Tote, was a friend of Margaret Thatcher's as well as Murdoch's, and thus his frightful column, used by him to reward his friends and sanction his enemies, was sacrosanct.

So far as I was concerned, I had a problem with my job description. There were two possible roles that a deputy could play. He could be the main hour-to-hour force under the editor shaping the newspaper and its news coverage. Or he could be an intellectual force behind and developing its leader policy. It was not possible to play both.

It may have been impossible, but that was the remit I was given. I was to arrive early in the morning to shape the choice of news coverage. I was then to stay late at night, until I had had a chance to read the first edition and reshape it. Simon would leave in time to get to the opera, though never until the first interval lest anyone think he was slacking. I was not so lucky.

Meanwhile I was supposed most days to write a leader. Typically, I could hope to get a start at around 3.00 pm, but because of the demands of my other roles, I had to be finished by 4.00 pm. I thought in the circumstances and whatever my other failings, my leaders were quite good. Simon rarely seemed to agree.

At first, he was happy with his choice. I did have a measure of judgement, so, for example, he could remain relatively relaxed on a Sunday when I was left in charge.

However, we never established a warm relationship. My personality means I perform best when appreciated. His personality means that he is slow to praise.

Incidents accumulated. There was, for example, the terrible tale of the *Times* April Fool. Jenkins was away. I thought we, like *The Guardian*, might cheer up our readers with some April Fool stories. I held a competition among the staff for the best, which was won by a superbly wrought tale that the M25 was to be closed for road works, so everyone who used it would have to complete a 117-mile journey the wrong way round.

Jenkins was incandescent. I had destroyed, so I was told, the authority of the paper.

I was not the only one to fail his tests. He would from time to time turn on senior members of the editorial staff. He once told me to fire Mary Ann Sieghart, an accomplished leader writer, an effective executive and a public asset to the paper. I managed to find ways of not quite doing what he wanted until the whim passed.

In my eighteen months or so at the paper, I did achieve a few things. For example, we started to take complaints that we had got things wrong seriously, especially when they led to legal action.

I was called in when Brian Sedgemore, then a left-wing Labour MP, was suing Robert Kilroy-Silk, years before also a Labour MP, over something he had written in his column. This was potentially an expensive case and, if we lost, we would lose much by way of reputation.

'When's all this scheduled for court then?' I asked, expecting an answer in months or years. 'Day after tomorrow,' came the reply. When it was heard, we were lucky to get away with a legal draw.

This was sorted. Reporters for the first time were told to inform management if they got a threat to sue. Complaints were treated seriously. Both Simon and I were supporters of the self-regulatory Press Complaints Commission, warts and all, and we incorporated its code of practice into the handbook given to all staff.

Sometimes, I got the judgement calls right. On the night of the 1991 invasion of Iraq, I was rung in bed in the small hours. 'It's started,' reported Tim Austin, the supremely competent news editor. I hurried into my clothes and to the office.

At 2.00 am, the place was humming. I glanced at a proof on the news editor's desk. 'Iraq bombs Tel Aviv. Massive Israeli retaliation launched,' it said.

'Um, what is our evidence for that?'

'An agency report, David.'

'Perhaps hold it for a few minutes until we get confirmation?' And so a page which would have ranked with the Hitler diaries as an exemplar of the errors of newspapers narrowly did not appear.

I could make terrible errors, too, during my time as acting deputy. One Sunday morning, I came in to edit. I am ashamed to say that I had not taken an early cut the night before and was thoroughly hungover. This was when the panic about dangerous dogs was at its peak, and indeed, obligingly keeping it boiling, another dog somewhere had nipped a child to provide us with our story.

Clifford Longley, the senior leader writer, asked me what our leader line should be. 'Kill all the dangerous dogs,' I said. He gently demurred. 'No, kill them,' I insisted, and so 'Kill them' became the policy of the paper.

In fact I had no views on the dogs or what to do about them. My sole thought was that this would make a striking leader. It might even hit the broadcast news.

On Monday morning, or so it was reliably reported to me, Kenneth Baker, the Home Secretary, read Longley's persuasive leader. Cautious Home Office advice was swept aside and 'Kill the dangerous dogs' became government policy. By common consent, the resulting Act is one of the worst passed by Parliament in many years. I can plead nothing in mitigation. I apologise to the unfairly martyred dogs and their owners.

I had to serve for many years as a trustee of the Retired Greyhound Trust to live that one down.

My star had hardly risen when it began to sink. I was soon in a vicious circle. I wasn't enjoying things, my confidence was not high. As I looked gloomier and said less and erred more, my standing fell. Though I had supporters on the staff, the lovely leader team and key members of the news operation, I had the defect of not truly being a *Times* man. I was also seen as the agent of Jenkins, who was increasingly unpopular.

The end was nigh. My fate was sealed when a big international story broke while I was on holiday in the Scilly Isles. Every other journalist rushed back to the office to cover it. I made a vague enquiry as to whether I might get a flight back, which was difficult. Otherwise I ignored it, which was easy given that the papers on Bryher arrived two days late. It was a grave dereliction of duty, which had fatal consequences for me. But it is not one I regret. We had a great holiday.

Eventually, the axe fell. Simon came in one Sunday to tell me that John Bryant was returning as deputy editor. I was demoted to a kind of notional number three and would not even edit the paper on a Sunday. Alternatively, of course, a pay-off could be arranged.

I did not want to leave immediately for one reason: the 1992 general election was approaching. Despite the sacking of Margaret Thatcher and her replacement by John Major, the government was in trouble. Not a single poll was giving it an overall majority. Elections were a bit of a speciality of mine and so were polls. It was worth putting up with a little humiliation to be involved in this one for *The Times*.

That too turned out to be a disappointment. Our coverage of the election was, I think, quite good. The result, from my point of view, was not. Major won an overall majority. I can remember next morning sneaking into the deserted office to plan the post-election coverage. I was at least dutiful to the end. Then I left.

Whatever had been the state of our relations before he fired me, Simon could not have been nicer after. He thanked me for my 'tolerance of me and my idiosyncrasies. Having been one myself, I know deputising is not easy.' He also suggested he could deliver the editorship of the *Times Higher Education Supplement* to me if I wanted it. The *THES* was a curious beast, mixing news about universities and colleges with intellectual content by academics. The prospect was quite tempting but it turned out that the appointment was not entirely within Simon's gift after all. It lay with Andrew Knight, then chairman of News International in London. He had a good candidate in Auriol Stevens, who had the not inconsiderable advantage of knowing something about higher education.

As things moved in her direction, I was moving too. I had remained friends over the years with Rupert Pennant-Rea, who had succeeded me at the GMWU and had then become a journalist. He had risen to be a successful editor of *The Economist*. I had always liked what I had heard about *The Economist*, where Dick Leonard, Tony's parliamentary private secretary, had carved out his career after the House. So I asked him if he might have a job for me.

Luckily, he had. Daniel Franklin, coming back from North America to do the job, had just been appointed to be the Britain editor. Rupert saw that Daniel might benefit from a wizened hack with recent knowledge of Britain. Daniel was prepared to take on someone who was senior and might have proved challenging. In fact my relationship with him was as successful as any I have had in my journalistic career. He was endlessly encouraging, which reinflated my ego. He is one of the great copy editors and, while sound himself, open to wacky ideas. Daniel's successors, Emma Duncan and David Manasian, were similarly joys to work for.

To a now-hardened newsman, my first Monday at *The Economist* came as a surprise.

My editor poked his head round my door. 'David,' he said. 'I know this is a lot to ask in your first week here before you've got your feet under the table. But you couldn't possibly pen us 400

words on the dentists' strike for Wednesday evening, could you?'
This was evidently a different pace of life than that to which I had
grown accustomed.

A meeting was then held to discuss the content of the section.
This was not quite like the equivalent editorial meeting at *The
Times*. 'Where's the market failure then?' asked Emma Duncan,
then writing for the section. 'What's the case for state intervention?'
Forty-five minutes of good-level theoretical economics followed. I
had died and gone to heaven.

The Economist's standing in the world is legendary. It was brought
home to me later by a trip to Germany with Roy Jenkins's committee on electoral reform. We were meeting some senior German
politicians and Roy was introducing his team.

'I am Roy Jenkins, the former President of the European
Commission,' he said. Their heads barely nodded. 'And this is Lord
Alexander, chairman of the National Westminster Bank' – no nod
– 'and this is Sir John Chilcot, formerly permanent secretary of the
Northern Ireland Office' – nothing – 'and Baroness Gould, former
national agent of the Labour Party' – bored – and 'this', last because
least, 'is David Lipsey of *The Economist*.'

Heads shot up. Beams broke out. '*Ach so*, of *The Economist*,' said
the leader of their delegation as if he had suddenly discovered he
was in the presence of a superstar.

The Economist's circulation has grown from under half a million
when I was there to some 1.5 million today. With that kind of reputation, it is not surprising. And it does so despite the fact that it is
unremittingly upmarket, unyieldingly intellectual, short of pretty
pictures and in its internal workings gives virtually no attention to
tailoring editorial content to maximise reader appeal. It defies the
forces of journalistic gravity that dominate virtually every other
publication worldwide.

This is not the only singular aspect of the paper. Another is that
it is produced each week by a tiny editorial staff, no more than
forty in the London office. The prose is unmatched, for clarity if
not for show. The facts are invariably right, thanks to the work

of the unsung library which checks them all. The opinions are well argued.

I do not wish to give away trade secrets. For one thing, I am and remain a shareholder in *The Economist* – one of its tricks being staff shareholding, which builds loyalty. But one at least deserves to be understood: the paper's refusal to allow by-lines on stories.

At first sight, this is daft both for readers and for writers. Readers are deprived of a clue as to where a piece is coming from and how much it can be relied on. Writers are deprived of their moment of glory when the world can see what they have created. This undoubtedly has costs for the paper. There has been a leakage of top *Economist* journalists, to the *Financial Times* in particular, where they can strut their stuff under their own names.

The advantages, however, are great too. Because no names appear on the pieces, they can be rewritten as required without offence to the author's ego. Endless disputes about by-lines are avoided. It was literally true when I was at the *Sunday Times* that journalists would creep down to the 'stone', where pages were put together, take pairs of tweezers and reverse the names of authors on stories so theirs came first. No such nonsense could take place at *The Economist*.

Because every story is attributable only to the paper, every story is also the responsibility of the paper. Every member of staff has an interest in making the content as good as possible. Co-operation replaces competition and – rather contrary to *Economist* editorial philosophy – it turns out that co-operation can produce a better product than competition.

While writing for the Britain section, I was able to produce some stories which it would be inconceivable for any national newspaper to produce. For example, we did a survey to trace the origins of the (arbitrarily defined) top 100 people in Britain to see if social mobility was a reality. It turned out that they were the same public school-educated mob as before Margaret Thatcher came to power. We used an actuary to calculate the likely number of by-elections in the 1992–97 parliament and so the likelihood that John Major would be forced into an early election. This got me reasonably close to one of the few journalism awards I coveted: the George Orwell Prize. Three times I entered and three times I was runner-up. Bernard Crick, the chair of the judges, very kindly produced a memorial plaque to record this, though not the winner's generous prize money!

In fact, the only journalism prize I won was also prestigious: *The Guardian*/Hansard Young Political Writer of the Year for a brilliant column entitled 'Reinventing Michael Portillo'. As, however, the award was for thirteen- to fifteen-year-olds, something was clearly not quite right. And it emerged what it was: a young man called Richard Belcher had purloined my column.

Perhaps the judges thought it mature for his years or perhaps it wasn't one of my more mature pieces, I don't know. However, when it was reprinted in *The Guardian*, the plagiarism was exposed and poor young Belcher was threatened with expulsion from school. I wrote a forgiving letter to his mother and one to the school begging mercy, but I might have been less charitable had the column been given second rather than first place. *The Economist*, wittily, ran an ad exploiting Mr Belcher's chutzpah, with its strapline a quote from him: 'I didn't think *The Economist* was widely read.'

If working for *The Economist* is heaven, writing the Bagehot column is sitting at the right hand of God. Though there are no by-lines, *The Economist* has instituted a few political columns which are written each week by a single author – Lexington on America, Charlemagne on Europe, and Bagehot, named after the nineteenth-century editor who made the paper, on Britain. Some years after I had arrived, Xan Smiley vacated the slot, and I took his place.

Bagehot was widely read and – partly because no modern name was attached to it – respected. You could get to talk to pretty well anyone you wanted to talk to. Because it was an opinion piece, you could report what they said or ignore what they said or simply plagiarise what they said. You were allowed to show off with the style.

I read the broad political situation in Britain right – namely that after Britain had left the Exchange Rate Mechanism in 1992, the Tory government, hopelessly divided about Europe, was done for. That didn't mean that each individual minister was without merit, and though my deep sympathies were with Labour, I hope I gave credit where credit was due. For example, Bagehot had a high opinion of Peter Lilley, the social security minister who was widely derided. After I had left, Peter served for many years as a supportive member of my policy advisory committee at the Social Market Foundation.

It was hard not to get carried away with excitement as Tony Blair threw away the baggage of Old Labour, as I had been urging the party leader to do for many years. I even surreptitiously rejoined the Labour Party. This was wrong. Political journalists should not be members of political parties. But I was simply unable to resist.

This led to the only sour note of my tenure of Bagehot. *The Economist* had been critical of the Tories and supportive of Blairism. When the election came, it might have been expected that we would endorse Labour, as did *The Times* and the *Financial Times*. In fact, Bill Emmott, the editor, came out for the Tories. He did so on the grounds, which proved as wrong as could be, that there was a hidden Old Labour wishing to get out from under the New Labour exterior.

I had no trouble with the editor making any decision he chose in this matter. I had never found it hard to work with papers whose editorial policy was at odds with my own. I did find it hard that Bill came to his decision in private, without discussing it face to face with me as his political editor. (I should say this was a rare blip in our relationship for Bill was more than kind to me.) I was already starting to move away from *The Economist* at the time as journalism had less and less new to offer me. I was taking on attractive bits and pieces outside the paper.

Bill's decision led to an amusing election night. *The Economist* usually goes to press on a Thursday but we had arranged things to hang on into Friday morning so we should be able at least in part to report the result. A small gang was assembled in Bill's office, waiting to call it. As the early indications of a Labour victory came in, a pall spread over the gathering, and mostly notably over Bill and his wife, Carol. I sternly resisted the temptation to smirk.

Eventually it was obvious that Labour had won its landslide. We called it. I sneaked away from the mourners across the river to the Royal Festival Hall. The Labour Party and its friends were celebrating in style, Blair himself flying in in the small hours to join the throng. I enjoyed being among comrades.

Bill Emmott of course knew where my politics lay. He nevertheless generously gave me a sabbatical, mostly to work on my book on the Treasury.

My time at *The Economist* was not quite over. It was soon apparent that I was too close to the government to remain as Bagehot. I was found an appropriate slot as social affairs editor, working part time. There I might have remained for the rest of my working life if it had not been for an unexpected development. By long-established precedent, you could not both remain on the staff of *The Economist* and serve as a party political member of the House of Lords – which was where in 1999 I found myself headed.

CHAPTER 10

THE FUTURE OF SOCIALISM
1979–99

My years in journalism were not confined to journalism. I also wrote from a different perspective, that of a Crosland-trained apostle of democratic socialism. In the chapters to come I shall also cover in some detail the three government commissions of which I was made a member and which led to my peerage: the Royal Commission on the Funding of Long-Term Care of the Elderly, the Jenkins Commission on the electoral system and the Davies Panel on the funding of the BBC.

I started life knowing for certain that I wanted to be a politician. By the early 1980s I was certain I didn't.

Besides my dislike of canvassing, mentioned earlier, there were two reasons for this. One was working as a journalist. Yes, journalists were entitled to views, indeed some were paid to hold them. But blind partisan loyalty and decent journalism are not compatible. Having already a politically disabling tendency to treat facts as facts and keep an open mind, my journalism led me down a path which increasingly diverged from the path of politics.

The second, however, was the state of the Labour Party. I have briefly referred to Callaghan's disastrous last months as leader, to the rise of the Bennite left and to the SDP breakaway. All this I reported on for one paper or another. The result was to erode my commitment to Labour. I lacked a political home.

On the one hand, for biographical reasons if for no others, I could not join the SDP. Tony Crosland had taught me that Roy Jenkins was not a socialist. I still thought that I was, at least in the Croslandite sense of the word. 'Never underestimate the passion of the Labour movement for unity' goes the old saw. I still had it in my bones if not in my head.

Equally I could not remain in the Labour Party, still less actively seek a Labour candidacy. In those days, the chances of an overtly right-wing member of the party getting a seat were those of a snowball in hell. Matters were not of course assisted when some of Labour's right-wing backbenchers left for the SDP.

Someone more ambitious and with fewer intellectual scruples than I would not have found this an obstacle. Paris is worth a mass, and I no doubt could have summoned up some convincing neo-Trotskyist rubbish to impress a selection conference.

It is easy to forget just how far this tide advanced. I remember, for example, attending one meeting of the Battersea Labour Party to support Alf Dubs, the much-loved centre-left MP.

A motion was put forward for the Labour Party conference. Its thrust was that the police should be put under the control of supervisory authorities, democratically elected of course. The words 'people's commissars' did not appear, but you knew what was meant.

A voice spoke out at the back of the hall. 'Comrade Chair, I wish to oppose the motion,' the speaker said. Was this the start of the fight back, I wondered? Was the voice of reason about to point out that law and order would not be best served by removing the operational independence of the police? 'Comrade Chair, there is only one answer to the police problem. It is a bullet in the back of their head.' This was not a party of which I wanted to be an active member, still less a party on whose behalf I wished to seek the support of the electorate by fighting a seat.

The Labour/SDP split did, however, involve me in one bit of business that I had to resolve.

Tony Crosland had nominated me as an *ex officio* member of the Executive Committee of the Fabian Society. The Fabian Society was a socialist society of nineteenth-century origins. Early Fabians had included H. G. Wells and George Bernard Shaw, while in the twentieth century Beatrice and Sidney Webb were its central figures. The society is nowadays referred to as a think tank, but that term was not yet current.

Via co-option I had proceeded to election to the Executive.

The chair of the society was chosen by an excellent system called Buggin's Turn: Executive members got the job one by one, longest serving first, and my turn was due in 1981–82. This was the time of the great divide.

The split went to the heart of the Fabian Society. Shirley Williams, the most popular of the 'Gang of Four' which broke away, was our chair. But Tony Benn sat on our Executive. Fabian members, though capable of cantankerous rows, were essentially inclusive and voted a mixed ticket.

It was in my car outside the Fabian office in Dartmouth Street that Shirley Williams finally confirmed to me that the die was cast, and the breakaway was going to happen. That raised an immediate question. What would become of the Fabian Society?

This was no small matter. The society had prestige. It had also quite considerable financial assets. It would be a catch for the Social Democrats to capture it, and a success for the Labour Party to retain it.

I should have liked the society to remain open to full membership by SDPers and Labourites alike. I hoped that one day the rift could be mended. An institution which permitted intellectual dialogue between the two would in time be valuable. Besides, any other course was going to cost us members.

But emotions were running high. The SDP thought the Labourites were cowards. The Labourites thought the SDP were cowards. Tony Benn at that time was at his charged-up worst, smelling conspiracies everywhere: anyone who was not with him was against him. The prominent pro-Labour anti-Bennites on the executive, led by Phillip Whitehead, dared not appear sympathetic to the SDP. Dianne Hayter, the general secretary, had somehow to try to contain these tensions, which were not helped by her being at war with her deputy general secretary, Richard Twining.

I had been impressed back in 1975 by Harold Wilson's use of the referendum on Europe. That was an issue which had threatened to destroy the Labour Party, but thanks to his adroitness, it didn't. So I conceived a similar device to Harold's for the Fabian Society.

Members would vote – either to allow the SDP supporters full membership or to confine them to associate membership, without a vote on the society's affairs.

I voted for full membership, though this is the first time I have ever admitted it. So did 1,342 fellow Fabians. However, 1,544 voted for the more restrictive solution. The leading SDPers angrily announced that they were not going to be second-class citizens in the society and left.

This was not a perfect outcome. In politics, perfect outcomes are rarely achievable. It was a satisfactory outcome. Lots of SDPers did stay with the society, and the bulk of the membership, from whichever side of the divide they came, did accept the verdict. Think tanks come and go but the Fabian Society has continued to prosper. It remains a powerful party influence for progressive policies, and I am proud still to be a member.

I was now ceasing to be in any sense an activist in the party. At some point around the mid-1980s, I quietly let my membership lapse. I should perhaps at some point have settled down to write a new *Future of Socialism*. But I had to earn a living and, besides, I had no confidence that I was up to it. Instead, I wrote between 1979 and the early 1990s a number of shorter pieces analysing Labour's dilemmas and proposing ways forward. I think I can claim some modest success in influencing the ditching of flawed Old Labour ways. I had no success at all in substituting anything progressive. Blairism was a great deal better than Thatcherism, but it was never what I meant by democratic socialism.

Some of our finest political thinkers seem capable of coming up with a new philosophy every five years or so. I think of the former liberal John Gray and of David Marquand, the Labour MP turned Social Democrat turned philosopher of the public realm.

There is nothing necessarily wrong with this. After all, the greatest modern philosopher, Ludwig Wittgenstein, invented one system (in his *Tractatus*) and then a contradictory one (in his *Philosophical Investigations*) but no one much holds that against him. John Maynard Keynes famously said: 'When the facts change, I change my mind. What do you do, sir?'

Tony Crosland was not of that school. In my contribution to the volume of essays in his memory I co-edited with Dick Leonard in 1981*, I said of him: 'In *The Future of Socialism* Crosland had erected a towering castle. The rest of his life was devoted to defending it against all comers.' I suppose much the same was true of my own writings, though it was less a case of a towering castle and more of a flimsy palisade.

I put the stakes in place first with my 1979 *New Society* article 'Towards Fraternalism'. This was the one I wrote when I thought Paul Barker was soliciting an article, not offering me a job.

My thesis was that the old class politics had declined. The working class was less numerous than it had been in the days when it alone was sufficient to provide Labour with a general election majority. It had also changed. It was 'instrumentalist' in its aims, centred on material prosperity. Labour had 'frustrated' it in those aims by failing to manage the economy to produce sustained economic growth. The new instrumentalist working class didn't much like the fact that they had to pay taxes to support benefits for the worst off for example. The new child benefit scheme was 'a particular electoral albatross' for Labour.

Labour needed to do three things if it was to keep its place in the political race. Firstly, it 'will have once more to face up to the question of whether it does, or does not, wish to be a party of government'. My hope and assumption was that it would, though it was a decade or so before the party finally decided that it agreed.

Secondly, we needed to look again at what could be done to get growth without inflation. *Dirigiste* economic planning, as embraced by Tony Benn and his allies, was not, on the evidence, likely to be the answer.

Thirdly, we needed to develop an alternative philosophy to the 'somewhat selfish' instrumentalism that had taken office. 'Of the

---

*   *The Socialist Agenda: Crosland's Legacy*, Jonathan Cape, 1981

trinity of Labour movement values – liberty, equality and fraternity – the time has come to elevate fraternity to greater prominence.'

These were themes to which I returned in the socialist agenda essay, then again in an unpublished paper for a high-powered Fabian committee in 1987 and finally in *The Name of the Rose*, another Fabian pamphlet following the dreadful disappointment of Neil Kinnock's defeat in the 1992 election. Gloom of course was the general state of the Labour Party between 1979 and 1993. At first, gloom was because the party was all but taken over by the far left, and, as a result, it split. Then gloom was because, though no longer threatened by Marxists, it failed to change quickly enough to keep up with the electorate. 'If necessary changes are not made, the Labour vote will probably decline ... by about 2 percentage points at each successive general election,' Crosland had written in 1960. In 1992, six elections later, he was not far out, with our vote down to just 2 per cent less than Tony's prediction implied. The decline since has been nearly as fast, from 34 per cent of the vote in 1992 to 28 per cent in 2010.

Of course, the leftist assault on the party was part of the problem. So too were faulty policies. In particular, an enthusiasm for disarmament shading into neo-pacifism put off many patriotic voters. Too much of that remained for Neil Kinnock to be a serious contender at his first election in 1987. Harder to explain is 1992, particularly as the pollsters predicted that Labour would be the largest party. Some blame Kinnock's triumphalism and particularly his over-the-top display at an eve-of-poll rally in Sheffield. This seems unlikely as most people had decided how to vote by then. More likely, detailed redistributive tax policies put forward by the shadow Chancellor, John Smith, caused the calamity, though they did not stop Smith succeeding Kinnock as leader.

But there was a more fundamental factor at work. Labour was traditionally and essentially a political response to social reality: a large working class which was not sharing fairly in social wealth and welfare. As time went by, however, the working class was declining in number and increasing in prosperity. With Andrew Shaw and John Willman, I wrote yet another Fabian pamphlet, entitled *Labour's Electoral Challenge*, in 1987. It showed that, though Labour support among social classes AB had fallen only from 16 per cent to 13 per cent from 1964 to 1983, that among the skilled working class had plunged from 61 per cent to 38 per cent.

These were the stark political realities that led me to argue the case for change in Labour in *The Name of the Rose*. The policies I advocated included a less intimate relationship with the trade unions and a more nuanced attitude to taxes and public spending. But those, I said, would not go far enough. Labour needed some-how to symbolise the fact that it had changed before the electorate would fully believe it. And here I first proposed a change in name for the party:

'All names for parties are faintly absurd. Any combination of words such as "radical" "democratic" "liberal" and "social" would probably serve to replace Labour, though "socialist" would be risky. The word "new" would do no harm,' I said. On those words rest my claim to be the founder of New Labour.

Where New Labour and I always differed, however, is in what we put in place of Old Labour. I was as enthusiastic a dumper of silly policies as Tony Blair and his acolytes proved to be. But the Blairites came almost to define themselves by what they were against: not the Tories, not the unequal society that was modern Britain, but the old Labour Party that they were out to transform. Everyone knew what they didn't want, but what did they want? In the vagueness of their answer to this question lay the roots of failures of 1997–2010, and the drift to a government that flailed away without apparently any sense of domestic direction.

To a Croslandite egalitarian, this was a great loss. Indeed, the meaning of equality was distorted in front of our very eyes. For example, the New Labour government was enthusiastic for equal-ity of opportunity. So long as everyone had a chance to climb the ladder, it did not matter whether it was only a few rungs high or rather, reached into the stratosphere. This was a concept of equality so weak that it could be shared by most progressive Tories. The ladder got longer and longer so those at the top enjoyed sumptuous wealth – and New Labour did not care.

At least equality of opportunity was a real concept. So too were racial and gender equality, equality for people with disabilities and equality by sexual orientation.

Otherwise, however, New Labour seemed to be determined to downgrade equality – historically with liberty the most powerful political concept of all time – to insignificance. I have in front of me a pamphlet written for the think tank Demos which says on its cover, no less: 'Active equality means people having the power to act together to bring about change.' Eh? Giving people the power to bring about change is no doubt within reason a good thing, but to say that that is what equality means is linguistic homocide.

My own consistent belief was that any meaningful concept of equality meant a large and substantial shift of resources from the well off to the less well off. This was desirable in itself both because the poorer got more in terms of enhanced welfare out of an extra pound than did the rich and because, as the academics Richard Wilkinson and Kate Pickett have argued in *The Spirit Level* (Penguin, 2009), a more equal society was a happier and healthier society.

There were here issues of means and ends. For example, the Labour Party has tended to associate greater equality with an increase in public spending, assuming that the greater the share of such spending in gross domestic product, the more equal the country will be. But it has not turned out that way. Taxation bears increasingly on the less well off, who pay income tax on low levels of earnings and VAT at the same rate as the rich. Meanwhile, public spending often benefits the better off – as in the case of state subsidy to the universities. The explosion of public spending that accompanied the last years of Gordon Brown has had a number of consequences, but it is doubtful whether, overall, it has contributed to equality. That after all was not its aim. Its aim was to attract particular groups of supporters whom Mr Brown deemed important to a Labour victory.

For any national government, achieving greater equality has become more difficult. Globalisation includes the ability of talent to move globally, whether pop stars, footballers or managers. Tax top bankers or starring CEOs more heavily in Britain and there is a risk they will move elsewhere. There are balances to be struck here, but – until Alastair Darling finally introduced a 50 per cent tax rate for the rich – New Labour struck the balance on most occasions where it would favour the better off. A new New Labour would revive the concept of fairness in the distribution of income and wealth, concentrating less on higher taxes on incomes and more on inheritance tax, the elimination of tax loopholes and perhaps an annual wealth tax.

Any democratic socialist party has to balance doing what it believes to be right and doing what it believes to be popular. Labour was in power for thirteen years on a prospectus that tended to the latter. Indeed, unlike previous defeats, the 2010 failure owed less to philosophical and policy weaknesses and more to the choice of a leader who turned out to be a bully whom the people swiftly rumbled. Defending the palisade to the last, however, I am reluctant to believe that British politics must deteriorate into a contest between the Tweedledums and the Tweedledees, competing on competence rather than disagreeing over ultimate objectives. Though there will be much that all parties have in common, they ought to have some things which they do not hold in common. Otherwise what choice are the people exercising?

My most sustained piece of writing during the 1990s was my book *The Secret Treasury*, though it was not published (by Viking) until 2000, when I was in the Lords.

> This book is not a history of the Treasury, though it contains some history. It is not a book about public administration, though it contains a lot about public administration. Nor is it about politics, though it is shot through with politics. Nor even is it about economic policy, though it contains some economics. It is, put

simply, an attempt to paint in words a portrait of the Treasury as
an institution ...

The decision to write it reflected my contrarian streak. The Treasury
was universally loathed. The left hated it for 'stop–go' economics,
and its rigid control over public expenditure. The right deplored its
excessive macroeconomic interventionism, its failure to embrace
monetarism and its inability to stop public spending rising. Either
of these criticisms might be right, it seemed to me, but they could
not both be right. It was not easy to find anyone who would defend
the Treasury, but I was up for that.

I also fancied the work involved. In my years in journalism, I
had found that the shrewdest sources were frequently Treasury officials. They were, to be sure, discreet, more discreet than politicians.
They were also a good deal more reliable. They had a balanced and
sensible view of most things. Above all, I have never come across
a Treasury official who did not at heart believe that it was their
fundamental duty to do their best for the nation and its people.
That is a rare virtue.

Terry, later Lord, Burns, was permanent secretary at the Treasury
when I started work. He was and is an old friend. We had worked
together when he was at the London Business School and the *Sunday
Times* published its forecasts. He reacted warmly and bravely to my
suggestion of the book, based as it would be essentially on off-the-
record interviews with Treasury officials. Indeed he devoted many
hours of his time talking to me. Andrew Turnbull, his successor,
was equally supportive.

The book was something of a *succès d'estime,* reviews ranging
between polite and enthusiastic. The public failed to respond *en
masse* and it sold a mere 1,200 copies. I occasionally spot a copy in
a library or bookshop and get a warm glow.

Most interesting was the reaction of Treasury officials. 'A book
by a clever man writing too fast,' was the reaction of a senior
director – to my face. 'You were far too kind about us,' conversa-
tions started, as Treasury officials launched into criticisms of the

institution to which they devoted their life. Only the Treasury could have remained impartial when presented with a defence of what it did.

Perhaps I was too kind, but that was a fault on the right side. The book itself, however, was swiftly overtaken by a change of policy by the Chancellor. As Gordon Brown's long reign went on, he moved away from the continence over public spending that had marked his early days. By the end of his regime as Chancellor, the Treasury's function had almost reversed itself. It became the department for public spending – or at least the department of the minister for public spending. Even without the global financial crisis, at some stage Britain's fiscal discipline would have had to be reasserted. Sadly, as the coalition government seeks to extricate itself from the fiscal hole, its position is worse as a result of years of Brown's election handouts and budgetary gimmicks.

That may mean that *The Secret Treasury* will again come back into fashion. The main secret included in there – the secret of how to control public spending – will certainly be needed in the next decade. Indeed I am reliably informed that *The Secret Treasury* was a hit read in George Osborne's office in the run-up to the 2010 general election.

CHAPTER 11

THE VOTING REFORM
DEBACLE 1998–2011

I was not without ties to the Blair government that swept to power in 1997. I had, for example, participated in the work of the Fabian Society in preparing members of the shadow Cabinet for office. A desire to explain the civil service to the party and the party to the civil service had nagged me since I left government in 1979. Indeed I wrote a Fabian pamphlet on the subject in 1982, contributed to another edited by Ben Pimlott in 1987 and attended various seminars for the Labour front bench in the run-up to 1997.

However, we only half succeeded. We made the civil service even hungrier for a Labour government, as it saw that party leaders were approaching the preparation for government seriously. We were not correspondingly successful in persuading shadow ministers to look forward to the civil service.

Our earnest Fabianism was a trivial influence by comparison with a comedy TV series, *Yes, Minister*. Its portrayal of a manipulative civil service controlling ministers was not only funny but plausible. Relations between Labour and the civil service were never good, and when Labour got back into office, civil service influence continued the decline it had begun under Margaret Thatcher. Many of the faults of the Labour government – government by wheeze, excessive attention to the media, tribal partisanship, impatience with detail – stemmed directly from this.

Despite these connections, I had no reason to expect any personal advancement under a Labour government. Indeed I expected to end my days, enjoyably and blamelessly, at *The Economist*. The early days of the Blair government were uplifting, as the government showed both energy and an attention to evidence in its policy-making. I cheered quietly from the sidelines.

Having been one of the first generations of political advisers, I was flattered to find that the new advisers who flocked in with New Labour were keen to take my advice. I was called in to address them all at Number 10 – and they were particularly struck by my account of the efforts of the civil service to keep down what we 1970s advisers were paid. Some civil service traditions, it was apparent, had survived.

This link helped me in my journalism. I should say I (or Bagehot) was perceived at the time as a well-informed and sympathetic observer of the new government, but by no means as a lackey. At least I hope that was the case.

Famously, London buses do not come for ages, and then two arrive at once. In my case, it was three.

Some months after the government had taken office, quite out of the blue I was approached to sit on two commissions – one on electoral reform and the other on long-term care of the elderly. Before long, a third came along – a panel on the BBC licence fee.

In its early days, the Labour government was much given to setting up committees of inquiry. Tony Blair seemed to go off them rather, but Gordon Brown was also a great inquirer though often relying on a single individual. Derek Wanless's important inquiry into the health service published in 2004 is an example of a Brown committee. Adair Turner on pensions in 2004 is another, though its findings were supported by Blair and therefore opposed by Brown.

There is little or no academic literature on such committees. They report and their findings are either adopted or not adopted, wholly or partly. But little is known about how they go about their work, what makes for successful committees and what for unsuccessful committees, how they relate to government during their proceedings, whether they seek adequately to find out about public opinion and so on.

Each of the committees on which I sat was significant in its way. It never seemed to me terribly sensible to devote a lot of work to studying a subject – and all three of my committees required quite a lot of work – only to drop the subject once the government had opined on it. So in all three cases, I remained involved in the subject of the commission. Indeed, that follow-up constituted by far the bulk of my political work, before and certainly after I went into the Lords.

The first such committee was the Independent Commission on the Voting System, chaired by Roy Jenkins. Sadly it did not change the voting system, and the result of the 2011 referendum on the alternative vote has meant at least a further delay before we change the way we vote. It did, as it happens, mean a big change for me personally.

No one is ever told why they become members of the House of Lords. It may be of course that the Prime Minister, reflecting on my virtues and my contribution to his party, came to the conclusion that no one could be more suitable to join his benches in the Lords. It would be flattering to think so. But I do not for a minute believe this was the case.

Despite the Crosland/Jenkins *frisson,* Roy and I had struck up a considerable friendship during the commission. We both had minds that combined analysis with an acute awareness of political realities. We also shared certain nerdish quirks, particularly a taste for curiosities of political history. We could swap gossip on the history of certain seats, the majorities at past elections, the kinks of MPs past and ministers present and so on.

At any rate, I have no doubt whatsoever that the reason I got into the House of Lords is that Roy suggested to the Prime Minister that he put me there. Typically of Roy, he never once tried to claim the credit. We remained friends there, and he observed my successes and failures with avuncular interest. And I continued in the Lords to do everything I could to bring about voting reform, before and after Jenkins's death in 2003. So the Jenkins commission and voting reform must rank the greatest failure among a number of failures in my political life.

Margaret Thatcher had ruled magisterially, even dictatorially, though receiving, even in 1979, only 44 per cent of the vote.

Naturally, the Conservatives could see nothing wrong with a system which delivered them regular, comfortable majorities. But many in the Labour Party took a different view. Neil Kinnock, the leader of the party from 1983 to 1992, was a convert to reform. This feeling was reinforced by Labour's Europeanism at the time, as leading party members became aware that countries could be well governed by coalitions. Even before the 1992 election, the party set up a committee under a leading political philosopher, Raymond Plant, which reported in favour of limited reform.

While Labour was in opposition, its enthusiasm did not lead anywhere in terms of concrete progress. But it did leave a mark. This was reinforced by the relationship which developed between Roy Jenkins and Tony Blair – neither of them tribal politicians though Jenkins had left the Labour Party and Blair had become its leader. Jenkins converted Blair to the notion that there was a natural progressive majority in British politics. This, however, did not assert itself because it was divided between two parties: Labour and the Lib Dems. If the electoral system delivered to the two parties a share of parliamentary seats which accorded with their share of the popular vote they would dominate every parliament.

Not all senior Labour figures were convinced. Many trade unions favoured first-past-the-post. Their leaders were brought up to believe that the party of the working class must take power alone if it was to bring about necessary change. Other Labour leaders did not want their programme watered down (as they saw it) by liberalism, while others again thought that the Lib Dems would become serious rivals for the progressive vote rather than allies.

In the end, a compromise was reached. In its 1997 election manifesto, Labour promised to set up an inquiry into the electoral system, charged with finding the best alternative to first-past-the-post. The British people would then choose between that alternative and first-past-the-post in a referendum. That would satisfy the reformers while giving the opponents of change within the party their chance to try to kill electoral reform when the referendum campaign began.

Typically, there was a delay in setting up the commission, while ministers and Whitehall faffed around. To try to make up lost time, Jenkins was set a tight timetable – to report within a year of its starting date of December 1997. In this case, that was just long enough, though, as we shall see, a similar tight timetable was one of many reasons why the Royal Commission on long-term care was a failure.

I had a lifelong interest in polling and in voting systems. I did not, however, have immutable views, though I did have certain instincts. First-past-the-post was defective in that it gave voters only one choice. I was thus keen on the alternative vote. Under this system, voters numbered their selections in order of preference. The candidate with the fewest first preferences was eliminated and the votes redistributed according to the second preferences. This had the huge merit that, at the end of the day, the winning candidate in each seat had the support of at least half his or her electorate. AV *tout court* was eventually the alternative put to the people in the referendum of 5 May 2011, a decade after the referendum was supposed to happen.

I was instinctively less keen on proportional representation. I could see why people thought it was fairer, but the argument was far from clear cut. If, for example, proportional representation delivered an effective veto power over government to smaller parties, was there not here a disproportionality of power?

Anyway, I thought I was well qualified to be a member of the proposed inquiry, and let it be known. Evidently I was not alone.

The call, when it came, was curious. My old friend Jack Straw was Home Secretary, and thus in charge of setting up the inquiry. Jack, I knew was an AV man, but totally and irrevocably against proportional representation. He said that he was minded to put me on the committee but he wanted to know one thing: would I be willing to sign a minority report? I think he had in mind that the non-Labour members – Roy, Bob Alexander and John Chilcot – might opt for full proportional representation. Joyce Gould, the other Labour member, might not but she might like company, and I could provide it.

It seemed unusual to be concentrating at that stage on what would happen if the committee did not agree. But I could honestly answer 'yes'. If for example the committee had recommended the Israeli electoral system, which gives full proportionality and a fragmented polity, I should certainly have written a minority report. That evidently satisfied Straw, for shortly afterwards a letter confirming my appointment arrived.

The commission got off to a stuttering start. The Home Office had chosen one of its officials for the vital post of secretary to the inquiry. He came with a compelling CV: not only did he have a brilliant mind, but he was also already an expert on the commission's subject matter. He met Jenkins.

Jenkins reported to the commission. He could see this was a good man, but the chemistry was not there. Besides he was a teetotaller – not, Jenkins hastened to add, that there was anything necessarily wrong with that, but...

In the end, Ros McCool was brought in to lead the official team. She was an effective administrative head but the intellectual impetus came from a talented young Home Office official, Gus Park. Sadly, he left the public service for a management course and eventually a job in financial services – the sort of thing that happens when governments do not value public servants enough.

The commission got on from the beginning. Bob Alexander, a liberal Tory, was a man of charm and intellectual honesty. John Chilcot was used to negotiating with the IRA and his quiet good humour was tempered by toughness when it was needed. My friend and ally Joyce Gould was even tougher, having made her way up from the bottom through the minefield that was the Labour Party organisation. She was devoted to the party, but was also fair minded and keen to find common ground.

The way we worked together was primarily down to Jenkins. Although he had a reputation for pomposity, I think this arose from a certain shyness that could make him awkward with strangers. However, he treated us like family. He could be self-deprecating. He was very funny. He had a crystal-clear intellect, combined with industry. His command of language, written or verbal, was unequalled. Whatever you think of the arguments in the report, it has no equal among state papers as a persuasive essay.

We met every couple of weeks or so. No commission member missed a single meeting. We mounted expeditions to Ireland to see at first hand their single transferable vote system; to Germany for their additional member system; to New Zealand for the new mixed member system and to Australia, principally for the alternative vote system used for their lower house. Jenkins decided not to accompany us on the latter expedition, for it was a long way for a man in his seventies to travel. He came later to regret that he had not come.

In addition we traversed Britain, holding open meetings for voters. I had expected these trips to be a waste of time. In fact, they were anything but. Of course we got a few obsessives for electoral reform like vegetarianism and animal rights activists have their resident corps of nutters. But we were impressed by the seriousness with which most of the people who attended approached the subject. Their passions ran high.

These days went like this. We would board a train carefully chosen to have a dining car. Jenkins would order a bottle of wine for the commission and its staff, from which (not wishing to be thought to be teetotallers) we would each take a glass. Jenkins would then order a further bottle, which we left to him.

The Government Car Service would then convey us to our meeting place. Roy would maintain an erudite running commentary on our journey. 'Ah, David, the town hall, Pugin 1877 if I remember correctly. Such a pity they knocked down the Georgian parade over there to build those monstrous shops. Good new civic statue round the corner though.' He later wrote a book, *Twelve Cities: A Memoir* (Macmillan, 2002), which I read today with nostalgia.

The meetings generally started mid-afternoon. Jenkins presided with grace, noting every point made, occasionally injecting a facilitating observation, his concentration absolute even when faced with the madmen and the bores. After two hours or so, he would wrap things up with a masterly summary of the discussion, leaving everyone confident that their views had been heard and noted. We would get on the train, he would have a gin and tonic, and then he would go to sleep.

The task we faced was not an easy one. Our terms of reference required that the commission 'shall observe the requirement for broad proportionality, the need for stable Government, an extension of voter choice and the maintenance of a link between MPs and geographical constituencies'. These had surely been drawn up by a Cabinet committee on which both pro- and anti-reformers sat. At any rate, you did not have to be a genius to realise that the objectives we had to meet were in conflict. You couldn't for example have every MP sitting for an individual geographical constituency *and* assure broad proportionality.

In fact, this was less of a problem than might be thought. For the fact is that there is no such thing as a perfect electoral system. Electoral systems are designed not only to be broadly democratic but to deliver a variety of objectives. Some of these objectives can only be bought at the expense of others of these objectives. Our task was therefore not to design the ideal. It was to design a system that best balanced the various requirements. 'None of us are electoral absolutists,' said our report (or, rather, our chairman – in *The Report of the Independent Commission on the Voting System*, Cm 4090, 1998). 'We all of us believe that any system has defects as well as virtues. Some systems are nonetheless much better than others, and we have endeavoured to seek relative virtue in an imperfect world.'

In the eventual referendum, voters were to be given a choice: our recommended system or the existing first-past-the-post system. We could and did note that first-past-the-post was increasingly difficult to defend. It was 'peculiarly bad at allowing third party support to express itself'. This mattered less when (as in 1951) 97.8 per cent of people voted Labour or Tory, it mattered more when (as in 1997) 75.5 per cent did and mattered more still when it fell, as it did, to 65 per cent in 2010.

First-past-the-post meant that in most constituencies most of the time, most people's votes were wasted. The seats were safe for one party or another, and so they could have no conceivable impact on the result. They were thus permanently unrepresented by a candidate of their own party in Parliament.

First-past-the-post had a further defect: it had developed a heavy bias. Because (essentially) there were lower turnouts in Labour seats, it took fewer voters to elect each Labour MP. Labour was thus heavily overrepresented relative to proportionality in Parliament – so in 2010 the party only had some fifty fewer seats than the Tories though lagging eight percentage points in share of the vote. The Tories were well short of an overall majority, but if Labour had a similar lead over the Tories as large as the lead they in fact had over us, it would have enjoyed a three-figure overall majority. This matters since it seems a *sine qua non* of any electoral system that a party that gets more votes does better than a party that gets fewer.

In reaching for an alternative system, we rejected the single transferable vote. This was for one overwhelming reason. The single-member constituency is arguably the greatest virtue of the British political system, and one to which the public appears to be devoted. We could amend it at the margin, but to go over to multi-member seats would have been fatal. Quite apart from anything else, it would have zero chance of going through in a referendum.

That Britain would benefit from greater proportionality than was provided by the existing system was arguable. Equally clearly, we did not need full proportional representation. Broadly, our aim was this. When the British people spoke with a reasonably decisive voice – for example the victory of Margaret Thatcher in 1979 or that of Clement Attlee in 1945 – the resulting government should be able to enjoy an overall majority. When they spoke with a less decisive voice – as in say 1964, and the two elections of 1974 and in 1992 – a hung parliament should reflect that voice.

It is one thing for a government to have a majority with, say, 45 per cent of the national vote. It is another for it to achieve an overall majority with 36 per cent of the vote, as Labour did in 2005, especially when, including abstainers, that amounted to fewer than one in four of the electorate.

To achieve a somewhat more proportional outcome the commission thought Britain would need some kind of mixed system. Most MPs would be elected for constituencies, but some would come from 'top-up' lists, where extra seats were given to those who had done disproportionately badly in the individual seats.

Here there was a division in the commission. Alexander wanted more proportionality and more top-ups. Joyce Gould and I, mindful of Labour sensitivities, wanted fewer.

This partly reflected our lack of enthusiasm for proportionality. But it reflected something more important if our report was not to gather dust on some shelf: the need to get Labour support. As I wrote to Roy on 10 July 1998, 'My reason for wanting to avoid introducing a system that would damage Labour too much in relation to first-past-the-post is essentially political. I want electoral reform. I think we can only get it if it has the backing of Tony Blair, his Cabinet and the majority of the Parliamentary Labour Party. And making all allowance for the virtues of magnanimity, that means we cannot ask them to swallow too much.' Roy took the point but not undiluted.

Good progress was made as a result of a brilliant piece of thinking by Gus Park. Top-up seats need not be allocated on a national basis or even a regional basis, leaving the winners isolated from local voters. Instead they could be allocated on a county basis using existing counties, so that each top-up MP was only representing say four individual constituencies. That both reduced the effect of top-ups in increasing proportionality, as well as making the top-up MPs more local and therefore more legitimate.

Beyond that, we simply did a horse trade between the enthusiasts for and the sceptics about greater proportionality. In the course of this, we had our most dramatic confrontation as a commission. At the end of a long morning, we agreed the number of top-up seats at 15–20 per cent of the total: 15 per cent was Joyce's and my preference, but it was also the least the more proportionally minded members could accept. We thought we had done well in negotiation. We reported the outcome to Number 10, which was by then taking a close interest in the progress of the commission.

During the lunch break, Roy had second thoughts. He wanted more proportionality and sought to reopen the deal. I was genuinely annoyed at this – my trade union background had left me with a strong cultural disposition to regarding a done deal as a done deal. But I was nothing like as annoyed as I pretended to be. I didn't walk out, but I did shuffle my papers together in a way meant to convey that I might be about to. Roy, who in any case was deeply embarrassed at his wobble, picked up the signs: 15–20 per cent it was. Under the Jenkins proposals, the great majority of MPs would still represent individual constituencies.

Another fraught issue concerned how MPs for those individual constituencies were to be chosen. Again Joyce Gould and I were allied in favour of the alternative vote. Bob Alexander, however, was strongly against AV. He believed, in words he quoted from Winston Churchill in 1931, that AV took account of 'the most worthless votes of the most worthless candidates'. Our argument raged in a civilised sort of way, with Jenkins carefully refusing to reveal his hand.

At one point, however, we got an insight into that hand, and it revealed that it held a bizarre card. As a historian, he had probed deep into electoral systems. He had discovered that at one point in the nineteenth century, Britain had different systems in town and country: first-past-the-post in the country, multi-member constituencies which were more proportional in the cities. He thought the links between individual voters and MPs were more important in the country than in the cities, where voters identified with the whole urban area. So he quietly floated a 'compromise': single-members chosen by AV in the country, multi-members in the cities.

The arguments of substance against this were many and varied. For one thing, the chances of explaining it to the British people in a referendum were nil. But there was another argument against it which Jenkins more readily appreciated. It was deeply biased against the Labour Party. In rural areas, AV would squeeze Labour votes to the Lib Dems, who would gain. In the cities, multi-member constituencies would not be Labour monopolies, with the Tories the main beneficiaries. The result would be a slump in Labour seats. As we were looking to the Labour government, three-figure majority and all, to bring in change, it was readily apparent that this would not appeal.

That left us with AV everywhere, and modest top-up lists. Bob Alexander decided not to go along with the AV bit, as was his right, and attached a brief note of reservation to the report saying so. I was a bit worried that this might divert press attention from our report: 'Jenkins split' was not the headline we wanted. I told Roy that I thought we should take the wind out of Bob's note by leaking its existence before the report came out. This was naughty, and Roy did not like doing it, but politics is never a wholly clean sport. A small story appeared in the *Financial Times*. When our report was published, Bob's heartfelt reservation was hardly noticed.

I am sure we went the right way on AV. Of our two recommendations – AV to replace first past the post and top up lists – I have always felt more confident that AV was right than top-ups. Moreover, and this was to grow more and more apparent in the years which followed, I thought AV was a practicable change and one which would stand on its own. I was never sure that top-ups would happen.

There remained a serious political problem with our report. Before a referendum could be held, legislation was required. That required a vote of the House of Commons. The trouble was that this was not going to be easy to win. True, Labour had a manifesto commitment. But it was also true that every single member of the existing house had been elected under the existing system.

To create the 15–20 per cent top-ups, we were going to have to have around a hundred top-up MPs. If the House was to remain its existing size, that meant we were going to have around a hundred fewer constituency MPs.

It was not just that a hundred or so MPs would lose their seats. It was that they could none of them have a clue whether it was their seat or some other bugger's which would be lost. For, to reduce the number of constituencies, it would be necessary for the independent Boundary Commission to sit, and redraw the boundaries of every seat in the country. No MP, whether for a marginal or a safe seat, could be sure that such an exercise would not mean the disappearance of his or her seat.

There was one, and only one, way round this problem. Suppose the top-up seats did not replace existing seats but were in addition to them. Then the existing boundaries could be retained and existing MPs could breathe easy. However, that too had a downside. It meant that the size of the House of Commons, already regarded by many as too big, would rise.

Jenkins took this point. He wasn't sure if an increased size of the House would be saleable. Though mostly we got on with our work without reference to Downing Street, he decided to make an exception. He discussed my notion with the Prime Minister. Tony Blair was clear: an increase in the size of the Commons was not politically saleable. So our recommendations were bound to go to a Commons whose members had a self-interested reason to chuck them out.

The difficulty of getting a reform through had increasingly borne in on me as we proceeded with our work. Roy Jenkins had only taken on the commission after he had been convinced by Tony Blair that the government was serious about bringing about change. He was determined that his should not be yet another report on electoral reform left 'mouldering on the shelf'.

Of course I shared this view. I did not underestimate Tony Blair's assurances to Roy, and indeed I am sure the Prime Minister himself believed them when he gave them. However, Tony Blair had to watch his step. Peter Mandelson pointed out to me that the last thing the Prime Minister would enjoy was losing a referendum shortly before he went to the country at a general election.

I was also aware – perhaps more aware than Roy, who had not

been a member of the Labour Party for more than fifteen years – of the nature of the Parliamentary Labour Party. Without the support of the PLP, Blair could not go ahead – indeed without the support of the PLP Blair could not remain Prime Minister. The more I contemplated what we were attempting, the more difficult I thought it would be to pull off.

I set out my views in a personal note to Jenkins. To go through, our proposals needed to get through several hoops. First, the Cabinet had to agree to put them to Parliament. This was by no means assured. The responsible minister was Jack Straw, and though he was a pro-AV man, he was wholly opposed to PR. He might of course change his mind – he did a complete U-turn in favour of changing the House of Lords from an appointed to an elected body later in the government's history – but that did not seem likely in the case of electoral reform.

The whips hated electoral reform. So did most of the unions.

Then the Bill had to go through both Houses of Parliament. The Lords then had a built-in Tory majority, though by convention it would not challenge a specific election pledge. The Commons was a different matter. Even then many Labour MPs thought the Lib Dems were devils incarnate. They hated their air of moral superiority, combined with their ruthless campaigning style. They feared them as rivals. Add to that the problem of redrawing boundaries and it was clear our proposals would not be received with joy.

If there was a referendum, it then had to be won. The Tories would oppose change. The Labour Party would be split, and it would be hard not to allow Labour ministers and MPs to campaign according to their conscience. The Lib Dems would be for, but they could easily be portrayed as self-interested. Constitutional change is never easy to excite people with, and instincts in the country are conservative. The polls on the issue are usually divided depending on what question you ask: in favour of greater fairness but against breaking the constituency link. It would be the devil's own job to win, and it could not be done without the full personal backing of the Prime Minister.

Setting out these problems was the easy bit. I also needed to propose a solution. What I suggested to him – the matter did not come before the commission – is that we should propose reform in two stages. First, AV would be put in place. Like Straw, many first-past-the-posters could live with that, so it was much easier to handle than a fuller reform. Secondly, and at a subsequent election, the top-ups would follow.

Experience elsewhere in the world, notably New Zealand, shows that once you change an electoral system, you will often change it again. Experience also suggests that once you get rid of a lousy system it never comes back. I argued therefore for a patient, long-term strategy for change.

Roy was not convinced – not at the time anyway. He pointed to the example of Lords reform. Once stage one, expulsion of most the hereditary peers, was complete, the government lost interest. An elected house was as far away as ever – and a dozen years later that remains the case. Besides, for Roy at his age, the long game was less appealing. Like Gladstone, the nineteenth-century Prime Minister of whom he wrote the definitive biography, he was an old man in a hurry.

I suppose I could have produced an Alexander-type note of dissent on this point, but it would have seemed churlish. Those of us on the commission who were cautious about reform had achieved much. Full proportional representation was off the agenda. The chairman's fanciful anti-Labour scheme was gone. AV had triumphed over first-past-the-post in our report. In life you have to know when to hold out and when to settle. We settled.

After our report was published, all seemed set fair. The Prime Minister responded to Jenkins with what was close to a personal endorsement – the committee, he said, 'makes a well argued and powerful case for the system it recommends'. The report itself was received with enthusiasm in the bulk of the press. We had momentum.

But we did not have momentum for long. Straw reported it to the House on 5 November in mocking terms, making much of the supposed complexity of our proposed system. (I hate to think what he would have done had Jenkins's idea of different systems in town and country gone into it.) MPs, especially Labour MPs, naturally rallied to their self-interest. It was after all always going to be hard to make Labour come out against a system which had just delivered it such a satisfactory parliamentary majority.

By then, too, Blair was tiring of the idea of a progressive coalition. It had enthused him once and he was even prepared to offer jobs in his Cabinet to senior Lib Dem figures. But, paradoxically, he was made weaker by the size of his majority. As Labour had won well on its own, why should the party share power, and jobs, with the Lib Dems? He found Lib Dem thinking generally rather woolly and on some issues, well, too liberal. He liked Jenkins but then Jenkins was not the Lib Dem leader. He was decreasingly prepared to invest political capital in seeming to override dissenters in his Cabinet and in his party.

So, to Roy's disappointment, his report got stuck almost as soon as it was published. He himself continued to think about the matter. He came round to believing, as I had argued earlier, that AV on its own without top-up lists was both a worthwhile step forward and an achievable one.

The Jenkins committee was not a complete failure. It has defined the parameters of the British debate on voting reform ever since. When the hung parliament of 2010 brought the issue again to the fore, it was to Jenkins's arguments that the reformers turned.

As a member of the House of Lords, both before and after Roy Jenkins's death in 2003, I became involved in the ongoing campaigns for electoral reform. There seemed to me to be little point in spending a year and more of one's life in absorbing an important political subject just to move on to something else once the report was completed. Indeed, my advice to anyone asked to join a government inquiry is: 'Reckon to spend at least as long on the subject after the report is done as you did on it during your inquiries.' I met this rule with Jenkins, exceeded it comfortably in the case of the Royal Commission on the Funding of Long-Term Care, and was not that far short in the less successful case of the Davies Panel on the BBC licence fee.

Our report was published in October 1998, well within the year we had been given to complete it. In 1999, I became chair of a campaign group to promote it, Make Votes Count (MVC), and so remained for the next decade.

There was a long-established campaign group for electoral reform, called the Electoral Reform Society. Why have another one? The reason lies in the politics of the Electoral Reform Society. It was established by the formidable Enid Lakeman. Now Enid Lakeman was a great woman, but she was also borderline dotty. She was not simply in favour of electoral reform; she was in favour of the single transferable vote (STV). The society therefore was STV minded. Indeed some members of its executive were as dotty for STV as she was.

Its admirable director, Ken Ritchie, a former Labour parliamentary candidate, saw this was a problem. He has over the years edged the ERS back towards a more eclectic position. However, at that time he would not have been able to carry its support for a campaign for Jenkins so Make Votes Count was set up to maintain a broader coalition. It was heavily reliant on ERS funds but not dependent on ERS policy.

I was lucky to have as my director Nina Temple, the last-ever general secretary of the Communist Party of Great Britain, and as a result of that experience, the world's most committed pluralist. She was succeeded by Malcolm Clark.

I am too analytic a person to list campaigning among my favourite activities. I can manage articles in newspapers, letters to the editor, and debates on the floor of the House of Lords. I can work up a head of steam at a public meeting, and thoroughly enjoyed Make Votes Count's regular outings at the Labour Party conference in particular. Lib Dem conference meetings were too easy, and we never seemed to manage to recruit more than the odd – in some cases very odd – Tory. Make Votes Count's strategy was to make sure that the issue remained alive and appeared positively wherever possible in Lib Dem and especially Labour election manifestos.

Some of our team wanted a more active approach. They hankered after mass meetings, demos, marches by the people on Downing Street demanding reform. At one point, they even arranged at eye-watering expense for a barge to float past Parliament bearing a caricature of Tony Blair and the slogan 'Bliar', expecting this no doubt to convert the Prime Minister to share their faith and change our constitution. They got short shift while I was chair. However, they popped up again when the actual referendum was held in 2011, helping with their combination of fervour and silliness to ensure that the British people turned down the reform for which Make Votes Count had worked long and hard.

I constantly struggled with one important group within Make Votes Count. I thought that voting reform was an issue *sui generis*, to be treated on its individual merits. It was most likely to happen if there was a coalition of political interests that favoured it, and that would be best achieved if we campaigned for it and it alone.

Others took a different view. They saw voting reform as just one item on a constitutional agenda. This included the creation of an elected House of Lords (which I have always opposed), a written constitution, and lots of measures all designed to strip elected politicians of power and give it to the people. They did not see voting reform as a way of improving the way we elect politicians. They saw it as a way of punishing existing politicians for their alleged failings. I have never been so confident of the wisdom of direct popular rule to make me an enthusiast for this approach.

We were where we were in 1999. The government had reneged on its pledge to hold a referendum on voting reform. One thing always seemed to me transparently clear. The only chance of ever getting such a reform was a hung parliament, in which the Lib Dems and other minor parties made reform a condition of sustaining a government in office. The other thing that became clear was that we should not let the best be the enemy of the good. In all likely political circumstances, it was going to be a great deal easier to achieve AV than to achieve root-and-branch reform, so we should do nothing to suggest that reformers would be in favour only of the latter.

I was walking a fine line. Many who were in favour of electoral reform did not think much of AV. They were proportionality people (which I never was) and they pointed out that AV was not systemically more proportional than first-past-the-post. Indeed in some circumstances it could be less proportional. If Lib Dem voters had a strong tendency to make Labour their second choice, AV could actually lead to even worse results for the Tories than their national vote share implied.

There was another tendency among voting reformers which had the capacity to weaken our campaign. Not surprisingly, voting reformers are great lovers of system chatter. I have tried in this account to keep things simple. I have not for example mentioned (so far) D'Hondt, the greatest-ever Belgian, or Sainte-Laguë or the two different varieties of Imperiali system for dealing with least remainders. This is not only because I have long forgotten what any of this means. All I know is that, by comparison with the big prize, the choice between these and other details of reforms is not of the least significance.

I suspect most voting reformers agreed with me. However, they could not help themselves. Given time in a room, they would fall to disputation over these matters, like medieval monks debating angels on pin heads. If I had a role as chairman of MVC, it was to try to move them on.

The Tories were unwinnable for electoral reform. This was partly self-interest. They wanted an overall majority and they thought first-past-the-post the best chance of getting it. They were slow to appreciate the bias against them in the existing system, putting forward as a remedy equal constituency sizes, which will make little difference.

In any case, the Conservative Party is the conservative party. They thought first-past-the-post in single-member constituencies was part of Britain's great constitutional heritage. This was not historical, for (as noted above) Britain has not always had such a system, but it was near enough historical to make them resist budging. Indeed David Cameron remains an instinctive first-past-the-poster despite having been taught at Oxford by Vernon Bogdanor, a leading academic advocate of voting reform.

The Lib Dems were on board. All that needed to be done there was to stop them indulging in building system castles in the sky.

So it was Labour on which we had to concentrate. In essence, our aim was a single one. It was to ensure that we got words in Labour's election manifesto which left open the route to voting reform. Then, if suddenly a hung parliament meant that reform was possible for Labour, they would have cover for doing it. In particular, they would have protection against a Bill's defeat in the House of Lords.

This required a combination of public campaigning and private lobbying. On the whole, we did quite well. The manifesto for 2005 said, 'Labour remains committed to reviewing the experience of the new electoral systems – introduced for the devolved admin-istrations, the European Parliament and the London Assembly. A referendum remains the right way to agree any change for Westminster.' By 2010 we had made further progress, for, as defeat loomed, so Gordon Brown was converted to AV as a possible facilitator of a deal with the Lib Dems. It committed Labour to a referendum, on 'moving to the Alternative Vote for elections to the House of Commons…'.

We were still not back to a commitment as strong as that in the 1997 manifesto of course, but voting reformers have to develop a capacity for gratitude for small mercies. It was apparent that there would be no progress on making electoral reform a reality unless a hung parliament came about. So the task was modest: somehow to keep a small flame burning which could ignite a bonfire of the existing system in due course.

I cupped my hands round the flame until 2008, when I resigned as chair of Make Votes Count. I had had nearly a decade in the job and was losing freshness. New voting reformers with new ideas on how to progress were coming through, though they did not necessarily do any better than my old guard. I also thought that my public position opposing an elected House of Lords was not helping our cause, most electoral reformers being enthusiasts for elections everywhere they could get them. Chris Huhne, the Lib Dem home affairs spokesperson and later energy minister, succeeded me.

AV's chance came soon after I had quit with a hung parliament in 2010, though it was not the chance we reformers had mostly hoped for. We wanted a Lib–Lab pact, of two parties open to or enthusiastic for reform. We got a Con–Lib pact, one party enthusiastic for reform and much the bigger one wholly opposed to it. Nevertheless the coalition agreement did commit the government to hold a referendum to allow voters to choose between AV and first-past-the-post and some of the early polling suggested (though I was always sceptical) that such a referendum could be won for reform.

Victory was always going to be hard. Internationally in the past quarter-century, according to Alan Renwick, an academic at Reading University, there have been only six major changes in electoral systems. Reform referendums, especially reform referendums which would make for greater proportionality, have been hard to win.

So I did not exactly expect a 'yes' vote in the promised referendum. Unfortunately, the tactical incompetence of its most important advocate, deputy Prime Minister Nick Clegg, made defeat certain.

Clegg made a bad deal with the Tories. The Conservatives wanted a three-fold change in Britain's electoral system. They wanted a greater equality of the size of constituencies, so that they were nearly all within 5 per cent of each other in the size of their electorates. They wanted constituency boundaries to be revised every five years. And they wanted the number of MPs in the House of Commons reduced from 650 to 600. They made a principled case for each of these changes. Under the surface they had a different motive, namely that they thought that the reforms would serve to reduce the pro-Labour bias of the electoral system. The basic thinking was that if the Lib Dems agreed to those, the Tories would yield on AV.

The two changes – Clegg's referendum and Cameron's boundaries – were combined in a single measure. But it was not a balanced measure. If Cameron's boundary changes did not go ahead, neither did AV. But even if AV failed at a referendum, Cameron's boundary changes went ahead. Had Clegg had any negotiating nous, he would have insisted that both changes had to be made or neither. If AV lost at a referendum, the boundary changes would go down. At the least, the boundary changes should also have been subject to a referendum. Had Clegg done so, the Tory Party would not have been able to mount the programme of lies and abuse which they did, led by Cameron, during the AV campaign. They would have had to curb their instincts by opposing AV in a more measured way, and their leader would have had to keep his mouth shut.

That was a Clegg blunder but it was the lesser of two blunders. For his real mistake was in deciding that the AV referendum must be held on the same day as the local elections and the elections for the Scottish Parliament and the Welsh Assembly in May 2011.

This was madness. Two parties, or at any rate two party leaders, favoured AV – Clegg and the Labour Party's Ed Miliband. However, these two were head to head in crucial elections which could determine whether the coalition survived or collapsed. The result was a fatal divide within the 'yes' campaign. Clegg took a back seat – as he was by then the most unpopular politician in Britain, that at least showed some wisdom – but the two parties' campaigns never really gelled.

Initially Clegg's position could be defended on the grounds that, such was his standing with the great British public, voting reform could be carried on his say-so. The reverse, however, was the case after his great U-turn on tuition fees. He went from hero to zero in twenty-four hours.

By autumn 2010 it was evident that the confluence of dates would be fatal to the AV case.

I was involved in one attempt to prevent this. The Parliamentary Voting and Constituencies Bill had to pass the Lords. I was in fact opposed to the bit of the Bill which changed the constituency boundaries. I thought the combination of equal-sized constituencies, too frequent reviews and a reduction in the size of the House of Commons was toxic. Like a party game of musical chairs, MPs would spend their whole lives worrying that their own seats would disappear. They would be so busy competing with each other for the seats that remained that they would have little time left to do their jobs. In the end, the Bill took 108 hours to go through the House of Lords, and Hansard records that I made 166 contributions.

Labour was accused of filibustering on the bill. I tried hard to make my speeches relevant so that this charge did not stick. However, I hoped that, if the bill was held up long enough, it might not be possible to hold the referendum on 5 May.

Meanwhile I tried my best to persuade Mr Clegg's friends of the absurdity of his timing. One by one they came out with his reasons. One was that turnout in Scotland would be higher in May 2011 because of the Scottish Parliament elections.

There were two flaws in this argument. First, the polls showed that support for reform in Scotland was no stronger than that in the rest of Britain. Secondly, given that Scotland represents a relatively small part of the population, it wouldn't much help if it was. If turnout in Scotland was 10 per cent higher than in the rest of the country, and if the Scots polled ten percentage points more for 'yes' than the rest of the country, the advantage to the 'yes' campaign would amount to, wait for it, 0.1 per cent of the total vote. When this was pointed out it did not change Clegg's mind. The friends started muttering some argument about London, so obscure and irrelevant that, despite having heard it a number of times, I am simply unable to reconstruct it now. Mr Clegg, I think, is not one of the finest advertisements for the benefits of being educated at Westminster School. He would not budge. Having made his tactical blunder he was determined to get his way.

Any charge of filibustering against Labour was outweighed a thousand times over by the government's bad conduct. Consultation on the policy was minimal. The Commons proceedings were truncated. The Lords sat all night with the usual rising time, laid down in its handbook of procedures, abandoned. The government got its Bill just in time, thanks to Mr Clegg's insistence. The turkeys had won their vote for an early Christmas.

The 'yes' campaign was run by Mr Clegg's aide John Sharkey, and had persuaded itself that it had a chance. I was torn between a liking for Mr Sharkey – who was a good deal more competent than his boss – and an acute distrust of the organisation over which he was presided.

The tale of the campaign is well told in *Don't Take No for an Answer* by two reformers, Lewis Baston and Ken Ritchie (Biteback, 2011). It produced opinion polls showing it was in front. Some were genuine but reflected the fact that most of those asked had no idea what they were being asked about. Others were founded on questions designed to tell voters what was at stake. The chance to get that message across to real voters had, however, disappeared because the campaign period was so short.

The 'yes' campaign was also not helped by divisions in its ranks about whether AV was the right alternative. David Owen felt with logical force and tactical naïvety that full proportionality should be on the agenda and not just AV. Some Labour electoral reformers persuaded themselves that an alternative form of alternative vote, the supplementary vote, used to choose the Mayor of London, was superior. Again, whether they were right or wrong is irrelevant. By banging on about systems, they damaged the case for the only alternative system on offer. The 'yes' campaign was doomed.

I cannot personally give an illuminating account of the campaign itself. I was put on the steering committee for 'yes' as a peace-offering. Alas! it was dominated by constitutional reform fanatics, who lived on a different political planet to the one I inhabited.

It is hard to identify which of the series of mistakes made by the 'yes' campaign was most damaging. The campaign's slogan 'Make your MP work harder' was incomprehensible to the public (to me too, since you ask). But it was part of a general anti-politics thrust to the campaign, which also included using semi-celebrities to promote the campaign when the public was looking to hear from politicians they trusted.

Anti-politics caused the campaign to ignore the most basic strategy. The Tories (of whom there were lots) were bound to oppose change. The Lib Dems would support it, but there were few of them left. So the crucial appeal should have been to Labour. Instead, the Lib Dems sought to dominate the campaign. The harder they tried, the further the vote fell.

What turned defeat into rout was Mr Clegg's contribution. He devoted his main speech during the campaign before a leftish audience to an attack on Labour: 'An act of rudeness and ingratitude to his hosts as well as ineptitude if the aim was to win "yes" votes,' say Baston and Ritchie. Throughout, 'he put his ego before winning votes', they say. He hurt his cause, he hurt his party and he hurt what remains of his reputation.

Fortunately I missed seeing most of this at close quarters. Remaining to argue with the campaign committee had all the prospects of success of an atheist seeking to covert a convocation of Catholic bishops. I therefore decided to go ahead with a long-planned sabbatical in the United States as the campaign opened, and had not returned when the result was declared.

As a long-standing reformer, to whom journalists might naturally turn for copy, I did not want to have to answer questions as to whether I felt that 'yes' was doing well. I thought that the anti-politician message which lay at the core of the 'yes' appeal was absurd. I therefore chose to observe it only at a distance.

Everything that happened confirmed my initial instinct: that the 'yes' campaign never had a prayer. On 5 May, Britain voted by 68 per cent to 32 per cent against change.

I had expected the result, but when it happened I felt less regret than I expected. My support for AV deep down reflected a combination of factors: principle, because the existing system was indefensible, and partisanship, because I thought it would help Labour. By 2011 I was not so sure.

As for principle, I did have a growing worry about AV. It enabled people to vote for parties other than the big three without risking wasting their vote. Britain's traditional party system was already fractured, with the big parties' shares of the vote barely two-thirds of the total. Under AV, and especially in the light of the great MPs' expenses scandal before the election, there was a real danger of the multiplication of fringe parties, some relatively benign like UKIP and some malign like the British National Party. The share of the vote of parties of government might fall so low that the legitimacy of our democratic system would be injured.

I had also supported AV because I thought it would lead to more Labour or Labour-led governments than the existing system. Most projections of the results of most elections on AV suggested the following: a biggish increase in Lib Dem representation in Parliament, a small drop in Labour's and a big drop in the Tories'. So reform would mean that, when Labour fell short of an overall majority, we should expect to govern with the Lib Dems.

That was a fair shout at the time of Jenkins. It was impossible to conceive that the Lib Dems as they were then would ally with the Tories. The problem rather was to persuade the Labour Party, which did not much enjoy Lib Dem dirty tactics in elections, that the Lib Dems would be suitable partners. Indeed following Jenkins I set up with the Labour MP Calum MacDonald an organisation called LINC, which worked to counter Labour hostility to the Lib Dems.

That all changed with Clegg's accession. The party abandoned the Lloyd George radical tradition and its conversion to pale blue politics. Clegg and most his senior colleagues are more comfortable in the company of Tories than of Labour. Hence the current coalition government, which spends much of its time trying to bring down what were once pillars of the Liberal faith. It is hard to see the progressive alliance, once dreamed of by Blair and Jenkins, re-emerging.

So we have an indefensible voting system. At the same time, the only change to it that has been on the agenda brings major risks. How this will be resolved in the long run, I do not care to predict. What I can predict with some confidence is that it is unlikely, though not impossible, that we shall see electoral reform in my lifetime, just as we never saw it in Lord Jenkins's. I am sure that he has a bottle of fine burgundy ready to uncork on his cloud on the day of victory. Thanks largely to Nick Clegg's ineptitude, it will now have a decade or two more to mature.

CHAPTER 12

FULL OF CARE 1978–

The electoral commission was challenging but a joy. The Royal Commission on the Funding of Long-Term Care of the Elderly, on which I served in parallel, was hell. It ended up with my authoring a minority report, and then entering more than a decade of struggle to make sure it prevailed over the majority.

Back in 1999, when the invitation to join the commission came along, I freely confess I had not given five minutes' thought to its subject in my life. I have this in common with most of my fellow citizens, who understandably do not like to contemplate the last years of their life.

The majority commissioners put about a theory I had been planted on the commission as a government nark. Tony Blair, so they thought, had given me orders to persuade the majority to adopt the policy the government wanted and, if I failed, to thwart them by writing a minority report.

I cannot prove that this is not the case. If it was, no one told me. It resembles those bizarre conspiracy theories which whiz around the internet. They are groundless. They are irrefutable. They give pleasure to those who propagate them. However, there is a flaw at the heart of their theory. If the government knew what it wanted, why did it set up a commission in the first place? True, it had made an election pledge to do so. But the pledge was made because this was a tough and complex issue, and Labour in opposition did not have the faintest clue what to do about it. A commission, so it must have seemed to ministers, was a way of clarifying the issues and perhaps coming up with a solution.

In any case, no conspiracy is needed to explain why my presence on the commission might have seemed a good idea. I was an economist by training. There was no other member who knew much economics. I specialised in public policy and particularly in public expenditure. No other member had quite this knowledge. I served at the time on the Personal Investment Authority, which regulated financial products. With the exception of Joel Joffe, who joined me in signing the minority report, no other member had knowledge of the role private insurance products could play in paying for long-term care. It is true that I had long been friendly with Frank Dobson, the Health Secretary, but that was hardly a disqualification.

What were we supposed to be looking at? Simply stated, the problem was this. If you are unlucky enough to be ill, you get free treatment from the NHS. However, the costs of attending to the disabilities that go with later old age are not always treated free. If you are poor, they are paid for on a means-tested basis. But those with money have to pay for their own long-term care, in some cases selling their homes to do so.

This is harsh, but not without parallel. Food is a necessity too, but no one expects the state to provide it free, even for the old and frail.

However, with long-term care, a further problem gives rise to acute feelings of injustice. Not everyone needs long-term care. Only one woman in three and one man in five will ever go into a care home. Those who do, through no fault of their own, may find their assets, if they have them, stripped away. They will not be able to leave much of their money or their property to their children.

Faced with this situation, campaigners for the elderly had rallied under the banner of free care for all. Their demand was given political voice by the Liberal Democrats, who for years supported such a policy. It was this that the long-term care Royal Commission was to examine, and it was the easy conclusion that care should be free that I came to oppose.

The disaster that the commission proved had its roots in its setting up. First, there was the choice of chairman. My relations with the then Sir Stewart Sutherland have over the years fluctuated. Even when I was off him, however, I never doubted that he is a moral man. A philosopher of religion, he rose to be vice-chancellor of Edinburgh University and a senior figure in higher education.

What was curious was his selection for this particular job. We were not being asked to investigate long-term care in general, with all the manifold social, organisational and medical considerations which applied to it; or to discuss the ethical case for treating older people well. Our remit was 'to examine the short- and long-term options for a sustainable system of funding of Long Term Care for elderly people ... and within twelve months, to recommend how, and in what circumstances, the cost of such care should be apportioned between public funds and individuals'. The terms of reference further said we were to cost our proposals and take account of the government's long-term spending review. Yet there was nothing in Sutherland's record – this is not a criticism – which suggested that he was likely to be sensitive to such considerations.

Peter Mandelson later described to me the meeting between Dobson and Tony Blair to discuss the appointment of the commission, at which he was present. 'Sutherland's not right for this, I can just see he is not right for this,' Blair muttered. 'Oh but I assure you, Prime Minister, my department is convinced that he is,' Frank replied. In the end, the Department of Health was allowed to overrule the Prime Minister's reservation.

I cannot fault the seriousness which Sutherland brought to the role, the industry he applied to it and his personal touch with all the members. It is just that his mindset was not, in my view, the right one for the task the government wanted done, to reconcile the aspirations of older people and their carers with the realities of government finance.

If the appointment of the chairman was odd, so too was the selection of members of the commission. The issue, to repeat, was not the delivery of long-term care but its funding. You would have expected a commission packed with experts on funding. We were not that.

For example, the late Claire Rayner, who after our disagreements publicly expressed a statesmanlike wish that my gonads would drop off, was (like me) a journalist, a much-loved agony aunt on the *Sunday Mirror*. Mary Marshall was a professor of social work,

Dame June Clark taught nurses, and Robert Stout and Iona Heath were both doctors.

But to any impartial observer, it should have been apparent that there was a gross imbalance in the commission. It was packed with those with the 'soft' skills in life. The commission lacked a demographer, to oversee its projections of future numbers in receipt of care and therefore of future costs. In this absence, I was asked to oversee this work myself. It lacked a numerate professional economist, though again I did have some economic knowledge. It included no actuary. We did not (until I took on the role) include a hard man or woman, aware of the realities of limited resources and the problems that gave governments in determining priorities.

We were universally of liberal views, and not one of us was therefore likely instinctively to raise the question of the impact on taxpayers of what we recommended. Moreover, the people from whom we took evidence were heavily the professional representatives of older people, who naturally wanted as much as they could get for them, free of charge. The majority proceeded as if money grew on trees.

The final fatal flaw was the timetable. It was no shorter than that for the Jenkins Commission, to be sure, and longer than that for the Davies Panel on the BBC, my next inquiry. But for the funding of long-term care it was wholly inadequate.

Long-term care is perhaps the most complex subject I have ever sought to get to grips with. The demographics are complicated. First, there is the issue of how long people will live for. The actuarial profession specialises in this, but projections have tended to lag behind reality. Not only are people living longer but that extension of life has accelerated. Any estimates of the costs of supporting people in extreme old age therefore have tended to be overtaken by reality.

Then there is a debate about how things are developing. It is not in doubt that people are living longer. But are they also suffering disability for longer? One school, the 'compression of morbidity' school, believes that they are not. As older people stay fitter, their period of disability at the end of their life gets shorter. Another school believes that they are. The old merciful killers, such as pneumonia, have been eliminated, and so old people instead have to put up with longer periods of crumbling health. A third school believes that the period of disability remains roughly constant. Which was right? The answer made a major difference to long-term costs.

The sociology is complicated. Old people themselves are often torn between a desire to remain in their own homes and a desire not to burden their offspring with looking after them. The younger generation – the children of the elderly – is no longer available (as once women were) to care for the elderly. This generation finds itself torn between the burden of guilt, the force of love and the practicalities of giving expression to either. In this situation, it is easy to create incentives that distort behaviour – for example, if care in people's own homes is free, as proposed by Gordon Brown in 2009, old disabled people may remain in them long after the burden on themselves and their relatives is truly sustainable.

The economics is complicated. Costs of care are high, and they are rising and will continue to rise fast. But how fast? There are two key issues.

First, long-term care is a labour-intensive service. The bulk of the costs in care homes is incurred in paying the staff to look after the residents. So how fast will their pay rise in future – given that they are horribly underpaid for the work they do at present? To what extent, if any, will that increased pay be offset by higher productivity? Can they be expected to reel up the hoists more quickly or shovel in the food in less time? And there is a complication with immigration policy. Many care workers come from ethnic minorities, for members of ethnic minorities are willing to do the work for the pay. This is particularly so where the labour force constraints are tightest, in London and the South East. So the more the government cracks down on immigration, the harder it becomes to staff our care homes.

Secondly, old people in care have ever-rising expectations of what they should receive, and rightly so. A few years back, the old were shoved into geriatric wards in hospitals to wait to die. Today's elderly – and their relatives – reject such cruelties. Standards in care homes have risen, as they needed to, and will continue to rise. But these improvements come at a cost. And when the golden generation retiring now come to face their last years, you may be sure that they will not quietly put up with the so-so standards provided today. Again, quite rightly so, but it comes at a cost.

Those costs have to be met one way or another – either out of private pockets or out of the taxpayers'. These two possibilities have very different implications not just for the level of taxation, but also for the national distribution of income and wealth.

So we faced a task of the utmost complexity against a timetable which was absurdly truncated. I may be wrong about this, but my impression is that the majority of the commission, and perhaps the chairman, in effect decided to cut the corner. The verdict came first, the trial later.

There is a case for free care. It had been set out by an inquiry by the Rowntree Trust a couple of years before we began, which the chairman commended to us. It proposed universal free care, funded from increased national insurance contributions. It was a plausible sort of a report signed by some plausible people. Why reinvent the wheel?

Quite early on, I started to feel uneasy about this free care conclusion. Two strands in my past contributed to this unease.

Firstly, from Tony Crosland, I inherited my belief in equality and in the role of the state in increasing it. How would state-funded free care impact on equality? The answer is that it would add greatly to inequality.

The less well off got care free under the existing system. Indeed some two-thirds of care home residents were being paid for by the state in 1999, though the proportion is somewhat lower today.

This worked through a means test: you were only allowed to keep a pathetically small amount of your income, the rest going to pay for care, and your assets were run down to £20,000 or so. The means test was therefore far from ideal, and resented by many who felt they had saved all their life. Nevertheless, its brute result was that free care would not benefit the less well off.

Every single penny spent on free care by the state would go to the better off. Indeed, as these were people towards the end of their life, it was not they themselves who would benefit from the extra cash. The true beneficiaries would be their children, inheriting gratefully the assets their parents had left. As a Croslandite, I stood against sumptuary inheritance, which I considered unearned, unjust and inegalitarian.

Secondly, I had written widely about public spending, and I knew how the Treasury worked. In broad terms, there was a budget for older people, and within that, a budget for long-term care.

Suppose part of that budget – a large part – was diverted to provide such care free for all. The remainder of the budget would be reduced or restricted.

What was this bit of the budget for? It was for the provision of services. On this depended how often you might expect paid helpers to come to clean you up if you lived at home. On this depended what residential homes could pay their workers, and thus in practice the quality of those workers. On this depended what help the state could provide for carers, including family carers, often laden with the most appalling personal burdens and in need of support and respite.

You could not spend the same money twice. If it went on free care, the standard of care that old people would receive would be lower than it otherwise would be. As this standard of care was deficient in many regards, this seemed a wrong priority.

This was the argument that persuaded Joel Joffe to join me in opposing the majority. I have had the good fortune to meet many good men in my lifetime, but Joel would come high in my list. He was Jewish and South African, and, as a lawyer, he had defended Nelson Mandela when he was on trial for his life in 1963. He still has the piece of paper on which Mandela had written the speech he would have delivered had he been condemned to death. Eventually forced out of his homeland, Joffe had accumulated a small fortune through his work in the life insurance industry, but he was not a man for jewels and yachts. His was a life of public service. I first came across him as a doughty campaigner against the abuses committed by the big financial services companies, a campaign in which I assisted him. He was a man of integrity with the rare quality of genuinely listening to evidence and argument.

It was not a pleasure to have to be writing a minority report. Indeed it was hard graft, since Joffe, with his lawyer's regard for precision and accuracy, made me go through some thirty-two drafts before he was satisfied. But in the end every hour of this process of revision was worth it. It made me confident that we had a solid argument every bit of which would stand up to scrutiny. Joel's steadfast and determined support made the whole thing possible.

As the commission majority sailed on down its course, and the minority reluctantly went its way, personal relations deteriorated. Sutherland, once the thrust of the majority report was clear, set off on a tour of Whitehall to persuade ministers of his case. I thought that I should, in these circumstances, similarly talk to those I knew with influence to try to persuade him of mine. The majority did not agree, and a meeting of the commission denounced me.

Then there was the press. Hints of the disagreement on the commission appeared first in the *Financial Times*. The majority of the commission thought I had leaked it. This is not true, but neither is it wholly untrue. I did not initiate any leak at any stage, but I did not deny it when a journalist rang to ask me if it was right that there was a division on the commission. I might even have explained, off the record, why I took the view I did. It seemed to me, and indeed still seems to me, that the public had a right to an insight into the arguments. Moreover, if the majority got first run with its case the contrary case might never get a hearing. That after all was what happened to Bob Alexander's minority note to Jenkins. By now, this was war, and I was not proposing any unilateral disarmament while the majority pushed its offensive forward.

I saw at this stage a different side of the saintly Sir Stewart. In one conversation he totally lost it, addressing me with a 'listen here, laddie', like an Edinburgh policeman dealing with a recalcitrant drunk. This did not have the effect of bringing me into line.

All this was hard on the staff of the commission. Alan Davey, our secretary, went on to be chief executive of the Arts Council and is a public servant of high ability. He had to reconcile his loyalty to his chairman with his duties to minority commissioners. He also was looking to fashion a report that could be adjusted to fit whatever route ministers eventually wanted to go down. Meanwhile, his staff, most of whom went along with the majority, had to perform professionally in an atmosphere which was hardly conducive to that.

I, too, tried to the end to find some common ground. At one point I wasted a good deal of effort drafting a report which tried to combine as much as could be combined of the majority and minority reports. The chairman on behalf of the commission dismissed my efforts in a single sentence.

Towards the end, majority and minority were barely on speaking terms. In a last throw, Sutherland tried to stop the minority report. This was not the title given to it for, by convention, minority reports to Royal Commissions were described as 'dissenting notes'. However, Sutherland sought to suppress it, or failing that, to make changes in it. If I were a more Machiavellian soul, I would have let him win this battle, refused to sign the majority report, and printed and distributed the minority report privately. That would have put him and his fellow commissioners on the back foot instantly. Instead, I appealed to Chris Kelly, the permanent secretary at Health, and the dissenting note appeared with only trivial changes to my original draft.

Sutherland took particular objection to the use by the minority of the phrase 'free care for all' to describe the majority's proposals, pointing out that it was 'free care for all with a proven need for it'. I took some pleasure in making sure that the phrase 'free care for all', shorn of Sutherland's otiose gloss, appeared in every public utterance I made on the subject. As I said, relations were not good.

The minority report was not merely a refutation of the majority's proposals. We set out detailed proposals for the future of long-term care. One set of proposals was designed to mitigate the most severe impact of the means test. So we suggested making not all personal care free but strictly nursing care in nursing homes free since this sort of care was closely analogous to health care. We advocated a scheme whereby old people never had to sell their homes in their lifetime to pay for care – the local authority lending them money against the value of the house, repayable only on their death. We wanted somewhat higher limits on assets before people had to pay.

I, though Joel did not agree, even floated a scheme whereby care would become free after five years for people who needed it. The logic was that it was reasonable to expect people to pay for care for up to five years – the average time for which people required it was two years – out of their own resources or by taking out private insurance. However, to live long in care was an unforesee-able eventuality against which it was unreasonable to expect people to provide.

Our main reason for not making services free was that the money would be better spent on better services. The better off could afford to buy these for themselves, but the worse off could not and only the state could pay for what they needed.

We were struck by the plight of carers and wanted a £300m fund set up to help them, including with respite care. In 2009–10, the Lib Dems, the original political advocates of free care, pleasingly came round to making this their priority too.

Finally we gave some attention to a subject that simply hadn't occurred to the majority, governed as it was by its money-grows-on-trees philosophy. We thought there were areas in which savings could be made. For example, Audit Commission evidence said that care in homes owned by local authorities was neither better nor worse than care in privately owned homes. However, it (then) cost on average £366 a week as compared with £238 in private homes. We wanted local authorities to give more attention to efficient purchasing and to use expensive social workers more effectively. We believed that savings could result from an integrated holis-tic approach to care. Whatever might be thought of our overall argument, I would maintain that in these recommendations, we were ahead of the game.

The launch of the report in February 1999 went well – from the minority's point of view. This was not a matter to which Sutherland had devoted much attention. He did not, I think, much like the press. The launch of the Royal Commission's report was ill planned and it got correspondingly little news coverage.

We did better. I took steps personally to brief the key leader writers and the acknowledged opinion leaders among journalists – Nick Timmins of the *Financial Times*, Malcolm Dean of *The Guardian* and others. Mostly, their comment sided with the minority.

I also prepared carefully for broadcasting opportunities. Modern news depends on the soundbite. You may well need an hour or ten minutes or a minute to explain your case properly. You are not going to get it. At the time, the soundbite length was eleven seconds though I understand it has come down since. So I rehearsed. 'The commission's proposals would cost a huge amount of money, all of it going to the better off and not one single penny going for the better services old people so desperately need.'

After tens of repetitions on every programme that would have me, I got pretty bored with this. I had no idea if anyone was listening. Then I discovered a strange phenomenon. People would come up to me. 'Weren't you on that Royal Commission?' they would say. 'Don't know what you thought but seems to me it would cost a lot of money, all of it going to the better off without providing better services for the poor old things.'

I do not claim we won total victory in the battle for public opinion. Ask voters about anything – prescription charges, TV licences, winter heat, roads – and they will always want them free. Ask them if they want higher taxes and you get a very different answer. However, the danger to the minority report was always that a populist campaign would take hold and that the government would be unable to resist. At least we avoided that.

Royal Commissions have gone out of fashion. After their experience with ours, ministers were not attracted by the model. The government commissioned many reports, of course, but from less formal bodies.

So my last word of advice may be redundant. It is this: if asked to serve on a Royal Commission, write a minority report. If you look through the history of Royal Commissions, these have been common enough. More important, it is only minority reports that get anywhere. Who for example remembers the majority report of the Commission on the Poor Law of 1906–09? It is Beatrice Webb's minority report that comes down to us, the begetter, before Beveridge, of the modern welfare state. Quite why only minority reports get anywhere is anyone's guess. Perhaps it is because you have to feel strongly about something to write one, and if you feel strongly about something, you are probably prepared to argue for it and fight for it.

Writing a minority report comes at a high cost. If you go down that route, expect public acrimony and private obloquy. But if your aim is to make a modest difference to public policy, a minority report is the way to do it.

I thought that with the publication of the report, my role in long-term care would come to an end. Ministers would deliberate and (so I felt reasonably confident) would reject the majority's central recommendation. Debate on the matter would of course continue over the years and no doubt from time to time I should be tempted, publicly or privately, to opine. But it would become less absorbing.

The commission had been horribly bruising. I had fallen out with those whom I liked and respected – Robin Wendt, for example, an ex-civil servant, Iona Heath, a splendid GP, and Paula Ridley, an all-round public servant – as well as members for whom I had no time at all.

Moreover being involved in it had one large personal disadvantage. The last years of one's life and those of those near to us don't really bear thinking about. Yet I had had to think about them, day in, day out, week in, week out, month in, month out and – as it transpired – year in, year out. Perhaps it was the effect of that which caused Joel Joffe to become the inspirational leader of the Dignity in Dying campaign, which seeks to change the law to allow people who are terminally ill to end their life with medical help.

I strongly support this campaign. Indeed, I would go further. Generations used to autonomy are not going to put up for ever with leaving the end of life to fate. Christians of course will kick and scream but in Europe they are a diminishing force. In the end, older people will win the right to end their lives at a time of their own choosing. I just hope it comes in time for me.

As things turned out, the publication of the commission's report was just the beginning of my involvement and not the end. On and off, I became involved in the subsequent debate. It was to terminate in 2009–10 with the biggest battle of my House of Lords career.

Some of this work was quiet and behind the scenes. Ministers did not take long to reject the majority report, and they did so with little public reaction.

Care ministers under the Health Secretary came and went. I had an implicit deal with them. They might share my views, but it was not always expedient for them to express that agreement. So whenever this, that or the other body again came up with a free care proposal, I stood ready to parade myself in front of the cameras, take to the microphone or write the article refuting the argument. I must over the years have said 'These proposals would cost a huge amount of money, all of it going to the better off and not one single penny going for the better services old people so desperately need' several hundred times.

I also had a forum for restating our position in various legislative debates in the Lords. My interventions were delivered with a good deal more passion than is generally regarded as appropriate in that august assembly.

The most satisfying part of this work was campaigning for the minority's positive proposals. We had some successes. The government gave more help to carers. It agreed to our proposal where nursing care, strictly defined, would be free. We did get the local

authority loan scheme off the ground. Unfortunately the government botched its implementation so that it was not specifically
compulsory for a local authority to offer a loan in every case. Some
cases went to the courts, which generally ruled that it must do so.
However, it remains the case that some old people are forced to sell
their homes to pay for care. That must end.

A particular bugbear of mine was the poor pay of residential
care workers. Though most care workers tried their best, they were
undertrained and, to use an Old Labour kind of a word, exploited.
Liam Byrne, an energetic care minister, asked me what I would
do if I had a restricted budget to improve elderly care. I replied
unhesitatingly that I would magic-wand care workers' pay up by
£1 an hour, and improve their training. Byrne listened and was a
strong supporter of efforts to upgrade the workforce.

I also tried to promote private insurance for care needs. People
ran a risk of having to pay for long-term care, just as, say, they run
a risk of having their house burgled. No one suggests that house
content insurance should be provided by the state. The state was
not going to provide long-term care cover either, so why should not
private insurance companies fill the gap? Indeed there were such
policies to insure against long-term care. More than 30,000 were in
existence when the commission reported.

We of the minority thought that a serious obstacle existed which
stopped people taking out such policies. They were not subject to
regulation by the Personal Investment Authority, or its successor,
the Financial Services Authority. People had been sold pensions
which did not deliver what had been promised. They feared they
would be mis-sold long-term care products too. They needed the
protection of law-backed regulations as to what might be sold
and how.

As with everything in government, this seemingly self-evident
proposition was the devil's own job to force through. The FSA was
overworked, so was the Treasury, and it was difficult to get this on
anyone's priority agenda. It took years of hard lobbying – I traipsed
in and out of the offices of distinguished economic secretaries to

the Treasury to make the case – before finally, in 2004, the regulations were introduced.

From insurance companies' point of view, there are problems about offering long-term care policies. One is the argument about morbidity discussed above. You simply do not know, and even your actuaries do not know, how long you are likely to have to pay out for. Naturally, a cautious insurer prices the policy on the basis of the maximum likely payout period. The cost, however, puts people off buying.

Another is moral hazard. People who are insured may look after themselves less than if they were not insured and had to stay fit to keep hold of their assets.

I have never found this latter argument compelling in the long-term care case. I have never thought many people were likely to do their best to damage their health so they could get into a home and claim against their policy.

Another more serious problem for insurers is adverse selection. Those who think or know they will stay fit won't take out policies. Those who think or know they won't, will. This too forces up the price of policies. But none of these arguments against long term care insurance seem decisive. They apply in much the same way to life insurance, which is a mass product.

I have done everything I can to promote private insurance. In the run-up to the 2009 Green Paper on long-term care, I persuaded ministers to set up a working party with private insurance experts to see if anything could be done to get it off the ground. Sadly, however, fewer and fewer companies offer products. They are not competitively priced. The market is shrinking not growing as it should.

Why? For the same reason that made my own involvement in long-term care a net burden rather than a joy: that, on the whole, people don't want to think about extreme old age. There is nothing nice about it. So they prefer the ostrich posture. Or, alternatively, they give money to Age Concern or Help the Aged (now amalgamated as Age UK) to campaign for free care, and persuade themselves it will actually happen. Long-term care insurance, in the insurers' jargon, is a policy that has to be sold. It will not generally be willingly bought. From the insurers' point of view selling it is hard, unprofitable work.

This may change with time. In 2008, I became honorary president of the Society of Latter Life Advisers (SOLLA), a body of independent financial advisers specialising in the elderly. It is to be hoped that, with time, independent financial advisers will persuade more of their clients to take out care insurance. They could be assured of alleviating much worry, and begetting much gratitude from the children whose inheritance would be protected.

These by-ways of the main issue kept me busy over the years. However, it turned out that the main debate – free care or not? – was by no means over. This came up in an unexpected way.

For Scotland, long-term care was a devolved matter. Policy was a matter for the Scottish Parliament and Executive. For a while, this was a distinction without a difference. The Scottish Parliament took the same view on free care as Westminster.

However, Scotland is more devoted to universal state services than is the rest of the UK. Moreover, following devolution, the Scottish government was basking in a Jacuzzi of cash provided by the British taxpayer under the Barnett formula. This enabled the Scots to enjoy better services without paying higher taxes to fund them.

The Lib Dems were particularly active in campaigning for free personal care in Scotland, and in the end, they got it. From 2002, personal care was not to be free exactly, but generous weekly grants were to be given to those in need of it. These applied whether they were in residential care or not.

I was somewhat inhibited in participating in the Scots debate by the fact that I am not a Scot. The Scots were not eager to take English advice on long-term care or anything else. However, the Scottish opponents of free care – and they included a majority of Labour members of the Parliament – were lying low. It was poor politics to oppose it. So I had to take a public position.

It was wildly expensive, I said. I repeated my soundbite that it only helped the better off. It would do nothing to improve services, especially services to the worse off.

As it was happening in only one part of the kingdom, there was one fresh point I deployed. The English would flock north of the border to avail themselves of free care at Scottish expense. Tongue in cheek, I envisaged a world where Edinburgh was converted into thousands of care homes – for which there would be adequate accommodation, so I said, since all the Scottish banks would have fled to England to avoid the unsupportable taxes needed to pay for them.

I do not think I made myself popular in Scotland. On one phone-in programme, a caller worked himself into a lather. 'I'm no' havin' Pipsqueak Lipsey telling us what Scotland should do,' he said. Some of my friends know me as 'Pipsqueak' to t his day.

For all my public protestations, the social scientist part of me welcomed the Scottish decision. The majority had made its recommendations on free care. The minority had dissented. Who was right? We were now getting something rare in social affairs: a controlled experiment where the two policies were run alongside each other. The jeremiads of the minority were now being tested in practice.

The most important issue was cost. Would the economic law by which if you price something at zero, demand for it increases apply? Or would care still only go to those who needed it, with the cost remaining stable?

On this, the evidence is unambiguous. The facts are exactly as the authors of the minority report expected them to be. Costs for free care at home went up 112 per cent in the first five years of the policy.

Even this was not the full story. Hard-pressed local authorities in Scotland were reported to be delaying assessments for free care so as to keep the burden within bounds. Services themselves were being cut to pay for free care, as we had predicted that they would.

Scotland's most senior social worker recently called for the free care policy to be re-examined.

Even the cloth ears of the SNP government picked up this concern. They decided to set up an inquiry into the workings of free care. And who did they choose to chair that inquiry?

Step forward Lord Sutherland, whose policy it was! I did not find it necessary to hold my breath in anticipation of his conclusions. Free care was working splendidly, he reported. However, it was not being funded as fully as it should be. An extra £40m or so on top of what was provided would be good.

Where was this to come from? Lord Sutherland, with a straight face, came up with his answer: the English taxpayer. Disability living allowance, a national benefit, was paid to Scots. Those getting free care would not need it. So the national Exchequer would gain. That money should be given to the Scots to pay for free care. The absurdity of the notion that English taxpayers would be happy to give a further subvention to the Scots to pay for a benefit of which they themselves were unable to take advantage seemed to have escaped him.

Whitehall declined the good Lord's suggestion. A little later, a remarkable turnaround occurred. Lord Sutherland himself, in the new post-crunch financial climate, questioned whether free care was affordable. In 2011 he called for a radical overhaul of free care in Scotland, after the bill rose to £319m. This turnaround took real courage on his part. Better the sinner who repenteth!

So the Scottish evidence has proved that free care was an expensive folly. No English political party supported it. How on earth did it – or at least a version of it – resurface on the political agenda, as it did in 2009–10? The answer is a salutary lesson in how to make and how not to make public policy, and a horrible warning to the public to be wary of politicians who seek to bribe them with their own money.

The care debate had never gone away completely. Mankind is divided into two tribes on long-term care: the vast majority, which declines to give the matter any more thought than it has to, and a tiny minority, which returns to it obsessively. Most of them were free-care advocates, so I also had to return to it obsessively to combat their arguments.

One significant contribution to that debate came in 2006. The King's Fund commissioned a report from Sir Derek Wanless, formerly a banker. Sir Derek's analysis was well worth it, both in updating and in improving significantly on the work of the Royal Commission. I could not agree with his conclusions, however.

He did not endorse free care. But he came near to it. First, the state would pay in full the cost of a basic level of personal care for all. Then, on top of that, it would match pound for pound the contributions individuals made to their own care. I could see what led him down this path, for it seemed to combine two *desiderata*: minimum free care to all and a big incentive to save towards long-term care costs. But it was far too expensive, almost as expensive as free care. Indeed, the King's Fund later recognised that, in the light of the credit crunch, the solution was unaffordable and put forward a less costly variant.

I sought to extinguish every attempt to breathe on the embers of free care, and indeed spoke out against the Wanless conclusions. However, as the decade went on, my own position was softened in two regards.

First, I was seized by one argument which, I must admit, completely eluded me when I drafted the minority report. Our argument was that there was a choice. Either you spent money on better care – our preference – or on free care – the majority's choice. You could not have it both ways.

However, and I owe this to Julian Forder of the London School of Economics, we had missed something. It turned out that the cost of care to the better off had resulted in a cut in the volume of care.

There were better-off people who needed care. Perhaps they needed paid-for help around the home. Perhaps – too often – they were really beyond remaining in their own homes. But they were not so short of money as to qualify for free care. Perhaps they owned their own homes. If they went into residential care, they would no longer be able to pass the value of those homes to their children. Even if they bought the care they needed, that inheritance would be eroded. If they were prudent, they might fear being reduced to the level of penury at which they were forced to be dependent on the state. They might even find this morally reprehensible.

These people coped in the only way they could cope – they did without. So they were not getting the care which they really needed.

This argument did not mean that they should get free care. That was unaffordable. It did mean that, for the first time, I could see a case for an element of state subsidy for the better off. This was particularly so since the pick-up in private insurance, which I had hoped would fill the gap, had failed to materialise.

The second modification of my position was more fundamental. In essence, I did not resile on any of the arguments in the minority report. Andrew Turnbull, who had been permanent secretary at the Treasury at the time we came out, had said that we had had the better of the argument, and I valued his endorsement. However, it is not always enough in life to be right. You have also to persuade others that you are right. And the fact remained that, for a variety of reasons, many were not persuaded.

Long-term care policy is not something that can chop and change. You are asking people to make decisions for themselves today which will impact on them many years in the future. Ministers too are taking decisions which will fundamentally affect public policy in general and levels of taxation in particular many years after they are gone and forgotten. As with pensions, you do not need only the right policy framework. You need a stable policy framework.

Meanwhile, long-term care policy was more and more of a mess. For example, councils' budgets for care were increasingly restricted. They understandably chose to spend what little money they had available on those with the greatest need. Those with lesser needs, particularly those still in their own homes, got no help. This was all very well, but a lesser need unmet today is a greater need to meet tomorrow.

As house prices rose, more and more people had to fund their own care. This in turn meant that more and more people were adversely affected by the means test. They and their offspring did not like this, and would put increasing pressure on the politicians. The danger was that, sooner or later, they would succumb to the electoral attractions of free care. Scotland was a warning. Some movement was needed if a sustainable position was to be secured.

These considerations led me to think that there was another imperative as well as those of avoiding free care and improving service standards. That imperative was to create a system which attracted consensus support, including, if possible, the support of all three main British political parties.

Care ministers came and went. Some, Liam Byrne among them, pushed hard for progress. Phil Hope in particular, who lost his seat in the 2010 general election, deserves credit for producing his July 2009 Green Paper. Others were defeated by the problem.

The Green Paper was never intended to be the last word. It was a statement of options. For example, there could be an insurance solution, whereby everyone had the chance to contribute a fixed sum in return for free care. The state could contribute a share of everyone's cost, irrespective of means. Or there could be a comprehensive option, whereby taking out insurance was compulsory. Free care paid for out of taxation was explicitly 'ruled out' on the grounds it would benefit a generation that had done well at the expense of the hard-pressed working population. There was to be a National Care Service, whatever that meant. There were some attractive minor proposals too, including one that would have ended for ever the necessity of anyone selling their home to pay for care. The minister got that one from me.

The Green Paper of course was never likely to determine policy. The Conservatives were working on their own alternative, based on a private insurance scheme whereby everyone would be covered for their care costs if they went into a home, for a one-off contribution of just £8,000. Labour did not look likely to win an election majority and so this Conservative proposal was, in its way, as relevant as the government's.

Still the Green Paper was a sound one. We were on a good course. I remained in that happy state of mind until I attended the Labour Party conference in September 2009 and sat in the hall to hear the Prime Minister's speech.

Gordon Brown was not (unlike Tony Blair) a great conference orator. He was not a phrase maker nor naturally funny though his speeches have a cumulative effect, like a hammer knocking on a recalcitrant nail. I was barely awake when I suddenly realised that he was referring to long-term care.

'The people who face the greatest burden are too often those on middle incomes, who have savings which will last a year or two, but then they will see their savings slip away. And the best starting point for our National Care Service is to help the elderly get the amenities to do what they most want: to receive care and to stay in their homes as long as possible,' the Prime Minister said. 'And so for those with the highest needs we will now offer in their own homes free personal care.'

I could scarcely believe my ears. This was free care, which the Green Paper had 'ruled out'. But it was a particularly pernicious variant of free care for its effect was as follows. While a person was at home with moderate care needs, they would get no help from the council or the state. When, however, they had deteriorated so they had 'the highest care needs' they would get their care completely free.

However, they might then continue to deteriorate. If they did so, they might have to go into a care home. If they did, they would then have to pay every penny their care cost.

How did the Prime Minister, usually a cautious politician, come to make his statement? I do not know. I made no fewer than five attempts to speak, not to him because that would have been beyond my pay grade, but to his advisers about the subject. I did not have the courtesy of an answer. They spoke to me only after I had attacked Brown publicly.

I can make an informed guess as to what happened. Firstly,

Brown, a Scottish MP, had observed that free personal care in Scotland was popular. Indeed it was, save with those, principally the English, who had to pay for it. Secondly, Brown, who was close to Paul Dacre of the *Daily Mail*, was much in favour of handouts to the middle classes. Thirdly, his advisers did not know much about the subject, but had picked up some gossip suggesting the Isle of Wight as a model. (It later emerged that IoW was cutting services including to the disabled to pay for its experiment.) Fourthly, he faced an election he was looking certain to lose. He did not have many game-changing ideas, but this bribe, of breathtaking size at any time, but particularly so at a time of fiscal stringency, looked as it if just might be one. Besides, his speech was short of head-line grabbers. The passage was slipped into the speech at the last moment, without due consideration, and in direct contradiction to the government's own Green Paper. It caught the Department of Health by surprise and the briefing round it was ramshackle even by the standards of party conference briefings.

I didn't know quite what to do. The Prime Minister was given to making dramatic-sounding pronouncements to secure a day's headlines, only for them afterwards to disappear without trace. My decision seemed to be made for me when I was asked to go on the *Today* programme to comment; then unmade when the item was dropped to accommodate the more newsworthy story of *The Sun*'s endorsement of the Tories.

Over the days that followed, however, it was clear that the proposal was not going to disappear. I had no doubt that I should campaign against it. My problem was that such campaigns only work if they attract the attention of the media. In this case, by not responding instantly, I had missed the boat.

There was one possibility, however. Bashing Brown was a popular pastime in which all the newspapers were keen to join. If, somehow, I could encapsulate my disagreement in a single flashing phrase, perhaps something could be done. In the middle of the night it came to me. I wanted to show that his statement contradicted what up to then had been his government's policy. That came out as: 'This is perhaps the first instance in recorded history where an admiral has launched an Exocet into the flagship of his own fleet.'

I tried it at a conference held by the Social Market Foundation on long-term care, with all the relevant journalists present. No one reported it. I tried again at a bigger conference a few days later. Nothing.

I then received an invitation to speak at a breakfast meeting on long-term care. Now I never attend breakfast meetings, holding the old-fashioned notion that that meal is best taken at home over the papers with one's wife. To have one more crack, I made an exception of this. I was assisted by the fact that Lord Norman Warner, a former health minister, was similarly infuriated by the Prime Minister's proposal, which he correctly declared at the same meeting to be 'insane'.

To his credit, Sam Lister of *The Times* had got up early too, and did notice. It was a quiet news day. *The Times* was short of a splash. So it was that my views, and Norman's, led the paper. The next day was spent jogging from studio to studio setting out the case Joffe and I had made in our memorandum.

Brown did not retreat. Rather the reverse. Norman Warner had said that he doubted a Bill was ready. On Downing Street's orders one was instantly produced. The consultation on the Green Paper had not yet ended. Very well, on Downing Street's orders, it would legislate first and publish the government's full proposals afterwards. An election was pending. Very well, the legislation would be rushed through, under procedures designed for emergency legislation, so it was on the statute book and the orders to give effect to it laid before Parliament was dissolved.

This bordered on the unconstitutional in its disregard for proprieties as to what a government could or could not do in the period just before polling day. Indeed Lord Robin Butler, a former Cabinet secretary and not a man given to exaggeration, described it as 'an act of national economic sabotage'.

We were powerless to do anything in the Commons. Brown's policy might have been mad but it might be popular. He had the chutzpah to force its detailed Commons examination through in a single day on the floor of the House. Neither the Tories nor the Lib Dems dared oppose him.

However, the purpose of the House of Lords, and an important one, is to act as an inhibitor of bad government behaviour. Had their Lordships simply disagreed with the free care policy, they would still have let the Bill go through as the expression of the will of the elected house. Brown's perfectly disgraceful disregard of the principles of good governance changed that. The Lords had a backstop role as guardians of the constitution. Norman and I set out to persuade it to play it.

We soon won the support of the Lib Dems, who had turned more and more against the free care policy; and the Tories, who did not fancy picking up the bill for Brown if they won the election. They wanted us to block the Bill, but they did not want the blood on their hands. More subtle amendments were needed to achieve our object without too obviously being seen to do so. Their Lords' spokespeople, Liz Barker (Lib Dem) and Freddie Howe (Conservative), were wonderful allies, as were the crossbench peers Richard Best and Elaine Murphy.

Such revolts are not uncommon in the Lords but they rarely succeed. We had an advantage over most of them as the media coverage had alerted their Lordships to the issue. Even on the Labour benches, we had strong support – though few would wish to carry those views to the logical conclusion of voting against the government. We needed a wider constituency.

I had noticed one thing in my Lords years. When any piece of legislation is before the House, we are heavily lobbied by outside interest groups, seeking to persuade us to support their chosen amendments. However, peers pretty well never issued written briefs to other peers. If we were to get our case over, it seemed to me, it was not sufficient to rely on corridor chats. Still less would speeches in the chamber do the trick, as relatively few peers would be in to hear them. Consequently Norman and I wrote a series of letters to peers setting out our case. We were greatly helped in that Glenys

Thornton, the industrious minister responsible for the Bill, felt she had to reply to them, replies which merely exposed the thinness of the government's case. This was not her fault, but that of Brown's policy.

We could not have succeeded if the election had not been so near at hand but it was. When an election is called, pieces of legislation that have not completed their parliamentary passage are submitted to a process called 'wash-up'. In wash-up, in effect, they have to attract consensus support or fall. So if the government hung in tough, it would lose the entire Bill.

Much of the minutiae of the campaign is on public record in Hansard; and much of what is not should and will remain private to the participants. The outcome, however, is no secret. The government's headlong rush was stopped. Ministers were forced to give an assurance that the Bill would not take effect until April 2011. More significantly, the Bill was amended so that it could not take effect before a commencement date agreed by a positive vote of both Houses of Parliament. That vote in turn could take place only after the general election. In other words, Labour could not use its majority in this parliament to seek to force it through in the next parliament.

Shortly after the general election, the coalition announced it would not be proceeding with the policy. The Act remains on the statute book as a monument to prime ministerial folly but it is most unlikely ever to come into force. Instead, a small commission under the economist Andrew Dilnot was created to come up with a policy which might at last end this long-lasting saga.

It was a satisfying victory. It is not often a backbench peer gets the better of a Prime Minister. It had, however, one sad consequence. I came reluctantly to the conclusion that Gordon Brown, for all his strengths, had demonstrated by his abusive handling of this issue that he was not fit to be the Prime Minister of our country. I therefore abstained from participating in Labour's 2010 election campaign – the first campaign since 1964 in which I had taken no part.

I did do something concrete to try to put flesh on the bones of the case for consensus. I attended a dinner arranged by the British United Provident Association (BUPA), major providers of long-term care. I was struck by how much agreement there was among the participants about the way forward.

I proposed, and BUPA kindly agreed, to set up a group to explore this consensus. Its membership included Sir Derek Wanless. It also included a member of each of the political parties. Norman Warner sat on it and so did Stephen Dorrell, a former Conservative Secretary of State for Health who had in office proposed a private–public insurance partnership to deal with the problem. Julia Neuberger, a peer and a former chief executive of the King's Fund, was the Lib Dem. Dorrell and Neuberger joined with the full support of their Commons party spokespeople. With considerable amity and little angst, we drafted in a few weeks a consensus statement, building on the Hope Green Paper.

Dilnot reported in July 2011. His splendidly argued case involved a 'cap' on the care costs that individuals had to bear, so making it affordable for people to insure privately against the cost. My friends were kind enough to tell me that Dilnot's proposals bore a remarkable resemblance to those set out in the minority report more than a decade earlier. I could not possibly comment.

The government has promised a White Paper by spring 2012. It may or may not be out by the time this volume is published. Either way, I hope, though I cannot yet be confident, that the Holy Grail of consensus on long-term care may materialise.

CHAPTER 13

AUNTIE'S CAKE 1998–99

There was no hidden agenda for my first two inquiries, the electoral system and long-term care. Ministers had not got a clue what to do about either. They sought informed independent advice. Things were not so simple in the case of my third inquiry, that into the future financing of the BBC, chaired by Gavyn Davies, which reported in 1999.

BBC funding was a controversial subject. The BBC licence fee was not a popular tax. It amounts to quite a lot of money, £101 a year at the time of our inquiry and £145.50 in 2011. It was a flat-rate tax with a minimal and controversial scheme of concessions to some of those in need. You could only avoid it by doing without a television – a virtual impossibility in today's world – or by breaking the law. I calculated that it would take a taxpayer on the minimum wage two weeks' work a year to earn what it cost.

The BBC understandably wanted a lot more money to fund its advance into the digital era, including its online presence. The BBC's competition – Murdoch's Sky and the increasing number of alternative online and TV services – wanted it to have a lot less money, so they would no longer face publicly subsidised competition. Ministers were walking a tightrope.

The dilemmas were made more acute by the coming of digital. Until that time, just about everyone received all the BBC's services, which meant that it was not wholly unreasonable to expect just about everyone to pay. However, the new BBC services, both online and additional digital services, were not universal, in coverage or in take-up. There was a perceived danger, not least in the BBC itself, of a revolt against the licence fee which could turn into a revolt against the corporation itself.

John Birt, its director general, came up with an ingenious solution. The licence fee should remain but on top of it an additional digital licence fee should be levied, to pay for these extra services. This was analogous to what happened when colour TV was introduced, with those who had it paying a supplement on top of the black-and-white fee.

This plan required the approval of ministers at the Department of Culture, Media and Sport (DCMS). Chris Smith, the Secretary of State, was a brave and progressive minister, but he was unsure whether this proposition could be made to fly politically. Rather than adopt it himself, he set up an inquiry. He hoped (as he quietly communicated to the inquiry) that it would recommend a digital licence fee. He could then gauge the reaction to our proposal and decide whether it was politically viable.

It would not have made sense simply to set up an inquiry into the digital licence fee. For one thing, there was a prior question which could not be ducked. How much money did the BBC need? For if the answer was, broadly, what it got at the time, there would be no need to introduce a new source of revenue.

It would also have been wrong simply to focus on the BBC's preferred solution. Other people had other solutions: pay-per-view, subscription, direct taxpayer finance. A few wild men of the right would have liked to wind up the BBC and leave broadcasting to the free market. Sensibly, Chris Smith asked us to proceed on the basis that the licence fee would remain the main source of funding for the remainder of the BBC's charter, which expired in 2006. Even so it was not possible in practice simply to ignore the question of other funding options.

Finally, there was the question of whether the BBC was appropriately organised. Should it own its own production facilities through its subsidiary, BBC Resources, or should it (as most private companies would have done) contract these out in the marketplace? Why should the BBC provide internet services free to the world outside Britain? Were its commercial activities outside Britain appropriately carried out as they were, by another subsidiary, BBC Worldwide? Were the BBC's rules for its trading behaviour sufficient to stop it behaving unfairly towards commercial competitors? Even if they were, did the BBC in practice police them adequately?

Was it efficient in collecting the licence fee? Should something be done to subsidise the licence fee for vulnerable groups, such as the elderly or the poor?

Our terms of reference were cast wide. They were so wide that the Secretary of State was in peril of being accused of chucking the whole thing into the long grass. He reacted as, in my experience, all Secretaries of State react: by giving us an absurdly truncated timetable. Starting work in January 1999, we were to report in July. We did, though with the benefit of hindsight, we might have done better to decide to treat his deadline with a modicum of flexibility.

In the case of the Davies Panel, the reason for my own presence was simple: Gavyn asked me. We had worked together on broadcasting in Number 10. He trusted my judgement as I trusted his and he rightly felt the need for a chum in the work ahead.

The inquiry, like that on the electoral system, was a harmonious one. It was made more harmonious by Gavyn's open style of conducting business. We were all-party – the Labour peer Jimmy Gordon, with broadcasting experience in Scotland, balanced by the Conservative peer Tony Newton, a former Health Secretary, and Julia Neuberger, a Liberal Democrat. Heather Rabbatts ticked various career boxes which included chief executive of a local authority. Helen Black was a trade unionist. Ruth Evans was a consumerist. Sir Alan Budd was an economist.

The workload on the panel in general, and on its chairman in particular, was considerable. I do not share the general view that DCMS is a weak department. I have dealt with it over a number of matters over the years – on broadcasting, on arts and heritage policy, and on sport because of my interest in racing. I have found its officials of high quality. It is sometimes suggested that it should be disbanded and its functions reallocated to the Home Office, where they originally lay, or to the industry department. This would have the advantages of having Secretaries of State with more perceived Whitehall clout. The countervailing disadvantage is that it would compete for the attention of those Secretaries of State with other and urgent issues. On balance, this would be a negative development.

However, being under the wing of a smallish department had its disadvantages for our inquiry. We were allocated a competent secretary to our work in Paul Heron, who had a small and dedicated team. But Heron continued with his normal broadcasting responsibilities. So much of the work that would normally have fallen to the secretariat in practice fell to the inquiry members, and to the chairman in particular.

It would not be true to say that everyone made an equal contribution. It never is. Some members were distracted by personal crises. Some took lines on particular issues but were less inclined to follow these up in detail. Shortly before we were due to report, it turned out that one member, who had promised to work up a proposal on which they had been particularly enthusiastic, had in fact neglected to do so. Fortunately, as a trained journalist, I was good at drafting fast.

We had also to take on board that we were not merely dealing with a government department. We were also dealing with the BBC, to whose future our recommendations would be crucial. The BBC is one of Britain's few world-class institutions, of which as a nation we are rightly proud. But like all world-class institutions, it had a strong ethos of its own, and a strong leader in John (now Lord) Birt.

This led to some comical incidents. One concerned an early decision of the panel. As we were inquiring for the public, it seemed right and proper that we should commission research designed to tell us what the public thought about some of the issues before us. We proposed to commission MORI, the opinion-polling company, to conduct such a survey.

This caused a tizzy at the Beeb. A senior BBC official rang Paul Heron. We were planning a survey, he was told. This could not be allowed. We would not know the right questions to ask.

The BBC commissioned polls of its own. Being a world-class

institution it had become experienced at this. In particular, it was experienced in phrasing the questions it asked to get the answers it wanted – for example on whether the licence fee represented value for money. By polling independently, we threatened to undermine this useful (to the Beeb) tradition. We simply ignored its objections.

On some of the issues facing us, we made no real progress. The concessionary scheme for example provided free licences for residential homes for the elderly. This was not easy to justify. Many poor people were not in residential homes. Many people in residential homes were not poor.

We received more evidence on this subject than on anything else. It did not amount to much. We as a committee were supposed to be well equipped to analyse broadcasting issues. The issue of the concessionary scheme, though important, was not one on which we could boast any particular expertise. In the end we concluded 'that the BBC's funding mechanism is not well suited to solving problems of income distribution and that the BBC should not be used as a benefits agency'. The only change we recommended was half-price licences for the blind, since they could not enjoy the full benefits of television.

Gordon Brown filled the gap for us. He decided that the TV licence should be free for over-75s. As so often, the Chancellor saw the opportunity to buy a few votes.

This was not a ridiculous decision, as older pensioners were clearly poorer than pensioners generally, both because they had had less opportunity to accumulate pension wealth before retiring and because they had been running down the wealth they did have for longer. At the same time we are living through an era where old people are no longer universally the poor in society. Indeed, having benefited from house price inflation, many pensioners are quite well off.

Free TV licences for the old proved a popular policy which no doubt tempted Brown to introduce a further universal benefit to the old in the form of the winter fuel allowance. Like all such concessions, once they are made they are not easily unmade. Giving new benefits to people is one thing. Taking away benefits they receive, and to which they then naturally feel entitled, is another. I am glad that free TV licences for pensioners over seventy-five was not the result of any recommendation of ours.

We did endorse the proposal for a supplementary digital licence, at a rate of £1.57 a month, but we were not confident that it would withstand the political process. We thus took the wise precaution of recommending that, should it not be adopted, the normal licence fee should be increased rather faster than inflation to produce the same amount of revenue.

The main dividing line in the committee was on how much extra the BBC should get. It wanted additional annual income of some £650m. None of us bought that, which we viewed as a sighting bid. But beyond that, our individual views were aligned along a spectrum. Some of our members, left to themselves, would have confined the increases in the licence fee to inflation, leaving the BBC effectively to give itself more scope by efficiency savings. Others, including the chairman, thought that this represented 'the BBC on a diet' and wanted much more than that.

There was no objective criterion on which to decide the answer. In the end it was a matter of judgement. We horse-traded. In the end we supported measures designed to increase its income by around £150m–£200m a year, an increase of 2–2.5 per cent a year in real terms from 2002 to 2006. Anything else would have to come from 'self-help' – what it could save through efficiency and what it could earn through commercial exploitation of its assets.

The report does not match Jenkins as a literary construct though, on the whole, it still seems to me a solid piece of work.

We were not so skilled in handling the aftermath of our report. We launched our report in July and then we went on holiday. While we were away, the rats got at our recommendation of a supplementary digital licence fee. Commercial interests objected. The rival broadcasters objected. So did those in the digital equipment business, who thought our recommendation could discourage take-up of their new products. The politicians wavered. Number 10, which had warned us against launching when news was short during the summer, took fright. The digital licence fee never came about. A relatively modest real increase in the licence fee was the outcome – better than nothing, but not as much as we should have liked.

Fortunately, the BBC managed to surpass itself in self-help. Indeed, with the benefit of hindsight, it got too much money rather than too little. This led to dangerous increases in the amount it was prepared to pay for rights, sports rights in particular; to scandalously high salaries for talent; to excessive rewards for its own top executives. For a while, under Greg Dyke's incumbency as Birt's successor, it led to an alarming rise in staffing.

There were other recommendations in the report which did have a positive effect. One such was the role of the National Audit Office.

The NAO is the independent parliamentary body charged with auditing the effectiveness with which government money is spent. The BBC World Service, which is directly funded by the taxpayer, was subject to NAO audit. However, the rest of BBC expenditure was not. The chairman of the Commons Public Accounts Committee had written to the inquiry pointing out this anomaly. I was inclined to agree and after the inquiry, by now a member of the House of Lords, I pursued the matter.

The BBC was utterly opposed. They constructed an argument that licence fee income was not public spending. As that crumbled, they tried a more plausible argument, that NAO audit would compromise the independence of the Beeb. As audit was a parliamentary function, it could be used by politicians as a weapon to pressure the corporation to change its editorial policies.

Though this was superficially plausible, it did not stand up for long for it mistook the role of the NAO. The NAO does not seek to determine policy. It seeks to determine whether the way in which policy is carried out is efficient in its use of public money.

An individual member of the House of Lords has little power. All you can hope to do is, on occasion, identify a winnable battle and fight it with all the weapons at your disposal. This means campaigning in the media as well as speaking in the House. It means using lobbying guile with ministers and the opposition parties. It requires, even if your case is sound, persistence.

Over the years, many members of the Lords achieve the occasional victory. This was mine. Tessa Jowell, an old friend who succeeded Chris Smith as Culture Secretary, was persuaded.

We formulated a compromise. The NAO would be allowed to audit BBC spending but with the topics it investigated being chosen by agreement with the corporation. The NAO, wisely, decided at first to investigate relatively minor issues, on which it invariably gave the BBC a clean bill of health. As time went on, the NAO's teeth have become sharper and it is no doubt on occasion a thorn in the corporation's flesh. However, even the BBC knows that the clock cannot be turned back. Indeed, *sotto voce,* BBC officials have been known to concede that on this, the panel was right. NAO audit is not now controversial, though the BBC continues to resist giving it full powers.

On this issue, I was at loggerheads with the BBC, though I generally regarded myself as supporter. I wrote an introduction to a Social Market Foundation pamphlet on public service broadcasting by Gavyn Davies. There I said we were both fans of the BBC but 'he is the sort of fan who would travel 300 miles on a wet Saturday and I am the home-only sort'.

The issue of public service broadcasting refuses to lie down. There are those who believe that public service broadcasting should be confined to certain kinds of programming – grand opera for example or classical drama. That would mean the end of the BBC as we know it. You could not expect Joe Public to voluntarily contribute enough to an organisation which produces programmes he does not wish to watch. Indeed a big problem has been those who are 'underserved' by the corporation, i.e. who do not get the programmes they want from it. Keeping the BBC presence in sport is important to them, and therefore that too constitutes public service broadcasting.

In the subsequent argument, too, we were able to make the case that the BBC generates a consumer surplus. That is to say, people watch its programmes because they are free whereas they may not be able to afford to pay-per-view or even rising subscriptions for alternative providers. This too we regarded as public service.

The BBC's standing in Parliament ebbs and flows. Just when it is on the up, some disaster seems to come along which erodes its position. The Jonathan Ross scandal (after he insulted an innocent ageing actor) was one example, especially since Mr Ross was particularly richly rewarded. Another concerned the Middle East. I have rarely seen parliamentarians more angry than when the BBC refused to broadcast an appeal for Gaza on the grounds it would prejudice its independence.

The Conservatives in particular have blown hot and cold on what they will do to the BBC. The controversial Culture Secretary, Jeremy Hunt wants the BBC to concentrate on serious programming, but no firm and final announcement has been made about the future of the BBC Trust, which replaced the governors, and which he has threatened to get rid of. Still, the appointment of Lord Patten, a well-placed Tory, must make revolution less likely.

Meanwhile the corporation has been subjected to eye-watering cuts. It now has to pay the cost of the World Service, which used to be borne by the FCO. Mark Thompson, a steely director general, seems confident that this can be achieved without decimating services. It is a formidable challenge.

The Davies Panel did not lead to everything it would have liked to lead to, and the future remains in doubt. In general the BBC has managed the transition to the digital era with skill and a foresight remarkable in a public enterprise; indeed, it has had a good decade since we reported. Let us hope it can weather cuts and the gibes of its competitors in the decade to come.

CHAPTER 14

LIVING LIKE A LORD 1999–

On the day my peerage was announced in the papers, the phone rang soon after 7.00 am. It was Derek Gladwin, my General and Municipal Workers' boss and now a Lord. 'Congratulations, David, well done. And don't let them sell you a coat of arms.' He told me that new peers were sent off to see an official called Garter King of Arms to settle their title. Garter was eager that they agree to buy a personal coat of arms, which cost £3,000. Don't be conned, said Gladwin.

A few minutes later Bill McCarthy rang with the same message. And then... well, and then and then and then. It must have been approaching 10.00 when I got a call from Peter Hardy, once Tony Crosland's Commons parliamentary private secretary and a Yorkshire MP, who was also now a peer.

'Hello Peter. I expect you've rung to tell me not to buy a coat of arms.'

There was a silence.

'You haven't got a coat of arms, have you?' I asked.

'Aye, I've got a coat of arms,' the puzzled Hardy responded.

I was desperate to end this part of the conversation. I remembered that Hardy had a great love for dogs and was also an active and passionate campaigner for badgers. So I thought I'd make a joke of it.

'The badger couchant and the retriever rampant, I suppose.'

'Aye, t'badger couchant and t'retriever rampant.'

I am not moved by tradition. So I was not in a positive mood when I visited Garter for the advertised conversation.

'Now, your title. Not as big as a big city, not as small as a hamlet. What's it to be?' he said, in an accent that made the Queen sound estuary.

'Tooting Bec, perhaps?' Tooting Bec Common was where I had

lived for many years, but, besides, I liked the echo of the Tooting Liberation Front in a peer's title.

'Tooting Bec, Tooting Bec,' said Garter, his scarlet face turning even more puce. 'That doesn't sound quite appropriate for a peer of the realm.'

'It's Tooting Bec or nothing. What are you going to do about it?' I am afraid I responded.

As I well knew, there was nothing he could do, and Tooting Bec it was. I later called my racing greyhound Tooting Becky after my daughter and my title. Before I accepted the peerage I had had a conversation with Denis Carter, Labour's much respected chief whip. He told me about my duty to vote and also about the hours.

The latter came as a shock to me: I had thought there would be a division most nights at around 10.00, as in the Commons. I had no idea that the Lords were essentially on a running whip, with votes possible from 3.00 into, in rare cases, the small hours.

Then he went on to money. This was important since I should have to leave my job. *The Economist* rightly would not allow a practising politician to write for it.

'Have you got a second home?'

Yes, I said. I had. Indeed, I spent much of my time in my home in Wales though not as much as I did once a member of the House.

'Good. You claim your daily overnight allowance on that as your main home.'

I later checked that I had heard right with Derek Gladwin. I also checked with a member of the Top Salary Review Board that this was their understanding of the rules too. Both agreed. I therefore claimed.

I later figured briefly in a *Sunday Times* exposé of peers' claims for main homes. Others were more comprehensively done over, and some were nearly prosecuted.

As it happens, my claim was in order not only according to custom and practice at the time, but according to the rules set out after the 'scandal' had broken. They specified that your main home was where you spent most nights when the House was not sitting and that, for me, was always my home in Wales. But I can understand why others who might not have passed that test claimed. We were told to, by those who were supposed to know.

In this there was an element of what might be called convenient hypocrisy. The time required of Lords had increased over the years. In 1959–60, the first session for which figures are available, the House sat for 113 days, for an average of 3 hours 59 minutes a day – 450 hours a year in total, or, say, thirteen normal 35-hour working weeks in a year. In 2007–08, the latest full session for which figures are available, the House sat for 164 days, for an average of 6 hours 46 minutes. This equates to a total of 1,059 hours or the equivalent of thirty full working weeks. In the process, it has become impossible for any working peer, however industrious, to hold down a full-time job outside the Lords.

But we had to live. The obvious course would have been to pay us a modest salary. That would have been straightforward. However, that would not have been how it appeared in the popular newspapers. 'Tony's Cronies cash in' – the *Daily Mail*; 'Peers pick your pockets' – the *Express*. The powers that be thought that would not please voters. Instead it was decided that we should enjoy reasonably generous expenses and get by like that. So we did, not noticing that the ethos of public life was changing round us. The *Sunday Times* stories, which caused immense pain to many peers and their spouses, finally sent out a signal we could no longer ignore.

I was introduced to the House on 13 October 1999. It was a delightful occasion, a small lunch attended by family and by my lordly friends the Gladwins, the McCarthys and Joyce Gould.

The introduction ceremony used to involve a good deal of walking backwards and tipping cocked hats. All the while, the performance of the new peer was marked by Maurice Peston, a Labour peer with a sense of humour, which made them all the more nervous. Even I could manage today's simplified ceremony. I was now The Lord Lipsey, a Labour peer. When asked, I said I was a Tony Crony.

I would like to say I settled in quickly. Formally I did, managing for example a maiden speech on the euro which got applause for being delivered without notes. Except when I have not had much time to prepare, I never read speeches, and try so far as possible to minimise my use of notes. Speeches which are not read out don't seem so fluent in Hansard, but they have much more impact on the floor of the House.

I did not have an office at first. I camped in the enormous Royal Gallery, lined on one side with a picture of Waterloo and on the other of Trafalgar. I used to joke I have the biggest office in the world, which may have been true. I also joked that we always asked French visitors to meet us in the gallery, which wasn't true – or at least it wasn't until, with a certain lack of tact, the House authorities chose to accommodate President Sarkozy there when he addressed Parliament. Later I got a shared office, where my desk was next to my dear lordly friend Baroness Golding, an ex-MP who shares my interest in racing, betting and our fellow peers.

I found the hours difficult to get used to. I was accustomed to getting on with work, and going home when it was finished. That was not possible. I resented in particular a duty imposed by the whips called 'roster'. This meant that chosen Labour peers were ordered to stay each night until close of business. This was purely precautionary. If a vote was called and fewer than forty peers were present the House was inquorate. The whips could not risk that. But I did not like sitting in the gloom of the palace, where the catering then was boarding school plus, while business droned on. I wanted to be at home with my wife.

At first, I assumed that I would want to become a minister. Just as my desire for a political career had eroded, so too did this desire. For one thing, if you wanted advancement, you needed to be impeccable in your attendance, as well as loyal. Your duties were wide – you were responsible for every bit of legislation your department brought forward including subjects on which you might know nearly nothing. You were torn between peers who expected you to bow to reasoned argument, and Commons ministers who expected you to concede nothing. The hours were long, the pay (for ministers were paid) modest, the reward exiguous. I guiltily remembered the contempt with which we in the Department of

Environment had treated poor Baroness Birk all those years ago. Within a couple of years of arriving, I had decided that a ministerial life was not for me and wrote what may have been an otiose letter to Tony Blair to say so.

No ministerial career was in prospect, so what was I to do with the Lords? I enjoyed in moderation the respect it brought, though I did not much use the title. It provided a comfortable place to hang out. The attendants in particular went out of the way to look after us, and the library was like having a private research staff.

There is one less obvious yet considerable pleasure in lordly life. Most of those who are there are past the peak of their active lives. They are no longer competing with each other. And so, instead of the catty gossip that pervades practically everywhere else I have worked, peers tend to speak well of each other. They are kind to each other, friendly to each other, informal rather than formal and restrict showing off to a minimum. It is something we no longer feel the need to do. All that makes the Lords a most agreeable place – the best club in London, it is often said, and I am not surprised that people are prepared to go to some lengths to try to become members. I made one good decision on arrival: only to speak on things I knew about. This meant, in particular, on the subjects of the government commissions on which I had been involved, though I dabbled in economics.

I only once allowed myself an exception to this rule. It was a disaster. The government was proposing to cut back the universal right to jury trial. Its plan seemed to me to be, in limited cases, sensible. You could not have criminals getting off because they intimidated juries or fraudsters running free because the jurors could not understand company accounts. The House of Lords was high on one of its civil rights kicks and few were willing to support the government. So I did.

I thought I had written a good speech. I was wrong. In a crowded House, I was bombing. And then I made one huge error.

What I said was this. 'It is said that black people do not trust magistrates and that if they cannot opt for jury trial they will lose confidence in justice … Some of them may opt for jury trial in the hope that they will get an "O. J. Simpson". They hope that there will be enough black jurors who are fundamentally hostile to the criminal justice system."*

This seemed to me, indeed it still seems to me, likely to be true, though I have no solid evidence. It was also unwise and was interpreted as racist.

'Never explain, never apologise,' said Benjamin Disraeli. This seems to me to be silly advice. I did not seek to explain but I did apologise. For a day or two, I felt utterly wretched. Then I realised that no one but me remembered it, and got on with life.

There are as many ways of being a member of the House of Lords as there are members. Some speak on everything. Others speak rarely. Many regard question time as the centrepiece of their day. Others think it is a waste of time. Some spend hours in the chamber. Others don't. Some spend hours being talked at by lobbyists. Others prefer to make up their own minds. Some attend many of the valuable all-party committees which play an important part in linking Westminster with the world outside. Others find them beneath their dignity.

For me, I am an all-party committee man. I do not spend much time in the chamber and speak less often than many. I try to concern myself not on what effect my activities have on other members of the House but on what effect they have on the things that matter to the public.

I think that being available to broadcasters is an important part of the role peers play in our polity, less partisan and more analytical than members of the Commons as they usually are. I have always written a good deal for newspapers and believe that, in terms of impact, a good piece in *The Times* is generally worth ten great speeches in the House. I have even achieved, occasionally, the epitome of public prominence. I have appeared on the *Today* programme.

---

* Lords' Hansard, 20 January 2000, c. 1257.

As the example of the National Audit Office and the BBC shows, as a peer you can occasionally change things. You cannot change big things which are the prerogative of Prime Ministers and Cabinet ministers (and God). However, what seems a small thing to say to a national newspaper editor may be a big thing to the group directly affected.

Another example of something that I shifted is the super-casino. The Labour government under Blair had eventually decided that there should be one and an independent inquiry had determined it should be in Manchester. In the Lords, however, there was strong opposition. One set of opponents were the religious, a strong force in the upper chamber, who did not like gambling. Another set of opponents were those who did like gambling, but thought the super-casino should be in Blackpool not Manchester. Another set of opponents, who included me, had no firm view where it should be, but thought the decision for Manchester had been taken with inadequate parliamentary consideration.

The matter was complicated by the fact that Blair – a liberal on gambling – was about to leave Number 10 and Gordon Brown, who was against it, was about to arrive. The super casino had to be got through before Tony went.

We desperately sought a deal with Tessa Jowell, the Culture Secretary, which would extinguish the Lords revolt. She just needed to add a little more parliamentary procedure and give Blackpool a glimmer of hope, and we could face down the antis. Now I am devoted to Tessa, who is a committed and principled woman, but quick decisions are not her greatest strength. She made concessions but always too late. By the time she was willing to say what was needed to get the super-casino through, it was too late to call off the dogs. The order establishing it was defeated in the Lords, and before anything could happen, Brown had taken over at Number 10. If I had not got involved there would probably be a super-casino under construction in Manchester.

There are some secrets to being an effective peer – that is to say, a peer who occasionally gets things changed. The first is that you have to work in a bi-partisan way. No single party has a majority in the Lords, though the present coalition comes close. Moreover the House of Lords listens most closely to opinion which comes from more than one group of peers within the House.

Secondly, you have to work behind closed doors as well as on the floor of the House and in debate. In particular, it is a help to know and to be able to talk directly to Commons ministers. Commons ministers tend to despise the Lords but this is born as much of ignorance as anything else. Put forward a well-argued case in a moderate way, be open to compromise and be willing to give all the credit to the minister if a problem is solved, and you can, not often but sometimes, make a difference.

As I write this, a potentially huge change in the House of Lords is in train. Indeed, opponents of the change refer to it as 'abolition' of the Lords, not reform. The Conservative/Lib Dem coalition is committed to bringing forward plans to make the Lords an elected chamber.

The Tories would have put Lords reform on the back burner had they won the election. Having lost the AV referendum, however, the Lib Dems want Lords' reform to compensate. My own Labour Party is committed to election, too.

I am not many years off the age at which I should be contemplating retirement anyway, so I hope I may be acquitted of self-interest when I say that I think this is not a desirable development.

One day, Britain might sensibly dispense with having a second parliamentary chamber. For that to happen, the following conditions would have to be met. First, the electoral system for the House of Commons would have to be reformed so no future government (as did the Labour government between 2005 and 2010) could enjoy a large overall majority in the House when it has the support of just over one-third of those who voted, and of one elector in five. Second, with that would have to go a change in the style of the Commons so it no longer consisted of two large parties yaa-booing at each other with a few others yaa-booing from the sidelines. Third, the Commons would have to undergo a thorough reform of its procedures so that legislation was properly and fully debated. Fourth, and to have time for this, MPs would have to stop spending most of their time acting as Citizens' Advice workers for their constituents. Fifth – most important and least likely – governments would have to cure themselves of their addiction to legislating, an addiction that is leading to more and more, longer and longer legislation, much of it useless or worse.

These conditions will not be met in my lifetime and I hazard a guess that they will not be met in my 28-year-old daughter's lifetime either. So for now we shall continue to need a second chamber.

What do we want it to do? Who do we want to sit in it? I put these questions in this order because this is the order in which, logically, they must be answered. The last government chose not to do so in its White Paper on Lords' reform – or at least it did so only in the sense of asserting, without argument, that the second chamber should do precisely what it does now, and with precisely the same powers as it now enjoys. Fortunately, however, with the two houses now at loggerheads – the Commons voting for a 100 per cent elected Lords and the Lords for a 100 per cent appointed Lords – the debate is still live. The 2007 vote in Parliament brought headlines crying 'The End of the Peers Show'.

But the 2007 vote merely brought the curtain down on Act 1. The election of the new parliament raised it for Act 2. I should be surprised if this did not turn out to be a five-act drama, with many a twist in the plot yet to come.

What are the roles of the Lords? First, it revises legislation. Second, it assists the Commons in holding the executive to account – sometimes going as far as to act as one of the checks and balances in Britain's constitution by delaying half-baked measures.

Its contribution to revision is essential because the Commons fulfils this function poorly. MPs divide on strictly partisan lines. Ministers treat committee proceedings as a chore. Members do their post during proceedings or pop out, returning only for divisions. Votes are whipped. If a vote does perchance change a Bill (a rarity), the change is often reversed on the floor of the Commons again by application of a whip. Worse, huge chunks of Bills are simply not considered by the committees as legislation is now invariably timetabled.

Many Bills are only scrutinised in their entirety because the Lords does so. Lords' procedure for the scrutiny of Bills is itself flawed, as we shall see.

In 2009–10, 2,031 amendments to Bills were considered by their Lordships, of which 565 were carried. These are crude figures, but there is no perfect truth to be had here. An amendment made in the Lords may be entirely rejected or entirely accepted by the Commons. However, frequently, a Lords amendment might be largely rejected but with some concessions, or largely accepted but with some limitations, or a 50–50 compromise of sorts might be achieved. Moreover, the government, sensing mounting pressure in the Lords, might bring forward their own pre-emptive amendment in the Commons. According to the Constitution Unit at University College London, around four out of ten Lords defeats lead to Lords 'wins' over the Commons.

The seemingly ridiculous process of ping-pong on a Bill serves a useful purpose. The Lords amend a Bill, the Commons disagree, the Lords try again, the Commons vetoes again, and so on. In general, the Lords ultimately bows to the will of the elected House, though it is becoming increasingly stroppy, as its resistance to restricting jury trial and its stand on terrorist detentions shows. It is so particularly when the government decides (as all governments decide) to put liberty second to expediency and to play fast and loose with the spirit of the constitution. In 2007–08 in the course of ping-pong, the Commons accepted thirty-three Lords amendments.

That is public stuff, but less generally known is the process of negotiation that precedes ping-pong. For example, in the case of the important Communications Act 2003, in the end there were sixteen amendments of substance that the Lords wanted and the government resisted. I gathered the peers involved in a room, we chose four of the sixteen to press, rang the minister and told her that she must accept them or continue deadlock. The minister graciously acceded. The eventual Act was much better for this process.

The second well-known function of the present Lords is in holding the executive to account, and occasionally in forcing it to think again before it acts. The Lords adds value to the Commons in this function for several reasons. First, although most Lords belong to parties, it is not a partisan place. Cross-party alliances are the norm. Second, and consequentially, this means ministers cannot answer questions with insults. They are expected to display detailed and accurate factual knowledge of matters within their remit. Third, for reasons we shall come to, the Lords concentrates on different matters than the Commons: foreign affairs in particular, and also defence, in which today's Commons is singularly uninterested. The same is largely true of agriculture, where the Lords contains a well-informed group of practising farmers. The Lords also goes in for debates on matters that otherwise might never get a parliamentary hearing: in 2001, for example, eight peers participated in a short debate which I initiated on greyhound welfare.

There is, however, a third function of the House of Lords: not one noted in the constitutional texts, but which is at least equally important in our nation's affairs. It is simply this: the House of Lords provides a body of men and women, mostly of some distinction, who have a duty to attend to public affairs and who are available to contribute from a largely non-partisan perspective to national debate, and to the resolution of intractable problems. These men and women are also available to lead or participate in the gamut of commissions, public inquiries, panels, tribunals and self-regulatory and co-regulatory bodies, which form an essential part of our constitutional arrangements.

Horrible death caused by social service neglect? Send for Lord Laming. Languages in decline in our schools? Summon Lord Dearing. What should be done about pensions? Lord Turner is your man. Even reform of the Lords itself was addressed by a Lord, Lord Wakeham, who was joined in his team of twelve by three other peers.

Within Westminster there is a correlate of this in the work of the many all-party committees on specific issues, ranging from the BBC group to the brass bands group, with all points between. These are open to peers and MPs. Attendance, however, is dominated by members of the upper House by a factor of two or three to one. This is not surprising: MPs have competing duties and obligations, some of which are directly related to their need to win support in their constituencies. However, if the non-elected members of these committees were no longer there, most would go into abeyance.

These then are the central functions which (pending the Utopia of unicameralism) the House of Lords plays. If it is to do so effectively, who should be in it? Should it be (as the Commons wanted) an all-elected House or should it be (as the Lords wanted) an all-appointed Lords? Note 'be', not 'remain', since nearly everyone agrees that the remaining hereditary peerage should be abolished. Nearly everyone also agrees that appointments should mainly be made by a statutory appointments commission in order to prevent any risk of so-called 'cash for honours' scandals, with the Prime Minister's patronage correspondingly reduced.

For the revising role, there is no contest. Appointed peers bring to this task the expertise that got them their elevation in the first place. Of course, to deal with a much-heard canard, all peers are not expert in everything. What matters is that, on any serious matter of public policy, there are invariably between ten and twenty peers who from their professional or academic lives know a lot about the subject. Since the average age of a life peer is sixty-nine, they will have an accumulated knowledge, usually ending up in a top or near-top job in the field. It is not to denigrate MPs that they, having entered the House at a relatively early age, simply cannot compete. Moreover, appointed peers are not distracted with the 101 tasks that go with being elected: looking after constituents, servicing the local press and generally strutting their stuff. This applies *a fortiori* to opposition frontbench spokespeople, who are not (unlike their Commons colleagues) trying to sustain a progressive political career. If you doubt this, take any Bill and read in full the proceedings on it in each House.

Some believe that the House would still attract this talent and experience if it was elected. This is implausible. Its members now are (ex-MPs excepted) people who rejected a political career with campaigning at its centre; they are hardly likely to fancy flocking to the hustings. Age too comes into this: knocking on doors is hardly a pastime for your average sexagenarian or septuagenarian. And how would crossbenchers, without the support of party, ever hope to get elected? Lords' life, save if you are using it to propagate knowledge and experience, is not one for which many people would choose to go through the business of election.

There is one formidable argument for election and it is one from first principle: it is not right that people should legislate who have not been elected. This is a high-sounding sentiment, but lacks substance. First, the kind of things the Lords revises are not the great and political issues underlying Bills. They are the fine detail, in which neither the electorate nor its representatives in the Commons take much interest. Second, so long as the Lords remains a second chamber – namely, one which ultimately bows to the will of the Commons – it can only legislate where it persuades its Commons to agree with them.

The final role of the Lords, as a pool of notables for inquiries and so on, could not possibly be replicated from within an elected House. Whatever qualities lead people to seek election, they are not these. Moreover, it has to be said that elected members of the House of Lords would be unlikely to be of high calibre. Their career path is limited. On the government's proposal at any rate they would serve only a single fifteen-year term.

The House in which they serve has limited powers. Elected Lords would be those who had failed to make the Commons, failed to make the European Parliament, failed (if Scots or Welsh) to make the Parliament or Assembly, and failed to get far on their local council.

If you start from function, the arguments for a wholly (or at least overwhelmingly) appointed House of Lords are powerful. This, doubtless, is why the supporters of election resort so readily to rhetoric, to mockery of supporters of appointment. Are we not merely today's descendants of Lord Wellington, who denounced the 1832 Reform Bill as 'mere democracy'? One answer to this is that some of us at any rate, while favouring appointment over election, also favour a radical overhaul of the way the House of Lords works. It succeeds, when it succeeds, despite its manifold shortcomings. The procedure whereby most Bills are considered in debate on the floor of the House is absurdly antiquated. Evidence-taking committees would be much better. This would free up more time on the floor for general debates and executive scrutiny. There is too much speech-making and too little common conversation. Ways of organising scrutiny that do not always require specific amendments to be proposed could be added. Too much is whipped which could be left to free votes. The pomp and flummery are unnecessary and detract from the House's standing as a serious body. Secondary legislation is too easily approved. And so on and so on. Lots about the House of Lords needs to change if it is to fulfil its function better – but not its appointed nature, which must be the bedrock upon which its future rests.

CHAPTER 15

A JOBBING PEER 1999–

Y ou can't be a conscientious member of the House of Lords and hold down a full-time job. But being in the House of Lords is not in itself a full-time job. So, I have always held a portfolio of bits and pieces of other roles, paid and unpaid. This works well. No one minds coming to the Lords for a meeting, because you can profitably fill the *longueurs* between House business you are interested in and votes you have to be there for. Your outside interests inform your Lords work and *vice versa*.

If asked my occupation, I reply 'jobbing peer'. At one point I tallied up the number of bits and pieces of jobs, trusteeships and honorary this, that and the other that I had amassed and they totalled twenty-two. Not all need covering in this chapter. But some were very much part of my life during my Lords years from 1999 to the present.

One such was that, for a few years, I had a second life as a regulator. I enjoyed two regulatory functions: as a member of the board of the Personal Investment Authority (PIA), the predecessor of the Financial Services Authority in regulating personal financial products, and as a member of the Council of the Advertising Standards Authority.

I got on the PIA board by accident. My companion on the commission on long-term care, Lord Joffe, was also a doughty campaigner against the abuses of the financial services industry, particularly those firms selling pensions. I gave him a hand with press work. Colette Bowe, a long-standing friend back in my government days, noticed. As chief executive of the PIA, she probably welcomed a supportive chum on the board, and Joe Palmer, the chairman, took her recommendation.

The PIA involved a lot of hard pounding. This was especially so since Labour in opposition pledged itself to abolish the PIA. I was sent on a mission to Alistair Darling, then a shadow Treasury spokesman, to talk him out of it in favour of a 'twin peaks' solution, a retail regulator and a separate prudential regulator. I failed miserably. Now, however, the structure which Labour rejected is being restored in the wake of the pig's ear the FSA made of the banking crisis. We were right – but fifteen years too soon.

The most interesting work was on the tribunal which heard cases against erring financial advisers. Most people when they hear of bad treatment by independent financial advisers (IFAs) probably think of villains like Bernard Madoff. We saw the odd small-scale equivalent, but most miscreants were not like that.

Typically, an IFA would come before us accused of forging a client's signature on the paperwork. It sounded terrible but on examination it usually turned out that there was a nearly innocent explanation. The client had gone on holiday just as some important deadline had dawned or their car was out of petrol and they couldn't get round to get the client's signature. In other words, they were cutting corners rather than committing fraud.

Of course this could not be allowed. But I found it hard to deprive someone of their livelihood over such infringements. My style was to give the miscreant a nasty hour in front of the committee and then perhaps a few days in agony waiting for the outcome. I saw no reason to add greatly to that as a penalty. Proper penalties should have been reserved for the rip-off bankers, who made and then lost billions by ignoring the risks of the products they were selling. They, however, are big people, so they invariably get off scot free, pensions intact.

That was brought home to me because I also served under Tony Crosland's former private secretary, later permanent secretary of the Environment Department, Terry Heiser, on the PIA's pension review sub-committee. Those who perpetrated pensions mis-selling were not mostly small men. These were big institutions who had cut corners to sell pensions on which they levied unconscionable charges. They deserved everything they got and perhaps more.

The PIA board was a mixture of industry representatives and

those who represented no one but themselves. I certainly never noticed that the latter were any harder on those who had offended than the former.

However regulators try – and the PIA under Bowe tried – it is not easy to get it right. In theory, you should be working to broad principles, leaving it to firms themselves to put them into practice. In practice, one rule led to another – and besides you could never trust the firms entirely to get it right. The industry hated us for imposing too much and costing too much. The public hated us for imposing too little and knew nothing of the cost. Regulation has come some way since then and the secrets of good regulation are widely understood, thanks partly to the work of the government's Better Regulation Task Force and its variants. Whether in practice the problems have been overcome is less obvious.

My time on the PIA led to one subsequent episode in my life, as short as it was profitless. The FSA, the PIA's successor, was forced by law to set up a Financial Services Consumers Panel, to represent the consumer interest. This was a good idea, since the regulator was inevitably susceptible to capture by the large and powerful firms it supervised. A consumer-oriented counterweight could help it.

However, when in 2008 I was headhunted to chair it, I resisted. I had, as it happens, a friend who had been chair and others who sat on it. It was a ghastly body, understaffed, underpaid, regarded with a mixture of hostility and contempt by many at the FSA and with virtually no public profile.

But I was seduced. I was persuaded that the FSA now did want a strong and effective Consumers Panel and that I was the man for the job. I therefore approached it with a measure of excitement. It came as a bit of a shock that the FSA, once I had been recruited, went back to default mode in its attitude to the panel. It came as more of a shock that some panel members seemed entirely happy with this. Like hostages who become accustomed to the relationship with their captors, they did not have any ambitions save to comment at length on the lack of wisdom of the FSA's policies and then to slink off muttering when their comments were ignored. I stood this for six months and then quit.

Unlike the PIA, the Advertising Standards Authority struggled much less with what it was doing. The ASA could impose no penalties save banning adverts from appearing again. Often campaigns were over by the time it ruled on them. Yet its regulation was respected by the public, which constantly rated its effectiveness very highly. The advertising industry took it immensely seriously, and only partly because an adverse ruling from the ASA disqualified a campaign from winning any advertising awards.

Council consisted of a cross-section of the (fairly) great and the good, who got on and reached sensible verdicts. The staff showed what can be achieved by young people, with a task they believe in and proper respectful management. The chairs, successively (Lord) Bill Rodgers, (Lord) Gordon Borrie and (Lord) Chris Smith, were all of outstanding quality. It was always interesting. I remember the long debate about whether it was OK to describe a chicken as free range when the doors of its shed were left open, though it transpired that the chickens, sensible creatures, never ventured out. We saved the public from lots of lies.

Racing has been a big part of my life. Whether the role of one's godmother should be to introduce one to vice I leave it for others to debate, though, having failed with my children, I am certainly trying hard to educate my grandchildren into the mysteries of the turf.

In the Lords I had the great advantage that I could combine my passion with work, and indeed on occasion be paid for it. I even wrote a racing novel, a pastiche Dick Francis, called *Counter Coup*. (Forthcoming, with luck.)

My first job in racing was as an independent non-executive director of the Horserace Betting Totalisator Board – the Tote for short. I got the job by the simple expedient of answering an ad in the newspaper. In my time there, I was responsible for various tasks. For example, at every Cheltenham Gold Cup I was invited to the Tote box. There I had the task of holding the hand of Henrietta Knight, the great trainer of the leading steeplechaser Best Mate, who is the only person in my lifetime who actually described me as soothing!

I was close to Peter Jones, chairman of the Tote. We went through some hard battles together. One was when Peter Savill, chairman of the British Horseracing Board, was trying to get an increase in the money paid to racing by bookmakers. In a conflict of interests that should never have been allowed, he was a member of the Tote board. His tactics were simple. He would get the Tote to agree an increase; other bookmakers would then have to follow suit or do without the racing product in their betting shops.

Gerry Grimstone, a board member who later chaired Standard Life, and I took a different view. Yes, the Tote was there to help racing. All our profits went to racing. No, however, we were not there to interfere in the workings of the market to benefit racing. Our duty as directors was clear: to maximise the long-term profits of the Tote. That would incidentally help racing, but we were not there to turn the Tote into racing's weapon in its endless war with bookmakers.

I had a special Croslandite difficulty. Bets were mostly struck by small people, often poor people, in betting shops. Horses were mostly owned by big people, often rich people. I have never seen why the former should subsidise the latter. Nobody subsidises the rich man's yacht or his villa on the Med. Why should his horses be any different? Yes, bookmakers should pay a fair commercial rate for the product racing provides. But the moans of the wealthy merely reinforced me in my stubborn resistance to their claims.

We successfully resisted the Savill ('Jimmy Savile' as I christened him) plot. He blamed Jones, and the feud between the two simmered on for years.

Peter Jones followed a chairman, in Woodrow Wyatt, who was curiously engaging but at the same time outrageous. Wyatt had used the Tote to support the hospitality which sustained his political activities, sycophancy to Margaret Thatcher and his hobnobbing with royalty. Jones turned it round.

True, we had a bit of luck. We bought lots of betting shops when others were selling them. The others wanted to get into the internet side of the trade, but as a nationalised industry the Tote was inhibited in the degree to which it could make risky investments in that. So we bought shops *faute de mieux*. It turned out there was a deal of profit in betting shops, which continued to make good money long after their expected sell-by date.

However, our profitability had a downside. Gordon Brown as Chancellor saw that the Tote was worth something and made it government policy to sell it. He wanted to show he was a more determined privatiser than the Tories were.

Morally, Brown's decision was indefensible. It was purely by chance that the government owned the Tote. It had never put a penny into it nor did it contribute to it save by appointing the directors.

We could have resisted flat out. We did indeed examine the law to see if there was any way in which the courts would overthrow Brown's plan. Unfortunately, no fewer than four eminent QCs concluded that such an action would have no chance whatsoever. That did not stop racing's grandstanders continuing to demand that a challenge be mounted. A challenge would have poured money out of racing and into the pockets of the lawyers.

Instead, we sought to shift the policy to being one of selling the Tote to racing. The hope was that, if owned by racing, the loyalty of its customers would increase, it would improve its efficiency, get into businesses which government ownership inhibited it from getting into, and in the end make more money for racing. We sought a deal by which the government sold the Tote to racing half-price and this was accepted.

I was charged with running a new body, the Shadow Racing Trust, including representatives of the major racing stakeholders. This would be the board that would be the purchaser, and subsequently the shareholder, in the new model Tote. A more commercial board would be appointed to take the business decisions.

Unfortunately, we hit a snag – the European Union. Though the government had done nothing to build the Tote, it did formally own it. To sell the Tote to racing at a reduced price would represent, so the Eurocrats opined, illegal state aid to the racing industry. We banged at Brussels's door but it remained firmly closed. The hard work of the trust came to nothing and, sadly, we wound ourselves up.

Even as he left office, Brown was repeating that he wanted to sell the Tote. Sadly the coalition was equally determined to flog off the Tote, and in the summer of 2011, it was sold to Fred Done, a bookmaker.

One door closes but another opens and in my case that was in greyhound racing.

It was by the merest chance that I had got interested in greyhound racing. In 1976, after the humiliating defeat of Tony Crosland in the Labour leadership election, I thought one Friday I should go somewhere where I could be absolutely certain of not meeting anyone in politics. Wimbledon Stadium, just down the road from where I lived, seemed the best bet.

As I breasted the steps leading up to the grandstand, I saw coming towards me an unmistakeable figure. Matthew Oakeshott, who once beat me for the job as chocolate soldier to Roy Jenkins, was coming up the other side. Oakeshott was not new to the dogs. He introduced me to David Richardson, a Wimbledon bookmaker who had also been a cellist at the Royal College of Music, and one thing led to another.

Eventually Richardson and I became partners in a dog called Park Laddie. Park Laddie was one of the slowest dogs to leave the traps in greyhound racing, a trait usually fatal to success. But he had tremendous middle pace. To watch him fly past lesser beasts down the back straight brought whoops to the most cynical. He came within hundredths of a second of the track record at Wimbledon. We paid £600, but were offered £3,000 within weeks – and in those days £3,000 was better than a slap in the belly with a wet fish.

Alas! Park Laddie was unsound. He broke a hock a few weeks after that and was never the same again. We were told to retire him.

The chief kennel hand promised they would 'see him all right', which sounded like honourable retirement. But to my shame I never checked. He might have been adopted. He might have been put down by a vet. Or he might have been shot or worse.

Years later Margaret and I tried to make up for Park Laddie. We adopted a beautiful greyhound called Zak from Battersea Dogs Home. Zak soon afterwards galloped away with the Westminster Dog of the Year award given by the Dogs' Trust.

Suddenly, we found ourselves involved in greyhound welfare. I called a debate on it in the Lords, following one in the Commons instituted by Jim Fitzpatrick, a subsequent animal welfare minister. I became chairman of the Retired Greyhound Trust, the charity helping rehome retired greyhounds.

I used to have a poor opinion of animal welfare people. Why bother about animals when there are so many humans in distress? This is one subject on which I have changed my mind.

Yes, humans are in distress but they are so hard to help. They go from one misery to another. Greyhounds are all gratitude. Give them a sofa to lie on and a bone to chew and they are happiness from head to waggy tail.

From my welfare work, I knew that greyhound racing was in a mess. It was in long-term decline. Once the greyhound track was the only place where a working man could place a legal bet but now there were betting shops on every high street. Moreover the sport was identified with flat caps and beery proles, though in fact you can get a decent meal at virtually every track in Britain. The number of tracks, around a hundred after the war, had declined to twenty-six. Though it was still Britain's third biggest spectator sport – after football and horse racing – the audience was ageing and declining.

More immediately, it was in short-term crisis. The sport's governors, understandably, thought that there was an answer to their problems: to get the bookmakers to pay much more money to support it. They conceived the ambition of pocketing 4 per cent of every bet taken by the bookmakers. Incomprehensibly, they thought that they would be able to get it by muscle. At least when David took on Goliath he had a working sling.

I saw an ad to chair the British Greyhound Racing Board (BGRB) in the *Racing Post* and thought 'I could do that'. When I applied for the job, the governing body was in complete chaos. The chairman, a rear admiral, had resigned because he was not consulted about strategy. The general secretary had been sacked after trying to bully the bookmakers by saying greyhound racing was fixed. Jarvis Astaire, a former showbiz bigwig who ran the leading greyhound track owner, the GRA, was suing a harmless member of the board. The bookmakers were refusing to pay more. The government had the industry's poor welfare record in its sights and animal welfare legislation threatened to burden it with unsupportable costs. Meanwhile the BGRB, the trade body, was at loggerheads with the National Greyhound Racing Club (NGRC), which set the rules, as to which was top dog.

All of this would have led a sensible man to keep well clear. In any case, why would a jobbing politician with some intellectual pretensions want to get involved in a sport which Winston Churchill famously described as 'animated roulette'?

Phil Bull, who founded horse racing's Timeform (the betting man's bible), described his sport as the 'divine frivolity'. I haven't come up with a phrase that good for greyhound racing and some would say that for greyhound racing, the frivolity is more obvious than the divinity. But should one confine one's life to the higher things? In a famous phrase, Tony Crosland said that, with the passing of old grievances 'we shall turn our attention increasingly to other, and in the long run more important, spheres – of personal freedom, happiness and cultural endeavour; the cultivation of leisure, beauty, grace, gaiety, excitement and of all the proper pursuits, whether elevated, vulgar or eccentric, which contribute to the varied fabric of a full private and family life'.

It would be elevating matters to describe that marvellous sentence as the guiding principle of my life. But I have found that most satisfaction is to be gained and perhaps even modest good achieved by doing a variety of things ignoring the world's view as to their relative merits. More succinctly, variety is the spice of life.

Another principle has been to take on things in trouble. If you accept jobs in organisations that are going splendidly, before long something goes wrong and you get blamed. If you go for basket cases, sometimes you will turn them round, in which case you get great credit, and sometimes you can't, in which case you can blame your predecessors. It works like that in politics too.

In the case of greyhound racing, I did not think the short-term problems were insoluble. Welfare needed to be dealt with, not only for the dogs' sake, but to keep the politicians at bay. That required more money from the bookmakers but they could be reasoned into providing it, if they could be persuaded that it was necessary to maintain a profitable betting shop product. The board needed to be broadened so it did not comprise stakeholders at war with each other. The industry did not need two separate competing governing bodies. The strategy wrote itself.

It did not, however, implement itself. I have spent forty years in politics, but I have never known politics be so hard as it was in the five years when I ran greyhound racing.

Personalities came into this. Greyhound racing folk are singular people – conservative, stubborn, quarrelsome. They are also passionate in their devotion to the dogs and to their sport, and mostly friendly, loyal and determined. They reminded me of the qualities Tony Crosland so admired in his working-class Grimsby constituents. I developed a love–hate relationship with them, though the number I loved always exceeded the number I hated.

Factionalisation was a problem. Doggy people tend only to see part of it at a time: owners see the size of the prize money pot; stadia the help available to them to invest; and so on. The most important stakeholders, the bookmakers, did not sit on the BGRB, though they were Banquo at the feast. It was a shock after chairing many boards to come across one where the norms that usually govern boardroom behaviour were not understood by every participant.

So what should have taken about eighteen months took five years.

I immediately persuaded the bookmakers to agree a 50 per cent increase in the voluntary levy they paid for greyhound racing. Its yield trebled in five years. The politicians also demanded structural reform of the governing bodies. That was achieved not by me but by another Lord, Bernard Donoughue. Lord Donoughue agreed to chair an inquiry into the industry. The NGRC only went along with an inquiry when they were bluntly told it would go ahead whether they liked it or not. His eminently sensible proposals led to the setting up of the unified Greyhound Board of Great Britain. Meanwhile welfare was advanced, the threat of statutory regulation was fought off and relative harmony restored. I cannot claim it was easy – once the board came within an inch of sacking me. The bookmakers, as usual friends and allies of good sense, helped to persuade them that this would not be wise.

I was helped by what seemed like bad news: the exposure by the *Sunday Times* of a case where one individual in the North East was shooting dogs with a bolt gun when they should only be put down by a registered vet. This story could not have been more atypical. The paper hugely exaggerated it: observing two dogs were shot one day, it extrapolated that to say 10,000–15,000 had been shot over fifteen years. But the story was a rude awakening for those who believed I exaggerated the welfare threat. We had to react not just by condemning what had happened but by doing everything we could to make sure it never happened again. I try to remember this every time my blood boils at modern journalism and its excesses, for on this occasion a half-true story did a great deal of good.

A sub-theme was the threat from extreme welfarists, those who were in principle opposed to greyhound racing. I was personally a target. My home in south London was besieged by demonstrators who laid wreaths round the walls. I had to involve Special Branch. They advised that greyhound welfare organisations had been infiltrated by ever more extreme factions. Those who had been prevented by law from demonstrating against animal laboratories had turned their attention to greyhound welfare, in the hope of radicalising the many decent people involved in that cause.

It is a strange fact that those who love animals the most appear to make one exception: the human animal. I did not – indeed could not – let these people worry me, and I have been delighted to observe that their demonstrations today attract only a handful of diehards.

More important, the greyhound welfare problem is effectively solved. When I rehearse my lines for St Peter I now shamelessly include the fact (for it is a fact) that today, 8,000 of the something under 10,000 dogs who retire each year are rehomed compared with 2,000 when I first got involved. Zak is long dead, of bone cancer, but I hope he will appear by my side and yap 'Hear hear'.

Racing clearly was deep in my blood. Indeed, as will be seen from the picture of me taking on my mother on my pony at the age of about seven, if I had not been a politician, I should love to have been a jockey.

When young enough and light enough, I was not rich enough or fit enough. But in my late fifties, I found a way to fulfil my lifelong ambition – harness racing.

No, harness racing is not what Prince Philip does – a form of dressage with a carriage on the back. Harness racing is a fully fledged racing sport, in much of Europe as popular as thorough-bred flat racing. In Britain it is less prominent, but retains pockets of strength, for example in Yorkshire and in Wales where I live.

I went one day and loved it. I noticed one other thing about it immediately. Many of the drivers were men and women of, shall we say, mature years. I thought: I could do that.

I read in the *Brecon and Radnor Express*, the local paper, that a trainer was setting up in our village. So I went down, knocked on his door, and said I was thinking of having a horse.

Dick Price and his wife Frances beamed, as trainers do in such circumstances.

'And driving him...'

Dick looked at Frances and Frances looked at Dick and slowly he said: 'I think you will find, Lord Lipsey, that it is a young man's sport.'

An indirect approach seemed most likely to work. So I bought the horse. Then I suggested I might try it in the field. Stella Havard, the feisty local chairman, challenged me to a charity match and then... we were away.

I drove for four years, mostly on slow horses which were even slower given the incompetence of the assistance they received from the sulky. But I did win. Goldwood, my tiny game pacer, came from last to first to win at Walton. I completed a double that day on Radnor Mary-Ann. The greatest triumph was also the greatest disaster since some of my friends berate me to this day for telling them not to back Ithon Abbey when he trotted up at Boughrood. My wife, who knows I am a bad tipster, availed herself of the 12/1 liberally on offer.

Harness racing is a lovely sport, full of lovely people. It is completely classless, quarrelsome but always family quarrels usually made up. I retain an ambition to help gain it a higher national profile, which was advanced when William Hill, the bookmakers, put £25,000 into a harness series at Wolverhampton racecourse. I don't drive now, having scared myself half to death in a near-tumble, but I remain proud president of the sport's governing British Harness Racing Club.

Throughout the first year of the new decade, I had one other post of significance, this time more 'large P' political. I chaired the Social Market Foundation, which had a long, mostly distinguished, chequered history.

Its birth came as the political party to which its progenitors belonged was dying. David Owen was one of the 'Gang of Four', self-styled social democrats who defected from the Labour Party as it yawed to the left in the early 1980s. That act apparently fed the good doctor's appetite for fissure. When the bulk of their Social Democratic Party decided to amalgamate with the Liberals after the 1987 general election, Owen dissented. He discerned an ideological gulf between what the Liberals believed and what he and his followers believed. He and his disciples were social marketeers and the Liberals were not, so he left his colleagues who formed one half of the Liberal Democrats. In 1988 he set up his own party, the Social Democratic Party Mark 2, to carry the banner of the social market into the electoral marketplace.

Unfortunately for him, voters proved less moved by the philosophical distinction between the Liberals and the Social Democrats than he was. His new party was wound up in 1990 after finishing an ignominious seventh in the Bootle by-election, coming behind Screaming Lord Sutch's Monster Raving Loony Party.

It did have one lasting memorial: the Social Market Foundation. Set up by a mildly eccentric peer, Alastair Kilmarnock, and gifted substantial core funding by David Sainsbury, the SMF has long outlived its progenitors.

A tendency to follow the intellect rather than bow to the conventions of partisan politics has been a characteristic of leading SMF figures. My predecessor as chair, the distinguished historian and economist Robert Skidelsky, graduated from the Social Democrats to the Tories, then fell out with them and now sits in the Lords as a crossbencher. I meanwhile, expect shortly to complete my half-century as a member of the Labour Party but my egalitarian, non-liberal, deregulatory and anti-choice views had little in common with whatever it was that the Labour government under Gordon Brown believed in. Hope trumps experience, and I therefore hope for better under his successor Ed Miliband.

Two SMF directors, Danny Finkelstein and Rick Nye, also went the SDP-to-Tory route, though Finkelstein, who did not get selected for a winnable Tory seat, is now a senior journalist on *The Times*. Philip Collins, a later director, is also at *The Times*, via becoming an adviser and speechwriter to Tony Blair. Even by New Labour standards, he is hard to classify as a man of the left. The present and excellent director, Ian Mulheirn, has no overt political allegiance.

When Skidelsky decided to step down, the board approached two candidates for the job: Peter Jay, the economist and former British ambassador to Washington, and me. Jay took one look at the accounts and said no. I looked at the accounts, too. But I applied the same theory that I had applied to greyhound racing: that you should only take on organisations in trouble.

In fact the saving of the SMF owed more to Collins than to me. I am not sure that the courts would have taken the view that it had always traded legally had the matter been examined but it wasn't and we came through.

Skidelsky had been a hands-on chairman. Indeed he had even set up a subsidiary organisation to work on his main interest at the time: economic development in eastern Europe. I took the opposite approach. Think tanks stand and fall by the fertility of the minds of their directors.

Walter Bagehot, author of *The English Constitution* and the man after whom my column in *The Economist* was named, attributed to the British monarch three duties: the right to be consulted, the right to advise and the right to warn. That describes the ideal director–chair relation too. Chairs also have the additional duty of ensuring that the organisation does not spend money it does not have. So long as you also ensure that you run a tight board, which gets the corporate governance right, you are doing what you should.

We had lots of goes at defining precisely what the SMF did. As with all modern organisations, we craved a perfect mission statement. In the end we came up with 'The Foundation's main activity is to commission and publish original papers by independent academic and other experts on key topics in the economic and social fields, with a view to stimulating public discussion on the performance of markets and the social framework within which they operate.' This appears at the beginning of all our publications.

I contented myself with trying to ensure we did not stray too far from our original mission. That was to advocate the advantages of the market, suitably but modestly regulated, in producing things, but also concentrating on the social framework which made markets work and people happy. Brilliant directors being as they are, they made occasional darts to occupy new territory. Phil Collins at one point wanted us to become a think tank for liberty;

he did not, for example, rate highly the case for clamping down on 'secondary smoking'. Under Ann Rossiter, his successor, the government's agenda of public service reform tended sometimes to define our agenda. I did not take a Stalinist position of suppressing their instincts but I did try to lean against their prevailing winds.

I also got involved in detail in bits of the SMF's work. I ran a big inquiry into health. It was a lesson in the occasional futility of democratic politics.

We examined prescription charges thoroughly. Though we thought they were a good thing – no charges and the demand for medicine goes through the roof – we could not understand the exemptions from them. For example, pensioners, now on average quite well off, were automatically excluded. As they consumed more prescriptions than anyone else this was a flaw. We reported accordingly, to respectful notices. It took the adviser to the Health Secretary about five seconds to tell us that we had wasted our time. Change was not on, politically.

Even there we struck some gold. In 2011 all hell was let loose for the government when Andrew Lansley, the Health Secretary, decided to abolish primary care trusts in favour of new commissioning trusts which he described as GP led. There was a case for change. There was little case for big bang change, the imposition of a further national top-down solution.

Looking back at our report, I found that we had tackled this problem in the following way. PCTs would remain but GPs could choose which PCT they wished to belong to. This would have led to a gradual evolution where they deserted poor PCTs and joined better ones. The better ones would have evolved into just the kind of higher-powered commissioning bodies that Lansley wanted. The benefits would have been achieved in an evolutionary way. Lansley was not persuaded to adopt this sensible solution but it does show that the ideas that think tanks generate may be relevant long after the publicity of publication has been forgotten.

I also ran a programme on gambling and casinos, and on media. Both affected the intellectual climate, at the margin. In particular, being a pro-market think tank, the SMF's consistent support for the BBC helped hold at bay those who wanted to destroy it.

Did the SMF in the near-decade I chaired it revolutionise the world? No. Did it change it? Modestly, yes. For the better? Probably, on balance. At any rate, I feel privileged to have participated in its work and to have left my successor, the commentator Mary Ann Sieghart, something to work with.

One initiative from that decade deserves a mention. This one, I owe to *The Guardian*. Once too often, I exploded in my bath as that paper again confused millions with billions, a distinction – or so a number of writers on the paper appear to believe – without a difference. Opinion is sacred but the facts are free! I decided there and then to start a pressure group to campaign against abuse of statistics by politicians, the media, advertisers and companies.

The outcome, thanks to a generous grant from the Nuffield Foundation, was a group called Straight Statistics. Under its director, Nigel Hawkes, a former health editor of *The Times*, it became reasonably effective in campaigning against abuse. So, for example, the Advertising Standards Authority has ruled against imputed claims we investigated that certain vitamin pills will stave off Alzheimer's; against claims by Betfair, a betting company, that its odds were 40 per cent better than anyone else's; and against a claim by Bird's Eye that its frozen vegetables contain 30 per cent more vitamins than fresh.

We also sought to educate journalists in the correct use of statistics. Our meeting with the editor and senior staff at *The Guardian* was one of our best. We held to account fact-bending politicians and lying PR men. Our offspring, the All Party Group on Statistics, helps educate MPs and peers, and we intervened successfully to improve the process by which the new head of the Statistics Authority was selected and appointed. If we contributed modestly to reason and right in public affairs, it was a job well worth doing.

Straight Statistics did good work for the three years for which it existed. In 2011 we amalgamated with another body with similar ends but a wider remit, Full Fact.

Denis Healey, the former Labour Chancellor going strong into his nineties, remarked recently that, with age, he became less interested in politics and more in culture. This was part of his famous 'hinterland' which marked him out from more single-minded friends and rivals.

I can't claim that culture has taken the place of politics in my life, but I have as time has gone by got more and more involved in one aspect: music.

There was no one cause of the arrival but I owe a great deal to my young pianist friend Kerem Hasan. Our link came in a curious way. I was attending, from duty as much as expectation of pleasure, a concert given in aid of retired greyhounds by Annette Crosbie, the actress. It featured pupils of Marion Blech, who once ran the London Mozart Players. A little boy hoisted himself onto the stool, his feet miles from reaching the pedals, and began to play the piano. I can't remember what but I can remember my reaction: 'My God, this lad is the Real Thing.' Then I noticed a man looking excited and recognised him as my barber, Erol Hasan. Kerem, the pianist, was his son.

I tried to follow Kerem's progress as he went forward. We set up a concert for him to play at St John's Smith Square at which the audience, many of them parliamentarians, marvelled. He performed the Schumann Piano Quintet with the Sacconi Quartet – nearly as young, as brilliant – for my sixtieth birthday, and twice performed at home in Brecon. At the time of writing he is on a scholarship at the Royal Scottish College of Music, where he has had a course specially created to combine piano with conducting. Remember the name: you will hear it again.

As usual, one thing led to another. I took up the piano again myself. I was gratified to find I played slightly less badly than I had as a teenager – a rare case of getting better at something with age. In Wales, with a group of friends including local peers, we supported a new chamber orchestra, the first anywhere in that country between the extreme north and the extreme south. I became a trustee of the Sidney Nolan Trust, mostly devoted to the works of the great painter (known best but wrongly for his Ned Kelly series) which also promoted high-class music at his ancient and beautiful farm in Herefordshire. I gave a bit of informal public affairs advice to the English National Opera under its chair, Vernon Ellis, whom I had known at Oxford. And – a campaign I fought with some purpose – I was elected chair of the All Party Classical Music Group in Parliament. I am taking the chair of Trinity Laban, a fabulously progressive music conservatoire, part situated in the old Royal Naval College in Greenwich. And so I celebrate the dying cadences of my political life with my eye on something new and challenging.

CHAPTER 16

THE TRANSFORMATION OF
POLITICS 1970–2011

I t is now forty years since a callow, gauche, thin, neurotic geek of twenty-four first arrived in Parliament. This book has followed me as I have trodden the corridors of Westminster and Whitehall, then a young geek, now an oldish one. So it therefore seems natural to finish my life story with a few reflections on what has changed in politics.

On the face of things, the answer might appear to be 'nothing much'. Parliament is still Parliament and Whitehall still Whitehall.

True, Parliament Square is rather grubbier than it was back in 1972. That was because the 1997–2010 Labour government, in one of its rare moments of liberalism, got rid of the old law that stopped citizens demonstrating outside Parliament. The result of this is that Parliament Square has been for years packed with a crowd even more insalubrious than those who inhabit the Palace of Westminster, complete with cardboard boxes to sleep in and cardboard banners to wave: Bliar, no cuts, free the Tamils. As I write, the authorities are now trying to do something about it. They have been trying for months.

Picking your way over the wreckage, has anything much changed? There is Downing Street, home of the Prime Minister, and the Palace of Westminster, home of Parliament. Both have acquired ugly iron barriers to fend off terrorists. It is not easy to decide which shows the greater contempt for aesthetics, the state or the demonstrators. But the great centres of government are recognisable still, though requiring a physical protection which was otiose in 1970.

You could easily be deceived into thinking there is not much change inside either. For example, ask MPs about their partisanship and they still today would overwhelmingly reply 'Conservative', 'Labour' or 'Lib Dem'. It is true the latter were Liberals in 1972 but that does not seem much change to have to show for forty years of politics.

The House of Lords still wears ermine robes for the meeting of Parliament. Black Rod hammers on doors. And *mirabile dictu,* there is still a speech from the throne read at the start of the parliamentary session by the same woman, Elizabeth II, Queen of England, now aged eighty-five. So is this still the world of the nation Britain sometimes likes to think it is: a conservative nation, where nothing changes unless it has to?

It is not. The British characteristic which the appearance of no change celebrates is a different one: our peculiar genius at preserving the face of things. This is Wilde's *Dorian Gray.* Underneath, this period has seen a period of social and related political change as fast or faster than any other period of British history.

It has been a period of big and ongoing constitutional changes. The first dates from 1972–73, just as I was padding through the Commons central lobby for the first time. It was Britain's entry into the Common Market as it was then known (European Union implied a bit too much unity for British tastes). Importantly, it was a change to which British voters assented in the 1975 'stay or quit' referendum.

A central proposition underlying Britain's constitution was this: that Parliament was sovereign. After EU membership, and with lots of ifs, buts, denials and obfuscations, it clearly no longer was. The British courts would, in appropriate cases, give priority to community law over British law. Those cases have tended to expand in number over time with successive revisions to the European treaties, and with what many Brits perceive as the imperialist tendencies of the European Commission, its central bureaucracy.

Meanwhile the Labour government incorporated the European Convention on Human Rights into British law so that cases under it can be brought directly before the British courts rather than being heard, as before, in Strasbourg. A controversy raged in Britain in 2011 about a decision from the European Court that prisoners must be given the vote in British elections. The populace was outraged.

The government was caught between the fear of a media spanking if it obeyed the verdict and the fear of judicial sanctions, including hefty fines, if it defied Strasbourg.

The result of that change is that, for the first time in British history, the separation of powers between the judiciary and the executive/legislative arms of British government has ended. The courts used to keep out of anything that even sniffed of politics. No longer.

The origins of this change lay with European entry. Judges in a European context had to intervene in matters where previously they would have declined to intervene. But once the barriers were down for that reason, down they crashed too in areas which had little or nothing to do with Europe.

The social context determining judicial activism had also changed. And so too, recognisably, had the judges. Previously they were a sort of sect bound by iron doctrines largely cut off from the rest of the world. Increasingly they transformed themselves into a body of men and women practising a broad faith, embracing a range of judicial and indeed social philosophies not much less wide than that of the population as a whole. Efforts were made by government to make the judiciary less unrepresentative of the society in which it operated by bringing in black judges, female judges and judges who had not gone to public school. During the 2000s Britain even had a black Attorney General, Patricia Scotland. In consequence Home Secretaries, responding to public opinion, spend hours in the courts being overruled by judges who – who would have thought it? – have turned from the crusty old reactionaries of days gone by to the primary defenders of civil liberties.

The second big change was devolution to Scotland and Wales. This took two attempts. A first go in the 1970s failed because of the efforts of some hostile MPs, but the second in 1997–98 was successful, following referendums in the two countries concerned. Meanwhile, through a quite different process, a power-sharing administration including both Catholics and Protestants was set up in Northern Ireland. The process of devolution has continued, and the Scottish Parliament and Welsh Assembly have consolidated their status as governments.

A third change was the reform of the House of Lords. Essentially the 1999 reform abolished the great bulk of the hereditary peerage so the House was dominated by peers appointed for life. In the process the permanent Tory majority in the House was ended. The effect was to increase the status and the power of the Lords, which now often amends government proposals, or even stops the government doing what it wants. The House of Lords has, for example, in recent years prevented the government extending the period for which suspected terrorists could be held and has stopped it abolishing jury trial for fraud.

A fourth, regarded as hugely important by most people with direct experience in government, is the change, amounting almost to quasi-eclipse, in the civil service and its power. Many of its functions have been contracted out to quangos no longer directly the creatures of ministers. At the same time, the power balance between civil servants, ministers and civil society has shifted against the civil service.

One could add new electoral systems for European and some local elections; elected mayors for big cities including London; the erosion of the power of local governments; reform of the House of Commons to create more powerful committees to challenge the executive; the introduction of the use of referendums into British political decision-making; and the diminution of the role of the Lord Chancellor, a politician who used, curiously, to run Britain's judiciary.

The coalition government, of Tories and Lib Dems, has launched a new phase. The first big move turned into a setback, with the loss of the AV referendum dealt with earlier. The referendum led to one change though not the one it was supposed to lead to. The new system of parliamentary districting will make constituencies more equal in size, all but a handful of exceptions varying only by plus or minus 5 per cent from the average. Seat redistribution will generally take place every five years. Eight to twelve years was the previous norm. The total number of MPs will be reduced from 650 to 600.

A fixed five-year term for Parliament is now the rule, replacing the previous arrangement whereby a Prime Minister could call an election whenever it suited his or his party's convenience. There is legislation so the public can force Parliament by petition to debate certain legislative measures. All three parties are more or less committed to changing the House of Lords from an essentially appointed to an essentially elected assembly, though I do not think it would be wise for anyone to hold their breath waiting for this.

None of this was planned. No thought-through philosophy underlies them. The individual changes are largely unrelated to each other. No constitutional principle has emerged to take the place of the old centrality, the sovereignty of Parliament, though it is true that a more American philosophy, that of the sovereignty of the people, underlies some of them.

The great bulk of the constitutional changes date not from the seventies, when Britain was undergoing something of a crisis of confidence, or even the eighties, when they might have been painted as part of the attempt to tackle that crisis. They mostly started in the 1990s and 2000s when broadly things were back on an even keel. Historians, who tend to be dedicated to discovering large causes, deep patterns and broad movements, are going to find it all a puzzle.

It is hard to justify the sheer volume of change; the at best half-baked arguments that have been used for change; the way that one change has (or rather has not) related to another change; and above all the headlong rush from one set of changes to another set of changes without any assessment of whether the changes that have been made are for the better or for the worse. Net good or net bad, the whole thing, in Professor Tony King's words, has been a 'mess'.

These constitutional changes have of course altered both the context in which politicians work and the constraints upon them.

But if we look at the political scene today, they are nevertheless not the changes that have transformed the practice of politics and the business of governing.

They are dwarfed by a huge social change which has altered the substance and style of politics to its roots. Most if not all of the political change that has come about can be attributed directly or indirectly to a single factor – the effective decline of social class as the driver of British politics.

Peter Pulzer, a leading British political academic, writing in 1967, said: 'Class is the basis of British politics. All else is embellishment and detail.' That is not true today.

The Labour Party – my party – was then a class party in two senses. First it stood for the interests of something identified as the working class. It wanted that class to get higher real wages and better state welfare benefits. With that, a minority of the party embraced a quasi-Marxist theory of class war, in favour – in the words of the party's then constitution – of the 'common ownership of the means of production, distribution and exchange'.

This was not and continued not to be a viable philosophy electorally. As has earlier been outlined, Tony Crosland pointed out in 1970 that the Labour Party was losing on trend two percentage points off its share of the vote at each general election.

This was for two reasons. Fewer people were working class and fewer working-class people shared this class approach to politics.

These trends have continued. So, according to Peter Kelner, a psephological expert, in 1970 (an election Labour lost) the C2DE manual working class comprised 66 per cent of the population. In 2010 it comprised 43 per cent of the population.

In 1970, 56 per cent of the C2DE manual working class voted Labour. In 2010 only 33 per cent did.

So, taking these figures today, in 1970 Labour polled 10 million votes from people in social classes C2DE. In 2010 that had fallen to 4.2 million votes – actually fewer than the 4.4 million votes Labour polled from the middle class.

The Tories remained a largely middle-class party throughout

though one that also benefited from a large vote from less liberal members of the working class. They could afford to. The middle class was growing. Labour had to change its social base if it was to survive, and to change its social base it had radically to reform its politics. The change came to be known as New Labour, a change of name discussed earlier.

The change was not simply one mapped by demographers and psephologists. It was palpable. In 1971, the journalist Anthony Sampson published a revise of his much-remarked sixties book on Britain, entitled *The New Anatomy of Britain*. Some things had changed since the original but more hadn't. But if you reread *The New Anatomy of Britain*, it is still a description of a society dominated by class and class divides. Without claiming that class has disappeared in Britain – it hasn't – the change since then is remarkable.

It is in a British context that I am analysing this change, for this is a book about a life led in Britain. But it is important to recognise that it is not confined to Britain, global capital of social class though it long was. It is broadly true of all the main European countries. The change in class structure is a universal consequence of economic development into the twenty-first century. It is one reason among many why the victory of Marxism is not only no longer inevitable; it is impossible. As Eric Hobsbawm, the great Marxist historian, famously put it, the forward march of labour has been halted.

It is also important to recognise that the decline of class politics has created a challenge for the political class everywhere. For social democracy and for Croslandite social democracy it is more than a challenge. It is an existential crisis.

Social democratic parties have always represented an alliance – between a liberal intellectual corps and a working-class corps. However, this alliance, never without its strains, is becoming harder to sustain. To take an example, the liberal intellectuals want free movement of labour (and besides a Polish plumber to do a cheap job on your central heating is greatly to be desired). But those Poles arguably undercut the wages of the old working class, and live in houses that it would otherwise live in.

This phenomenon is well explored in a 2011 Policy Network publication entitled *Exploring the Cultural Challenges to Social Democracy*. It isn't new – Tony Crosland was always moaning about the insouciance of the Labour Party towards the genuine difficulties faced by his working-class constituents in Grimsby as a result of immigration – though actually Grimsby was largely immigrant free.

In Britain, these demographics were reinforced by another factor. As class loyalties eroded, voters became more and more instrumentalist. They wanted to know what their party – indeed any party – would do for them. If a working-class voter wasn't convinced by Labour's answer he or she would turn elsewhere. When John Major failed to deliver for Tory middle-class voters they tried Blair instead.

With this of course went a broader social movement of decline in respect for authority. If you want a single indicator of the social change that has affected Britain in the last forty years it is that the director general of the BBC, Mark Thompson, attends meetings with members of Parliament tieless. Even in the House of Lords, peers are now only required to wear ties after prayers have been read – a neat conjunction of the traditional and the modern.

The decline in social class directly impacted voting behaviour, so that Pulzer's law became moribund. In 1970, the two big parties polled between them 89.5 per cent of the national vote. That was already down on the 98 per cent or so they polled in the early 1950s, but nothing much had been seen yet. Between 1970 and 1974, their share plummeted to 74.9 per cent – a fifteen percentage point fall in under four years. It has continued to subside though more gradually since. In 2010, the Conservatives and Labour between them polled 65.1 per cent, with much of this fall coming between 1970 and 1974 alone.

The mirror image of this decline is the performance of the Lib Dems. In the 1970 general election, the Liberals polled only 7.5 per cent of the vote. In the election of February 1974, they polled 19.3 per cent. They have progressed much more slowly since, ending up with a disappointing 23 per cent of the vote in 2011, but a quarter of the vote is not nothing. It remains to be seen if after Jo Grimond, Jeremy Thorpe, David Steel, Paddy Ashdown and Charles Kennedy had marched them up the electoral mountain, Nick Clegg will have marched them down again.

At the same time, the national parties in Scotland and Wales increased their parliamentary representation from one in 1970 to nine today, though their vote is broadly unchanged.

The result of this shift away from class voting affects what has always been the central feature – and for some the central defence – of the British political system. That is, the system invariably generates majority governments with a mandate for change who can be held accountable for their performance by the electorate. That required two clearly defined and dominant national parties – and in accordance with Duverger's law, that is what Britain's first-past-the-post electoral system provided, as, for example, the American political system still does.

It is surprising that this system, with one or other party enjoying an overall majority, abided so long. You have to look at it election by election. For many years after 1979, the Labour Party had eccentrically rendered itself unelectable; and then from many years after 1997, the Tories did the same. The consequence – seven successive elections yielding parties decent overall majorities – may also owe something to chance. After all, every gambler knows that, if you toss a coin, sometimes if not often it will come up heads seven times in a row.

That sequence came to an abrupt end in 2010. The result was a hung parliament and one, moreover, from which it was not immediately clear what kind of government would emerge.

According to John Curtice's appendix to Philip Cowley and Dennis Kavanagh's *The British General Election of 2010* (Palgrave Macmillan, 2010), the hung parliament was facilitated by three factors.

Firstly, the Lib Dems and the other small parties were less severely punished by the electoral system in terms of seats they won than in the past.

Secondly, the number of seats which are marginal between Tory and Labour has declined sharply and so a swing in vote share between the two brings about a much smaller swing in seats than it used to. In 1970 a 1 per cent swing between Tory and Labour would lead to a swing of seats of 3 per cent (the so-called 'cube law'). That has now halved to 1.5 per cent.

Thirdly, the electoral system continues to exhibit a pro-Labour bias. Labour would win an overall majority in the Commons if it polled 3 per cent more than the Tories, according to Curtice, but for the Conservatives to do the same, they would need 11 per cent more votes. That is why after the 2011 general election they had to join with the Lib Dems to form a government.

An argument advanced by David Cameron and his Conservatives in the 2011 AV referendum was that AV would lead to more hung parliaments and more weak governments. Whether they think the present coalition which they lead is weak, they do not say. But the truth is that AV would have increased the likelihood of hung parliaments relatively little. According to Dr Alan Renwick of Reading University, under AV in 2010 the Tories would have won twenty-two fewer seats, Labour ten fewer and the Lib Dems thirty-two more (*The Alternative Vote: A Briefing Paper*, Political Studies Association, 2011). This of course would have greatly changed the post-election arithmetic and might even mean that Britain was now governed by a Lab–Lib coalition led by David Miliband. But we should have had a hung parliament with AV or without it. Indeed, the likelihood is that Britain in future will regularly, perhaps nearly always, end up with coalition governments, as is generally the case elsewhere in Europe. This is a change of enormous proportions, with political and constitutional implications the political class has hardly started to grasp.

This will be accompanied by a continuation of the decreased role that ideology pays in British national policies. It is now fifty years since Tony Crosland's friend and subsequently mine, Daniel

Bell – one of the great modern intellectuals – proclaimed 'The End of Ideology'. In Britain it has been a slow death though it has seen periods of revived ideological government, most notably under Margaret Thatcher. But Thatcherism has broadly completed its course. Labour no longer has a fundamentalist left wing. I, once regarded as a proto-fascist in Labour circles for my right-wing views, am now a dangerous leftie, without having changed my mind much on much.

The left of the Labour Party believed in nationalisation. No one does now. The party as a whole believed in increased public spending especially on welfare. It is now much less sure of that, for the public mood has turned from European to American in its hostility to welfare benefits. Public support for increasing taxation and public spending is at its lowest level since the early 1980s, according to the annual British Public Attitudes survey for 2010. This combination is supported by 39 per cent, down from 62 per cent in 1997. Huge inequality and the rise of a class of super-rich on almost an American (or Russian) scale have been tolerated.

Meanwhile the Conservative Party has abandoned being 'the Church of England at prayer'. It is no longer illiberal, nor anti-gay nor anti-feminist though it is still blundering about seeking a line on immigration and multiculturalism.

Labour has, I suppose, a residual bias towards public spending and to the public sector. The Tories have, I suppose, rather more respect for the power of markets. But these are matters of nuance where once they were great gulfs dividing the parties. The Tories have more faith in the self-righting properties of the economy, whereas Labour believes in a degree of state intervention. But these again are matters of nuance.

So, two related things have changed. Firstly, class has declined as the central divide in British politics. Secondly, and partly in consequence, the parties have become far less ideological. Politics is increasingly about what works and what doesn't work.

This has led to revolutionary changes in our politics. An example is the rise of media power. This is not new in British history.

Stanley Baldwin, an inter-war Prime Minister, once berated Lord Beaverbrook, the owner of the *Daily Express*, as one who exercised 'power without responsibility, the prerogative of the harlot through the ages'. The modern press is doing that again. Because politicians no longer command armies of voters loyal to their leaders' orders, they constantly seek to influence those who might determine voter opinion – and the press and TV are obvious candidates.

I will just illustrate the change with one quote. J. P. Macintosh, a former Labour MP and academic, said in the seventies: 'A phone call from Number 10 complaining about an article or news story tends to produce a reprimand for the journalist rather than a rude rejoinder.'

Not now it doesn't. John Major rang Kelvin Mackenzie, the editor of the popular *Sun*, to request sympathetic treatment of his devaluation of the pound. Mackenzie reportedly responded: 'Well, John, let me put it this way. I've got a large bucket of shit on my desk and tomorrow morning I'm going to pour it all over your head.'

The politicians of course and their advisers seek constantly to spin, and that includes berating editors. The difference is that the editors and their journalists don't give a damn. They know where today the power lies. A prime ministerial rebuke is a circulation-boosting accolade. Instead, therefore, as the Coulson–Cameron affair has laid bare, politicians devote themselves to courting the press. The master–servant relationship has reversed.

British politics is still less media dominated than American politics. By law political reporting on television, though not in the press, has to be unbiased. Rupert Murdoch is said to want to change that rule so there can be a British Fox TV. More important, political parties cannot buy TV advertising. The role of money in British politics is much less influential and thus corrupting than it is in American politics. It remains to be seen if the British political class can summon up the will to maintain these safeguards.

Another result of the decline of class voting is a change in the nature of the inhabitants of the political class. In 1970, the House of Commons still contained many people whom ordinary people would recognise as essentially the same as themselves. Many Tories were still running businesses. The Labour ranks were buttressed by ex-trade union officials of working-class origins.

Now the Commons is stuffed with people who are overtly professional politicians, many of whom have done little or nothing else but politics all their life. David Cameron (like me) is an ex-special adviser. So is Ed Miliband, the Labour leader, his shadow Chancellor Ed Balls, his shadow health spokesman Andy Burnham – and so one could go on. I do not say these are people without beliefs – they are not – but they are people whose beliefs do not reflect gut, class-based dispositions.

This is not all for the bad. The old House contained men and (not many) women of limited ability, lobby fodder for the government and if the truth be told, liable to spend too much time in the bars. It is at least encouraging that the number of MPs who sometimes rebel against government policy in votes has increased, as the research of Professor Philip Cowley of Nottingham University has demonstrated. Quite often, a combination of a rebellious House of Commons and a House of Lords where the government has no automatic majority forces the government to reverse major policies.

Nevertheless this cultural gulf between members of Parliament and members of the public is a substantial change which the electorate recognises. There was a fierce public reaction to the parliamentary expenses scandal of 2009 – a scandal incidentally which would hardly count as such in most countries – which threatened for a while the stability of the political system.

The political response to this has been to try to eliminate the worst abuses. MPs' expenses have been regulated so that many complain it is hardly possible to do the job. The way things are going, it will not be long before MPs are segregated from their families and forced to live in rabbit hutches where they are fed off mouldy lettuce leaves and travel to their constituencies in prison transports jeered by the populace. We shall see if the elected members dare to protest.

The final change is this. Britain used to be regarded as a parliamentary democracy, that is to say a land governed by an executive, responsible to Parliament. There are signs, however, that the political class, cut off as it is from the class base that nourished it, is losing its nerve and that we are moving instead to something which contains important elements of direct democracy.

One example is the rise of referendums – actual (for example on the EU, on devolution and on the voting system) and threatened (for example on any increases in the power of the EU). Politicians are reluctant to take decisions on these matters themselves and therefore contract them out to the electorate. That way the people have only themselves to blame.

Others are direct elections for all sorts of bodies which in the past were in the hands of locally and nationally elected politicians, with elections introduced for hospital foundation trusts, for schools and, coming shortly, police authorities. This is very American save the turnout is very British. The candidates barely campaign, the public takes no interest and therefore the gains to democracy are negligible. And voters show signs of election fatigue. Turnout, 72 per cent in the 1970 general election, fell to 65 per cent in 2010 and even that was regarded as a relief. Barely a third of voters can be expected to show up for local and European elections.

Another is the excessive influence of opinion polls on politics and politicians. These include both genuine polls and the proliferating surveys carried out for companies and lobbies with questions crafted to elicit the answers that suit those who are paying for them. The political class is not statistically sophisticated. For too many the polls, good, indifferent or rubbish, are the Old and the New Testament – for they pretend to tell what politicians most now want to know: what stances they should take to capture the transient allegiance of an electorate that no longer has much loyalty to any party.

Enough. I am not a golden ageist. I do not think all these changes are for the worse any more than I think they are for the better; and a new generation will have to try to create a new polity to fit the new circumstances. All one can safely assert is that the combination of a constitution changed largely by accident and a politics changed by profound social shifts is likely to produce interesting times – as interesting as the times through which it has been my privilege to live.

And, at the end of it, am I disillusioned with politics?

I don't think I have ever seen political life through rose-tinted spectacles. I am more of a realist than an idealist; and nothing in politics has changed that.

However, if I am not disillusioned, at least some of my illusions have been watered down. Two unrelated ideals have lurked behind the day-to-day fumblings of my career. One is a belief in the Labour Party as an instrument which aims and can hope to bring about a more equal society. The other is even wider: a belief that public policy should be based on accurate facts and serious analysis, rather than political (or any other) kind of prejudice.

So far as the Labour Party is concerned, it has on occasion talked a good game on equality in opposition but, since the Attlee government, these hopes have been disappointed in office. Both Wilson governments and that of Callaghan were mostly pragmatic, middle-of-the-road affairs; Tony Blair did not even pretend to believe in equality; and Gordon Brown did precisely that – pretend. I hope, and on good days believe, that Ed Miliband will buck that trend and lead a radical egalitarian Labour government. I wish to believe (with Roy Hattersley and Kevin Hickson in their *Political Quarterly* pamphlet *In Praise of Social Democracy*) that 'Labour's only tenable ideological position must be recognisably social democratic – particularly the pursuit of greater equality and the freedom it provides.'

But there are two problems. First, equality is a great ideal but not necessarily an election-winning one. The changes in the class system, and in particular the dominance of the emerging aspiring middle class, make equality a hard platform to sell. Hattersley and Hickson argue that it is because Labour politicians have failed to make the case that it today lacks public resonance. I just wish I was more confident that they are right.

Secondly, and even if there were to be a Labour majority government with equality as its central objective, a whole new set of difficulties arise. For the instruments of public policy which would bring about that equality are everywhere contested. High taxes on the rich, yes, though there are constraints on what is possible in a global economy, but taxing the rich more will not in itself bring about a social transformation.

Labour used to rely on public expenditure as its instrument for equality, but we are increasingly aware that it often favours the better off as it does the poor: witness the state pension, which middle-class people, because they live longer, go on drawing for far more years than their poorer counterparts. Meanwhile, some public expenditure which would increase equality – increased spending on welfare for example – is effectively ruled out in the face of the public's understandable hostility to hand-outs and something-for-nothing.

As for equality of opportunity, promoted for example by a more egalitarian education system, I am far from convinced that is a weapon for equality of outcome. The more people feel they have earned their good fortune by their good performance, the less they will wish to share the proceeds of that good fortune with the less fortunate.

For the Labour Party there is no alternative to social democracy. But there should be no illusion either: even if we get another Labour government in short order and even if Mr Miliband turns out to be the leader we hope, the prospects of a social transformation along social democratic lines are not great.

My second loss of illusion is that in the role of reason in public affairs. I have not lost my faith in its desirability. You could not sit in Tony Crosland's study, floor piled high with White Papers and research documents, and not develop a sense of awe at the role of reason in pointing the way to progress.

But in many of the developments I have discussed here – for example, the decline of the power of the civil service – I perceive a deep structural change. Lip service is paid to evidence-based policy but I fear that politicians mean by this that they want to be given evidence that supports their policy rather than have their policy be determined by evidence. 'Spray-on evidence', David Halpern of the Institute for Government has dubbed it.

The rise of the new political class, paralleling the political consultants who dominate American politics, is germane here. When I began my career as a political adviser, I simply could not have imagined that my successors would be as powerful as they are over policy nor the effect that would have on the quality of the policy-making process.

I fear that the political class is to blame for this. For every Tony Crosland today there are tens of politicians who are not really interested in policy, save as an instrument to get themselves on the *Today* programme. They therefore start from their prejudices. Those who work for them, if they want to keep their jobs, will provide such facts as they can to support those prejudices. Who today speaks truth unto power? Weaker voices I fear than used to be the case.

Personally, I am out of the advice business. One of the joys of getting older is that the ambition for political advancement disappears. Today, I can pretty well say things as I see them, not worrying too much if anyone is listening and certainly not tempering my views to the half-baked prejudices of some of the politicians I come across.

Being a politician is not easy. Being a successful politician is incredibly hard. I can't personally see the point of trying in order to end up a modern Ozymandias. 'Look on my works, ye Mighty, and despair!' – not.

Politics guided by moderate ideals and governed by reason is essential to a good society. I trust that a new generation will demonstrate that this philosophy is not doomed to end in disillusion.

INDEX